Using Spanish

Using Spanish

A guide to contemporary usage

R. E. BATCHELOR

Senior Lecturer in Modern Languages, University of Nottingham

C. J. POUNTAIN

University Lecturer in Romance Philology, University of Cambridge
Fellow of Queens' College

CAMBRIDGE
UNIVERSITY PRESS

Companion titles to *Using Spanish*

Using French
A guide to contemporary usage
R. E. Batchelor and M. H. Offord
[ISBN 0 521 44361 X hardback]
[ISBN 0 521 44821 2 paperback]

Using German
A guide to contemporary usage
M. Durrell
[ISBN 0 521 42077 6   hardback]
[ISBN 0 521 31556 5   paperback]

Using French synonyms
R. E. Batchelor and M. H. Offord
[ISBN 0 521 37277 1   hardback]
[ISBN 0 521 37878 8   paperback]

Forthcoming:

Using Spanish synonyms
R. E. Batchelor
[ISBN 0 521 44160 9 hardback]
[ISBN 0 521 44694 5 paperback]

Published by the Press Syndicate of the University of Cambridge
The Pitt Building, Trumpington Street, Cambridge CB2 1RP
40 West 20th Street, New York, NY 10011–4211, USA
10 Stamford Road, Oakleigh, Melbourne 3166, Australia

© Cambridge University Press 1992

First published 1992
Reprinted 1994

Printed in Great Britain at the University Press, Cambridge

A catalogue record for this book is available from the British Library

Library of Congress cataloguing in publication data

Batchelor, R. E. (Ronald Ernest)

Using Spanish: a guide for the advanced learner / R. E. Batchelor, C. J. Pountain.
    p.   cm.
Includes indexes.
ISBN 0 521 42123 3 (hardback). ISBN 0 521 26987 3 (paperback)
1. Spanish language – Textbooks for foreign speakers – English.
2. Spanish language – Grammar – 1950–   I. Pountain, Christopher J.   II. Title.
PC4128.B3   1992
468.2'421 – dc20   91-10240   CIP

ISBN 0 521 42123 3 hardback
ISBN 0 521 26987 3 paperback

Contents

Vocabulary

Authors' acknowledgements

Information for this book has all been collected from, or checked with, native speakers, and we are particularly indebted to the following for their generous giving of time and effort in this respect: José-Luis Caramés Lage, Teresa de Carlos, Carmen Melbourne, María Amparo Ortolá Pallás, Gaspar Pérez Martínez, Alfonso Ruiz, and innumerable students from the University of Valencia.

Richard King and Sara Palmer read the entire manuscript with an eye, respectively, to US English usage and Latin-American Spanish usage, and made many additions and amendments.

We would also like to thank Annie Cave, Peter Ducker, Julia Harding and Ann Mason of Cambridge University Press for their care, thoughtfulness and imaginativeness in bringing this material to the printed page.

Abbreviations and symbols

Note Spanish alphabetical order is followed in lists of Spanish words and expressions.

ADJ	adjective
Am	Latin-American Spanish
Arg	Argentine Spanish
Brit	British English
Eng	English
esp	especially
f	feminine
fig	figurative(ly)
gen	general
ger	gerund (eg Spanish **hablando**)
indic	Indicative
inf	infinitive (eg Spanish **hablar**)
intr	intransitive
IO	indirect object (**a**^{IO} introduces the indirect object)
lit	literal(ly)
m	masculine
Mex	Mexican Spanish
N	noun
pej	pejorative
Pen	Peninsular Spanish
PERS	personal (**a**^{PERS} denotes the Spanish personal **a**)
pl	plural
PP	past participle
PREP	preposition
R1★, R1, R2, R3	markers of register (see pp 3–4)
refl	reflexive
sb	somebody
sg	singular
sth	something
subj	Subjunctive
tr	transitive
US	US English
usu	usual(ly)

= is used in ch. **20** to indicate that the subject of the main verb in a sentence is the same as that of the dependent infinitive.

⟦!⟧ is used to indicate forms which are in regular use but which might be considered 'incorrect' in an examination.

> † indicates that more information about the word or expression is to be found in another section. Look up the word or expression in the Spanish word index at the end of the book.

Glossary

The page number in brackets indicates where the term is first used.

adjectival complement (p 271) 'Copular' verbs, such as English *be*, Spanish *ser* and *estar*, are usually considered to take **complements** rather than objects. When these verbs are followed by an adjective, this may be termed an adjectival complement.

affective suffix (p 111) Spanish suffixes (eg *-ito*, *-illo*, *-ón*, etc) which have an emotive or ironic overtone.

agent (p 188) The performer of a verbal action: in an active sentence, the agent is typically the subject of the sentence; in a passive sentence, the agent (the subject of the corresponding active sentence) is usually introduced by *by* in English and by *por* in Spanish.

anteriority (p 235) An earlier stage.

aspect/aspectual (p 234) Relating to the way in which an action or state is viewed: continuous, repeated, within fixed limits, etc. The difference between the Imperfect and the Preterite in Spanish is usually thought of as an aspectual difference, though several other verb-forms, and especially the **periphrastic** (see overleaf) verb-forms, have aspectual values.

cognate (p 19) English and Spanish have many words which are very similar in form, often because they are derived from the same Latin or Greek word (eg *sinfonía/symphony*). Such matching words are known as cognates. They are very often essentially the same or similar in meaning, but sometimes they are different in meaning (**deceptive cognates**). Deceptive cognates present hidden difficulties for the learner; and so they are traditionally known as 'false friends' (*falsos amigos*).

complement (p 202) See **adjectival complement**. The term complement is also used in this book to denote a sentence, infinitive or gerund which acts as the object or subject of a verb.

deceptive cognate (p 19) See **cognate**.

demonstrative (p 162) A pronoun or adjective which expresses proximity to or remoteness from the speaker (eg English *this*, *that*, Spanish *este*, *ese*, *aquel*).

diminutive (p 6) A form which indicates smallness (eg Spanish *-ito*).

disjunctive pronoun (p 280) A (personal) pronoun which is free-standing or the object of a preposition (eg Spanish *yo*, *mí*, *usted*). (In English all personal pronouns are effectively disjunctive.)

ellipsis (p 3) Partial expression of an idea.

falso amigo (p 19) See **cognate**.

gerund (p 15) In this book, the term is used to refer to the English verb-form in -*ing* and the Spanish verb-form in -*ndo*.

homonyms (p 46) Words that sound the same although spelt differently, eg English *bow* and *bough*. Standard Peninsular Spanish has relatively few homonyms, but Latin-American Spanish has a number as a result of the absence of a *c*/*s* contrast, eg *cima*/*sima*.

implied subject (p 202) A subject which is not explicitly stated by a noun, pronoun or the verb ending, but which is necessarily understood (eg in *Prometí hacerlo*, 'I promised to do it', *o*, 'I', is not only the expressed subject – through the verb ending – of *prometer* but also the implied subject of *hacer*).

instrument (p 212) The thing employed to carry out an action: eg *hammer* is the instrument in *I hit the nail with the hammer*.

interference (p 19) The influence of one's native language on the foreign language one is learning.

metaphorical (p 163) Relating to metaphor, a figure of speech in which a thing, person or action is referred to as something else which it resembles in some way (eg *a pain in the neck* = 'a (person who is a) nuisance'). The boundary between 'literal' and 'metaphorical' meaning is sometimes difficult to determine because words often change or extend their meaning metaphorically (eg *a shark* = 'a rogue').

mood/modal (p 234) Relating to the attitude which certain verb-forms express (eg *Serán las diez*, 'It must be ten o'clock', expresses supposition; *Me da un kilo de patatas*, 'Can I have a kilo of potatoes', expresses a kind of command). Traditionally, forms such as the Indicative, Subjunctive, etc have been distinguished on the basis of mood, but it is clear that modal meanings can be expressed by most verb-forms.

paronym (p 32) A word similar in form to another (in the same language).

periphrastic (p 240) Relating to paraphrase, and used here of structures in which a number of words are involved (eg *voy a ir* is described as a periphrastic future by comparison with the simple future *iré*).

pleonastic (p 268) Redundant, not strictly necessary (from the point of view of meaning).

positive imperative (p 281) An imperative which is not negated (eg English *Do it!*, Spanish *¡Hazlo!*).

topic (p 173) The most important element in a sentence in terms of interest to the speaker or hearer – usually what is being currently talked about.

truncation (p 3) Shortening or curtailing (of a sentence or word).

Introduction

The Spanish language today

Spanish is currently spoken by nearly 300 million speakers, and is the official language (or the principal official language) of some 20 nations. It is also widely spoken in the USA. The areas of Central and South America over which Spanish is spoken are enormous: for example, Mexico City is as far from Buenos Aires as Beijing is from London. It can quickly be appreciated that the task of providing a guide to contemporary Spanish usage is a daunting one. The linguistic consequence of the diffusion of Spanish in the New World has been the appearance of many local differences in speech; and within Spain itself there are also considerable differences from region to region. At the same time, speakers from different areas are generally mutually intelligible, and the written language, while sometimes reflecting differences in speech, maintains a high degree of uniformity.

Local variety and standard

The Spanish standard is generally taken to be the speech of Old Castile. Yet it is immediately apparent that, if that is the case, more than 95% of Spanish speakers do not speak 'standard' Spanish! In practice, the speech of any national capital or important regional centre tends to create its own 'standard'. An Andalusian or a Latin-American speaker would only under rather unusual circumstances adapt his or her speech and usage to that of the Castilian 'standard'. It is important to realize that in the Spanish-speaking world there is no stigma attached to speaking a local variety of the language. This can be rather difficult for English (as distinct from British) people to appreciate, since standard English is not identifiable with any local variety, but is rather the variety of a particular socio-economic class; furthermore, speakers of the English standard tend to look down on speakers of local varieties of English (or dialects, as they are often categorized).

Peninsular and American Spanish

A major distinction is often drawn in reference works between Peninsular and American Spanish, and it is one which will be used in this book. However, it is in some ways misleading. First, although 'American Spanish' does have a number of general features, it is not really a homogeneous variety of Spanish: there are many differences in pronunciation and usage from region to region, even within the same country. Secondly, so-called 'American' features are often

The Spanish speaking world: countries where Spanish is spoken, with an estimate of the numbers of native speakers

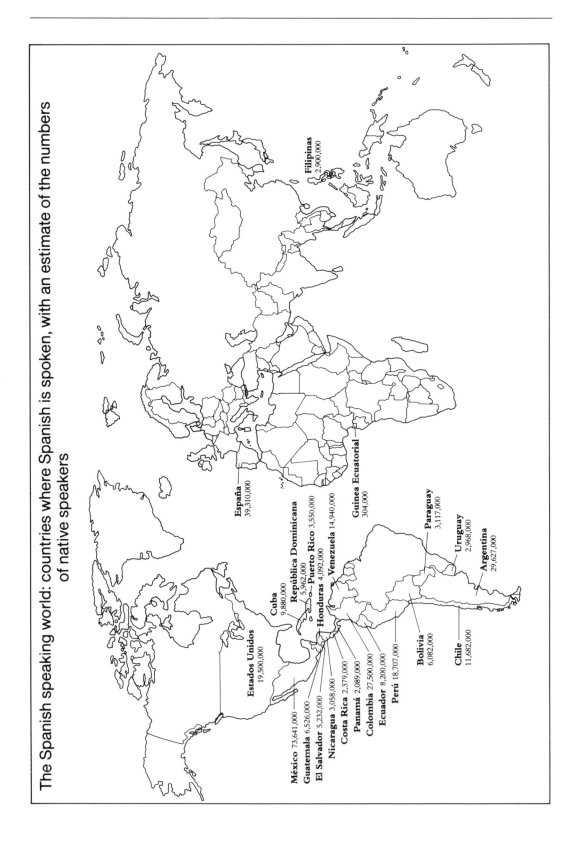

Filipinas 2,900,000

España 39,310,000

Guinea Ecuatorial 304,000

Cuba 9,880,000
República Dominicana 5,962,000
Puerto Rico 3,550,000
Honduras 4,092,000
Venezuela 14,940,000

Paraguay 3,117,000
Uruguay 2,968,000
Argentina 29,627,000

Estados Unidos 19,500,000

México 73,641,000
Guatemala 6,526,000
El Salvador 5,232,000
Nicaragua 3,058,000
Costa Rica 2,379,000
Panamá 2,089,000
Colombia 27,500,000
Ecuador 8,200,000
Perú 18,707,000

Bolivia 6,082,000
Chile 11,682,000

shared with local varieties of Peninsular Spanish, particularly with Andalusian.

Forms marked 'Am' (American) in this book are in fairly wide use in Spanish-speaking Latin America. Only the most striking of more localized usages (eg Arg, Mex, Chile) are given, and are marked accordingly. Forms marked 'Pen' (Peninsular) are not used commonly in Latin America. It is beyond the scope of this book to reflect finer details of local usage.

Register

Speakers employ a number of styles of language depending upon the situation in which they find themselves; even a single individual may regularly oscillate between a number of such styles, or registers. A formal letter to an unknown person, a chat in a bar, a scientific report – all call for quite different words and constructions, even pronunciations. Three basic registers, described below, are distinguished in this book.

R1

Informal, colloquial usage, characterized by slang expressions, vulgarisms, restricted range of general vocabulary and 'loose' syntax involving repetition, ellipsis and truncation. Vocabulary used is often ephemeral, since fashions in slang words come and go. R1 would probably be used in a conversation between family or friends. A special sub-register of R1 would be adults talking to children.

Within R1 we also distinguish R1★. R1★ words and expressions are those generally considered indecent or 'taboo'; they often sound odd on a foreigner's lips, and a foreigner should in any case be very circumspect about using them. We make no apology for including such terms – they are among the most frequent in colloquial Spanish, and must be understood!

R2

The 'neutral' register: careful, educated speech, characterized by the absence of slang and vulgarisms, and by the use of full sentences. This is also the informal written language register. R2 would probably be used by a teacher and pupils in a classroom, in a radio or TV news bulletin, in a letter to a penfriend.

R3

Formal written language, characterized by 'officialese', archaic expressions, rarer vocabulary and often very convoluted syntax. There are many identifiable sub-registers, such as those used in journalistic writing, financial reports, legal documents, business letters, formal lectures and addresses, etc.

This division between the three registers is rough and ready, but it seems unnecessarily complicated to refine it more. In any case, a piece of Spanish and its constituent elements rarely fall into one register exclusively; and the vast majority of words and constructions (unmarked for register in this book) can be used in all registers.

'Correctness'

There are two senses in which Spanish can be 'correct'. The first relates to a foreigner's command of the language – if what is said is unacceptable to a native speaker in any variety or register, then it is 'incorrect'. The second relates to the native speaker's attitude to his own language, and is a more complex matter. In both the popular and educated mind, there is a close association between 'correctness' and the 'standard' language: features of local varieties and registers which differ from the 'standard' are deemed in this way 'incorrect' even though they are regularly used by native speakers. The Real Academia Española has traditionally been recognized, even outside Spain, as the guardian of 'correctness' in Spanish. The Academia has generally been sensitive to changes in the language, although inevitably many judgments on 'correctness' are essentially arbitrary.

The problem in presenting contemporary Spanish usage is that sometimes actual usage does not conform to the accepted view of what is 'correct' in this second sense. This is a book with a primarily pedagogical purpose, to be used by learners who will take examinations, and since the assessment of what is 'correct' is sometimes stricter in examinations than it is among Spanish speakers, we indicate such 'incorrectness' by the sign $\boxed{!}$. Forms and structures marked in this way exist and are in regular use, but are not to be copied by foreign learners.

Passages illustrating register and local variety

Example of R1* (Peninsular Spanish): *Un encuentro en la calle*

Pepe:	¡Eh! ¡macho!
Paco:	¡Joder! No te había visto.
Pepe:	¿Qué hay? ¿Cómo te va?
Paco:	Psa, tirando… ¿y tú?
Pepe:	Yo, me voy tirao tirao.
Paco:	Joder, ya será menos.
Pepe:	Quita, tío, quita, que estoy de una mala leche.
Paco:	Bueno, a ver qué coño te pasa ahora.
Pepe:	Que me se ha escacharrao el coche.
Paco:	No, ¿otra vez?
Pepe:	Otra vez, joder, otra vez.
Paco:	Mucha pasta.
Pepe:	Coño, no sé…jo, pero como sea mucha lo tiene claro porque hasta que yo no cobre el mecánico no ve un duro.
Paco:	Va, tío, olvídate. Esta noche me voy al cine con unas tías. ¿Te vienes?
Pepe:	Hum, no sé. Tengo faena.
Paco:	Pero que coño vas a tener tú faena. Pero, macho, de que vas. Si es esta noche.

$\boxed{!}$ These forms are in regular use but might be considered 'incorrect' in an examination.

Pepe: Es que…no sé, joder, no sé.
Paco: Pero coño, tío, si es un rato. No me seas cabrón.
Pepe: Jo, tío, que plomo eres, pero ¿no te he dicho que no lo sé?
Paco: ¿Que tienes plan?
Pepe: Te pego un telefonazo.
Paco: Bueno, bien… Pero…jo, es que esta noche no ceno en casa.
Mira, yo te llamo y te digo lo que hay.
Pepe: Hecho.
Paco: Sobre las nueve.
Pepe: Muy bien, tío, nos vemos.

The R1★ forms are: the expletives †¡**joder!** and its shortened form †¡**jo!** (= *damn*, lit = *fuck*) and (**qué**) †**coño** (= *shit*, lit = *cunt*); the nouns †**tías** (familiarly = *girls*, though also = *whores* or *prostitutes*) and †**cabrón** (lit = *billygoat*, but familiarly = *bastard*), and the expression **de una mala leche** (= *in a foul mood*).

Apart from these R1★ forms, the conversation has many features which are typical of R1.

Pronunciation is not systematically represented here, but the dropping of **–d–** in the **–ado** ending is widespread in speech, and is often shown in the representation of R1, as here, in the spelling of spoken forms (**tirao, escacharrao**).

Vocabulary and idioms

¿qué hay?/te digo lo que hay	*how are things?/I'll tell you what's happening*
(voy) †tirando/me voy †tirao	*I'm OK/things have got me down*
escacharrarse	*to break down*
†pasta	*money*
ser (un) plomo	*to be a bore*
tener †plan	*to have a girlfriend, have sth arranged (with sexual connotations)*
pegar un telefonazo	*to give a call*

Forms of address

- †**macho**, †**tío**, used between men (= *mate, man*).

Syntax

- **me voy tirao/¿te vienes?** In R1 the reflexive form of verbs of motion is frequently used. The reflexive has an 'intensive' value by comparison with the non–reflexive form (see **29.4**).

- **a ver** A very common imperative form (see p 208).

- **me se** ⌷ **ha escacharrao** In standard Spanish, **se** is always the first pronoun in a sequence (see **28.1**).

- †**como sea mucha** = **si es mucha**

- †**hasta que yo no** ⌷ **cobre** NOTE: the meaning is *until I'm paid*; the **no** has no literal negative value. It is not used in standard Spanish.

- **pero/(de) que/es que/si** are all used in R1 as connectives.

- †**bueno** is an R1–2 connective which introduces the answer to a question.

- **te llamo y te digo** The Present tense is used instead of a Future (**te voy a llamar, te llamaré**). See **23.1**.

- Note the elliptical nature of many of the remarks, eg **mucha pasta** =
  eso te va a costar...

Example of R1 (Mexican Spanish): *¡Pélale! Que vamos al cine*

Mario:	Ahorita vengo.
Teresa:	¿Adónde vas?
Mario:	A la farmacia. Necesito unas hojas de afeitar y un rastrillo nuevo. ¿Se te ofrece algo?
Teresa:	No, gracias. Ah, sí, se me pasaba: unas curitas y un paquete de algodón.
Mario:	¿Es todo?
Teresa:	Creo que sí. No te tardes, gordo. ¿Ya viste la hora? La película empieza al cuarto para las seis.
Mario:	¿Al cuarto? Tenemos que salir en diez minutos.
Teresa:	Ya lo sé. ¡Pélale!
Mario:	¿Y Susana? ¿No iba a lanzarse con nosotros?
Teresa:	Sí, dijo que se caería por aquí como a eso de las cinco.
Mario:	Tu cuatita es la impuntualidad con patas. Dale un fonazo a su chamba para ver si ya salió.
Teresa:	Bueno, pero ¡vuélale! Ya sabes que a esta hora el tráfico se pone de la cachetada.
Mario:	Sí, y para acabarla de amolar está lloviendo. ¡Qué lata! ¡Vuelvo!

It is in R1 that specifically regional forms of Spanish are most frequent and apparent.

Vocabulary and idioms	curitas	*plasters (Pen parches, esparadrapo, tiritas)*
	rastrillo	*razor (Pen maquinilla de afeitar; Pen rastrillo = rake)*
	¿se te ofrece algo?	*do you want sth?*
	al cuarto para las seis	*at a quarter to six (**Pen** a las seis menos cuarto)*
	¡pélale!/¡vuélale!	*get a move on!*
	†lanzarse	*to go, come*
	se †caería por aquí	*she would come here*
	cuatita (*diminutive of* cuata)	*friend*
	impuntualidad con patas	*lateness personified*
	fonazo (*cf* ch. **4**)	*phone call*
	chamba	*job, work*
	se pone de la cachetada	*it's getting hopeless*
	para acabarla de amolar	*and for good measure*

Form of address

- †**gordo**, used between men. (Women would consider **gorda** an insult: they use **flaca**.)

Syntax

- †**ahorita/cuatita** Diminutives which are widespread in R1 but especially common in American Spanish. In the very common **ahorita** the diminutive is attached to an adverb rather than to a noun.

- **no te †tardes** Reflexive corresponding to Peninsular non-reflexive. See **29.3**.

- **¿ya viste la hora?** The Preterite is used extensively in Mexican Spanish where a Perfect would be expected in the standard language.

- **en diez minutos** Pen **dentro de diez minutos**.

Example of R1 (Peninsular Spanish): *Cosas de críos*

Carmen:	¡María! ¡Chissst! ¡María!
María:	Huy, ¡hola! ¿Qué tal? ¿Cómo estáis?
Carmen:	Bien, estupendamente, ¿y vosotros?
María:	Regular, tengo a la nena pachucha.
Carmen:	Sí, chica, ¿qué le pasa?
María:	No, nada, que está muy costipada.
Carmen:	¡Vaya, mujer!
María:	Vino ayer el médico y le dio un jarabe porque se ha pasado toda la santa noche tosiendo.
Carmen:	No te preocupes, cosas de críos.
María:	Oye, pero es que me asusté un poco. Bueno, y tú ¿qué me cuentas?
Carmen:	Pues me voy al cole a hablar con el tutor de Carlos.
María:	Sí, pero ¿es que tenéis algún problema?
Carmen:	Mira, no sé. Dice que el niño no atiende, que está en la higuera. Vamos, que pasa de las clases, y oye, con siete años es un poco pronto para empezar a pasar de nada, ¿no te parece?
María:	Y él ¿qué te dice?
Carmen:	¿Carlos? Bueno, según él, pues que se cansa, que se aburre, que le duele la cabeza.
María:	¿Habéis mirado si tiene algo en la vista?
Carmen:	Ya lo creo. Mira, pasó las revisiones médicas en el colegio y yo lo llevé además al oculista y el niño ve perfectamente.
María:	Se le pasará.
Carmen:	Eso espero porque ya me tiene frita.
María:	Huy, mira la hora que es. Me voy, que se me ha hecho tardísimo.
Carmen:	Me he alegrado mucho de verte.
María:	Yo también. A ver si pasáis un rato a tomar café, o mejor aún veniros a cenar.
Carmen:	Venga, a ver si encuentro un rato y nos vemos tranquilamente. Yo te llamo.
María:	Muy bien. ¡Que no se te olvide! Recuerdos a tu marido.
Carmen:	Gracias, igualmente.

The R1 features covered in 'Un encuentro en la calle', and also found here, are not dealt with a second time.

Pronunciation	• **Costipada** [!] reflects a common R1 pronunciation of standard †**constipada**.

Vocabulary and idioms	estupendamente	*fine*
	†nena	*little girl (= niña)*
	pachucha	*sick*
	toda la santa noche	*santa is an expletive (= all the blessed night)*

críos	*kids*
¿qué me cuentas?	*what's your news?*
el cole	*abbreviation for* el colegio. *Such shortenings are typical of R1.*
está en la higuera	*he's in a world of his own*
†pasa de las clases	*he's not interested in the classes*
¡ya lo †creo!	*I should say so!*
me tiene frita	*I'm sick and tired of him*

Forms of address ● **chica**, **mujer**, used to women by women or men.

Interjections ● This exchange has many interjections (ch. **11**): **¡chissst!**, **¡huy!**, **¡vaya!** (invariable for person), **¡oye!**, **¡mira!**, **¡venga!** (invariable for person).

Syntax ● Note the 'highlighting' of the pronoun (see **18.2**) in **tú ¿qué me cuentas?** and **él ¿qué te dice?**

Example of R1 (Argentine Spanish): from *Don Segundo Sombra*, by R. Güiraldes

Y yo admiraba más que nadie la habilidad de mi padrino que, siempre, antes de empezar un relato, sabía maniobrar de modo que la atención se concentrara en su persona.

– Cuento no sé nenguno – empezó –, pero sé de algunos casos que han sucedido y, si prestan atención, voy a relatarles la historia de un paisanito enamorao y de las diferencias que tuvo con un hijo'el diablo.

– ¡Cuente, pues! – interrumpió un impaciente.

"– Dice el caso que a orillas del Paraná donde hay más remansos que cuevas en una vizcachera, trabajaba un paisanito llamao Dolores.

"No era un hombre ni grande ni juerte, pero sí era corajudo, lo que vale más."

Don Segundo miró a su auditorio, como para asegurar con una imposición aquel axioma. Las miradas esperaron asintiendo.

"– A más de corajudo, este mozo era medio aficionao a las polleras, de suerte que al caer la tarde, cuando dejaba su trabajo, solía arrimarse a un lugar del río ande las muchachas venían a bañarse. Esto podía haberle costao una rebenqueada, pero él sabía esconderse de modo que naides maliciara de su picardía.

"Una tarde, como iba en dirición a un sombra'e toro, que era su guarida, vido llegar una moza de linda y fresca que parecía una madrugada. Sintió que el corazón le corcoviaba en el pecho como zorro entrampao y la dejó pasar pa seguirla."

– A un pantano cayó un ciego creyendo subir a un cerro – observó Perico.

– Conocí un pialador que de apurao se enredaba en la presilla – comentó Don Segundo – y el mozo de mi cuento tal vez juera'e la familia.

"– Ya ciego con la vista'e la prenda, siguió nuestro hombre pa'l río y en llegando la vido que andaba nadando cerquita'e la orilla.

"Cuando malició que ella iba a salir del agua, abrió los ojos a lo lechuza porque no quería perdir ni un pedacito."

– Había sido como mosca pa'l tasajo – gritó Pedro.

– ¡Cáyate, barraco! – dije, metiéndole un puñetazo por las costillas.

In this very famous novel of gaucho life, Güiraldes is concerned to reproduce the everyday language of the gauchos, and although written as long ago as 1926 it is still a convenient text with which to illustrate features of rural Argentine speech.

Pronunciation

- The **-d-** of the **-ado** ending is regularly lost: **enamorao, llamao, aficionao, costao, entrampao, apurao.**

- **d-** is also lost from **de** following a vowel: **hijo'el diablo, sombra'e toro, juera'e, vista'e, cerquita'e.**

- **f-** is pronounced very lightly, almost like English *h*, and is represented by **j-**: **juerte, juera.**

- **-ll-** is pronounced as **-y-**: **cáyate.**

- **i** and **e**, especially when unstressed, may be switched by comparison with the standard language: **dirición (dirección), nenguno (ninguno), corcoviaba (corcoveaba), perdir (perder).**

- **para** is **pa**; in **pa'l** the **e** of the article is also lost.

Vocabulary

- There are many Americanisms:

†paisano	*peasant (= compatriot; civilian in Pen)*
polleras	*skirts, and hence women (= chicken coop; petticoat in Pen)*
rebenqueada	*whipping (rebenque = whip)*
maliciar	*suspect*
barraco	*pig (here a term of abuse)*

- Some words denote local things:

vizcachera	*burrow of a vizcacha (type of rodent)*
toro	*a cabin made of branches*
zorro	*not fox here, as in Pen, but skunk*
pialador	*a gaucho skilled in using a lasso; the action is pialar*
tasajo	*jerked meat (ie meat left to dry in the sun)*

Syntax

- Diminutives are widespread here, not only with nouns (**paisanito, pedacito**) but also with other parts of speech (**cerquita**).

- **en llegando** This has only an R3 value in Pen (= *on doing sth*).

NOTE ALSO **naides (nadie)** and **vido (vio)**, which are found archaically in Pen, and **ande (donde)**, which is found dialectally.

Example of R2 (Peninsular Spanish): *Una agencia de viajes*

Señora:	Buenos días.
Señor:	Buenos días. Un segundo, si es tan amable, y en seguida le atiendo.
	…
	Sí, dígame.
Señora:	Me gustaría que me diera información sobre los vuelos de fin de semana a Londres.
Señor:	¿Para qué fecha tiene prevista la salida?
Señora:	Bueno, pues lo más pronto que fuera posible.
Señor:	Vamos a ver, ahora lo consulto con el ordenador… Me temo que no va a ser posible para este fin de semana. Está todo completo.
Señora:	¿Y en el siguiente?
Señor:	Sí, aquí sí que hay asientos libres. ¿Cuántos?
Señora:	Cuatro, por favor.
Señor:	Muy bien, hasta aquí de acuerdo. Vamos con los horarios. El avión sale el jueves a las trece veinte y tiene la llegada prevista a las catorce treinta a Heathrow.
Señora:	¿El traslado al hotel corre por nuestra cuenta?
Señor:	No, habrá un autobús de la agencia esperándoles a su llegada para llevarles al hotel y les volverá a recoger el domingo para trasladarles al aeropuerto.
Señora:	¿Y el horario de la vuelta?
Señor:	Salida a las catorce diez, llegada a las diecisiete veinte, hora local. ¿Ha estado ya en Inglaterra?
Señora:	No, es la primera vez.
Señor:	Ya sabe que tiene que personarse en los mostradores de Iberia con hora y media de antelación al horario de salida. Puede facturar hasta veinte kilos sin recargo por equipaje.
Señora:	¿Cuánto alcohol puedo llevar?
Señor:	¿Sin tenerlo que declarar se refiere?
Señora:	Sí, claro.
Señor:	Son dos litros de vino o uno de coñac o whisky y puede pasar hasta doscientos cigarrillos.
Señora:	Bueno, pues yo creo que ya está todo, muchísimas gracias.
Señor:	A usted, señora, y buen viaje.

This exchange contains some of the connectives which, as we have already seen, are typical of conversation in R1 (†**pues**, †**bueno**). But the speech of the people in this more formal situation is free of expletives and interjections, and is less prone to ellipsis. The need to be polite requires polite formulae, circumlocution, and vocabulary which is sometimes shared with R3.

Polite formulae

● **si es tan amable**, **me gustaría que** + Past Subjunctive, **me temo que** (see **26.3**), **por favor** (used much more infrequently than Eng *please*), **muy bien**, **muchísimas gracias**, **a usted**.

Circumlocution

● **¿Para qué fecha tiene prevista la salida?** = **¿Cuándo piensa salir?**; **¿corre por nuestra cuenta?** = **¿tendremos que pagarlo nosotros?** Such expressions 'soften the blow' of more direct expressions in making enquiries and giving information. Note how often expressions involving nouns rather than the corresponding verbs are used: **salida**, **llegada**, **traslado**, **horario**, **recargo**.

Vocabulary shared with R3 and 'officialese' in tone	● †**atiendo**, **personarse**, **facturar**, **se refiere**.
Form of address	● **Usted** is used here (but see **28.4**), and the formal **señora**.

Example of R2 (Latin-American Spanish): from *Resumen*, Caracas, 12 August 1984

Resumen:
Ha sorprendido mucho a la opinión, que un miembro de una organización que aparece ante la opinión pública como anticastrista, viaje a La Habana, y además los comunicados de la ODC (Organización Diego Cisneros) dicen que los ataques que ellos dicen recibir, son porque ellos son anti-comunistas. Luce como contradictorio que por una parte están furibundos, y por otra parte una persona que no vea nada de malo ir a Cuba con sus ejecutivos en su avión.

Oswaldo Cisneros:
Todos mis viajes han tenido un carácter familiar. Para nadie es un secreto que mi padre y la familia de mi padre eran cubanos y que yo tengo familiares allá a los que he tenido la oportunidad de ayudar en alguna forma cada vez que he ido. Cualquier otra interpretación es maliciosa y además en cierta forma risible. Ya aclaré con bastante amplitud en mi rueda de prensa del jueves, lo relativo a estos viajes. Sin embargo, como parece que a pesar de ello todavía flota en su mente alguna duda, déjeme aclarar que todos los días, por así decirlo, viajan a Cuba personajes de todo plumaje y color, sin que hasta el momento se haya tratado de estigmatizar a nadie por ello. Yo soy venezolano, demócrata y hombre de negocios, además que estoy convencido que únicamente se puede prosperar en un clima de libertades que definitivamente no existen en Cuba. Me fui a La Habana en mi último viaje y realicé allí una de mis habituales reuniones con mis ejecutivos, muchos de los cuales también tenían familiares allá. Sin embargo, el principal motivo de esta reunión en La Habana no fue la visita que cada quien hizo a miembros de su familia, sino mi interés más personal de que estos hombres, que manejan miles de trabajadores en sus operaciones diarias pudieran ver con sus propios ojos las proporciones del paraíso soviético-castrista. Lo demás es pura especulación.

The participants in this interview express themselves carefully: there is little difference between this style of speech and informal written style. Conversational connectives are few (we may note the emphatic **déjeme aclarar que** and the explanatory **por así decirlo**).

Syntax

- Complete sentences are used; there is no ellipsis. While some of the sentences are quite long, their structure is not unduly complex.

- **una persona que no vea nada de malo…** The 'highlighting' of **una persona** (which properly belongs to the **que** clause) is typical of conversational style (see **18.2**).

- **estoy convencido que** Omission of **de** is frequent in Am R2.

Form of address

- **Usted** is used; but notice how the interviewer refers indirectly to Cisneros (**un miembro de una organización**, **una persona**).

Vocabulary

- A minority of words used are perhaps more typical of R3 than R2:

†luce como contradictorio	*it seems contradictory*
furibundos	*furious*
con bastante amplitud	*at sufficient length*
†realicé una reunión	*I held a meeting*

Style

- Cisneros uses a metaphor (**flota en su mente alguna duda**) and his description of Cuba as **el paraíso soviético-castrista** is ironical.

Example of R2–3 (Peninsular Spanish): *Intercambio de casas*

Albacete, 7 de febrero de 1986

Distinguido Sr:

Me es muy grato dirigirme a Vd. en relación con el posible cambio de uso de mi casa de Lo Pagán, con otra de Nottingham de un colega suyo.

Mi propuesta consiste en brindarle el alojamiento durante un mes completo, cualquier mes del año, aunque junio, julio, agosto o septiembre son preferibles por hacer mejor tiempo. Junio y septiembre son más tranquilos, mientras que julio y agosto son más animados en el lugar.

A cambio, su amigo me solucionaría mi alojamiento familiar en Nottingham para 15 días de julio o agosto, pero para una familia de un matrimonio con ocho hijos.

Lo Pagán es un pequeño pueblo situado en la costa del Mar Menor que es un pequeño mar comunicado con el Mediterráneo. Hay playas muy tranquilas en el mismo pueblo (a menos de 150 m. de la casa).

La casa tiene 4 dormitorios, un cuarto de estar espacioso, una cocina de buen tamaño, donde se puede comer, un cuarto de baño, un aseo, una terraza amplia a la calle y un tendedero interior. Está amueblada sin lujo, pero con comodidad suficiente para uso vacacional. Son utilizables hasta 11 camas, una de matrimonio. Su situación es muy buena para mi gusto, en el centro del pueblo viejo, junto a la iglesia, un cine al aire libre, con comercio muy próximo de todas clases. Hay aeropuerto (el de Murcia–Cartagena) a menos de 5 km.

Le envío alguna documentación gráfica de la situación del piso y de la propia finca.

Quedo a su disposición para aclararle cualquier detalle, espero sus noticias sobre el respecto y le saludo muy atentamente.

Formal letters, even from one private individual to another, as on this occasion, tend to include many R3 features.

The form of address used on paper is **usted**, since the correspondents do not know each other, even though it is likely that they would soon be using the **tú** form in conversation on meeting.

Letter-writing formulae	●	Distinguido Sr	*Dear Sir*
		dirigirme a Vd.	*to write to you*
		espero sus noticias	*I look forward to hearing from you*
		le saludo (muy) atentamente	*yours sincerely*
Other polite formulae	●	me es muy grato	*I am pleased to*
		quedo a su disposición para	*I would be glad to*
Other R3 vocabulary and expressions	●	mi propuesta consiste en	*this is my proposal*
		†brindar	*to offer*
		solucionar	*to solve (lit); here, to provide*
		mi alojamiento familiar	*accommodation for my family*
		uso vacacional	*holiday use*
		documentación gráfica	*here, a map or diagram*
		sobre el respecto	*concerning it*

Notice how the register lowers to R2 as the owner describes the village and house in a style which he might well use in careful speech.

Example of R2–3 (Peninsular Spanish) from *San Manuel Bueno, Mártir*, by M. de Unamuno

Ahora que el obispo de la diócesis de Renada, a la que pertenece esta mi querida aldea de Valverde de Lucerna, anda, a lo que se dice, promoviendo el proceso para la beatificación de nuestro don Manuel, o, mejor, san Manuel Bueno, que fue en ésta párroco, quiero dejar aquí con-signado, a modo de confesión y sólo Dios sabe, que no yo, con qué destino, todo lo que sé y recuerdo de aquel varón matriarcal que llenó toda la más entrañada vida de mi alma, que fue mi verdadero padre espiritual, el padre de mi espíritu, del mío, el de Ángela Carballino.

De nuestro don Manuel me acuerdo como si fuese de cosa de ayer, siendo yo niña, a mis diez años, antes de que me llevaran al colegio de religiosas de la ciudad catedralicia de Renada. Tendría él, nuestro santo, entonces unos treinta y siete años. Era alto, delgado, erguido, llevaba la cabeza como nuestra Peña del Buitre lleva su cresta, y había en sus ojos toda la hondura azul de nuestro lago. Se llevaba las miradas de todos, y tras ellas los corazones, y él al mirarnos parecía, traspasando la carne como un cristal, mirarnos al corazón. Todos le queríamos, pero sobre todo los niños. ¡Qué cosas nos decía! Eran cosas, no palabras. Empezaba el pueblo a olerle la santidad; se sentía lleno y embriagado de su aroma.

Creative writers often manipulate register for stylistic purposes. In this passage, for instance, there is a striking oscillation of R3 and R2. To R3 belong the 'legalistic' resonances of the first paragraph, consistent with the deposition–like nature of its content: **esta mi querida aldea, que fue en ésta (aldea) párroco, quiero dejar consignado**. To R2 belong the parenthetical insertions of the fictitious authoress, which lessen the formal tone: **a lo que se dice, o, mejor…a modo de confesión, y sólo Dios sabe, que no yo.**

Other stylistic devices which belong to literary R3

- Imagery: **llevaba la cabeza como nuestra Peña del Buitre lleva su cresta**; **había en sus ojos toda la hondura azul de nuestro lago**; **traspasando la carne como un cristal**; the village began to **olerle la santidad**, and was **embriagado de su aroma**.

- In the first paragraph, mention of the writer's name, Ángela Carballino, is deliberately delayed so that it appears in the position of maximum stress, and hence of maximum surprise to the reader. **Mi** and **mío** are used in successive phrases which build expectations until the 'key' is given.

- The deliberately unexpected juxtaposition of **varón** and **matriarcal**.

Example of R3 (Latin-American Spanish): from *El Comercio*, Quito, 2 October 1985

Plausible desde todo punto de vista que la política agropecuaria implantada por el Gobierno tenga como metas específicas la producción de alimentos básicos para satisfacer la demanda interna y la diversificación y mejoramiento de los productos de exportación. Con lo primero se solucionará el problema de la escasez y el déficit de varios alimentos que inciden en la malnutrición de los ecuatorianos. Con lo segundo, el país obtendrá nuevos ingresos por concepto de la venta al exterior de frutos y materias primas que tengan acogida foránea por su calidad.

En ambos casos se estará contribuyendo positivamente a incrementar e incentivar la actividad agrícola que se vio afectada por varias circunstancias. Era necesario otorgarle toda la importancia que el campo ha tenido siempre en nuestro desarrollo y en el autoabastecimiento. Por desgracia, el Ecuador tuvo que convertirse en importador de productos que hasta poco tiempo atrás exportaba, con grave detrimento para la economía nacional.

Con satisfacción se ha venido anunciando que varios países se hallan interesados en adquirir flores, frutas frescas, hortalizas, varios elaborados, fibras y otros elementos utilizados en la agroindustria. Continuamente se suscriben convenios que tienen como fundamento estas transacciones e, igualmente, se buscan mercados para ampliar la venta de los mismos. Es así como ya se ha emprendido en la diversificación de cultivos cuya adquisi-

ción se ha asegurado. En este sentido, el trabajo rural con-
seguirá su justa recompensa que ha sido uno de los factores
que venían desalentándolo.

As expected in a higher register passage, there is little in this text that
is specifically Latin American, with the exception of the expression
hasta poco tiempo atrás (= Pen **hasta hace poco tiempo**).

Vocabulary

- The subject matter of the editorial necessitates a good deal of
  specialized R3 vocabulary from the field of economics:

agropecuaria	*agricultural*
demanda	*demand*
de exportación	*for export*
déficit	*deficit*
ingresos	*income*
actividad agrícola	*farming*
desarrollo	*development*
autoabastecimiento	*self-sufficiency*
importador	*importer*
elaborados	*produce*
agroindustria	*agricultural industry*
convenios	*agreements*
transacciones	*transactions*
mercados	*markets*

- More general R3 vocabulary:

implantada	*introduced*
†mejoramiento	*improvement*
†incidir en	*to affect*
por concepto de	*by means of*
foránea	*foreign (= en el extranjero)*
incentivar	*a neologism: to give incentive to*
†otorgar	*to grant*
detrimento	*detriment*
†se hallan	*(they) are (find themselves (lit))*
ampliar	*to widen*
†emprender en	*to embark upon*

Syntax

- Sentences are of medium length, though they contain many relative
  clauses. Many sentences are introduced by an adverbial phrase: **en
  ambos casos**, **por desgracia**, **con satisfacción**, **continuamente**,
  en este sentido.

- The first sentence has no main verb: (**Es**) **plausible...que...**, an R3
  affectation.

- Journalistic and academic writing in Spanish is making increasing use
  of verbal paraphrases. Here **venir** + gerund (= *to keep doing sth*, see
  24.5) is used: **se ha venido anunciando**, **venían desalentándolo**.
  Use of this aspect makes the meaning of the verb more immediate
  and hence more distinctive.

1 Misleading similarities

1.1 Similar form – different meaning

There are many pairs of Spanish and English words which are very similar in form (ie cognate) but which are different in meaning. Such pairs are known as deceptive cognates or '**falsos amigos**'.
Interference from one language to another is likely in these cases, and it is worthwhile giving special attention to them.

'Falso amigo'	**English equivalent**	**English cognate**	**Spanish equivalent**
actual	*present*	actual	*verdadero, auténtico,* †*real*
†**adjudicar algo a uno**	*to award sth to sb*	to adjudicate	†*juzgar, decidir*
agenda	*diary, appointment book*	agenda	*orden (m) del día (although agenda, an anglicism, is sometimes used)*
agonía	*death pangs*	agony (gen)	*dolor (m) intenso, angustia*
agonizar	*to be in the death throes*	to agonize (over sth)	*ponderar (algo) mucho, sufrir un suplicio (por algo)*
artífice (m)	*artist, craftsman*	artifice	*artificio,* †*estratagema (m)*
†**atender a**^PERS **uno**	*to attend to sb, to pay attention to sb*	to attend sth	†*asistir a algo*

---

† More information about these words or expressions may be found in other sections. Use the Spanish word index to find the page numbers.

R1★ vulgar or indecent
R1 informal, colloquial
R2 neutral
R3 formal, written
See also p 3.

The gender of nouns is only given where it is not predictable from the principles given in ch. **16**.

Am Spanish-speaking Latin America
Arg Argentina
Mex Mexico
Pen Peninsular Spain
See also p 1.

'Falso amigo'	English equivalent	English cognate	Spanish equivalent
barraca	*hut, cabin*	barracks	*cuartel (m)*
†**bizarro**	*gallant, generous*	bizarre	†*extraño, estrafalario*
bordar	*to embroider*	to board sth (transport)	†*embarcarse en algo,* †*subir a algo*
		to board (= to give board and lodging to) (tr)	*hospedar*
		to board (= to take board and lodging) (intr)	*hospedarse*
		to border on sth	†*lindar con algo*
carpeta	*file, folder*	carpet	*alfombra*
casual(mente)	*fortuitous(ly), accidental(ly)*	casual(ly)	*despreocupado (de manera despreocupada)*
cava	*digging, cultivation*	cave	*cueva, caverna*
†**cavilar**	*to ponder*	to cavil	*objetar, poner peros a (R1)*
collar (m)	*necklace*	collar	*cuello*
comando	*terrorist gang (but increasingly = commando, terrorist)*	commando	*integrante, miembro de un comando*
		command	†*orden (f), mando*
comediante/-anta	*actor, actress*	comedian	†*cómico*
comodidad	*comfort,* BUT *in Am = commodity*	commodity	*artículo de consumo, mercancía*
compás (m)	*beat, rhythm*	compass	*brújula*
concreto	*concrete (ADJ),* BUT *in Am = concrete (N)*	concrete (N)	*hormigón (m) (Pen)*
conductor (m)	*driver*	conductor	*Brit cobrador (on bus), US = revisor; director (orchestra); pararrayos (lightning)*
†**confidencia**	*confidential remark*	confidence (abstract)	†*confianza*

'Falso amigo'	English equivalent	English cognate	Spanish equivalent
consistente	*solid, thick (of sauce, etc)*	to be consistent with	*estar de* †*acuerdo con, ser consecuente con*
		to be consistent	*ser coherente*
estar †**constipado**	*to have a cold*	to be constipated	*estar estreñido*
†**contestar**	*to answer*	to contest	†*negar, poner en tela de juicio*
†**coraje** (R2–3)	*anger*	courage	*valor*
dato	*piece of information* (***datos** (pl) = data*)	date	*fecha (day); dátil (m) (fruit)*
decepción	*disappointment*	deception	†*engaño*
†**departir** (R3)	*to converse*	to depart	†*salir,* †*marcharse*
desgracia	*misfortune*	disgrace	*vergüenza,* †*escándalo (event); deshonra (moral state);* BUT *fall into disgrace = caer en (la) desgracia*
deshonesto	*indecent, lewd*	dishonest	*falso, tramposo*
desmayo	*fainting fit, faltering*	dismay	*consternación*
destitución	*dismissal*	destitution	*indigencia,* †*miseria*
†**deteriorar** (tr)	*to damage*	to deteriorate (intr)	*deteriorarse*
disgustado	*upset, annoyed*	disgusted	*enfurecido, repugnado, avergonzado*
disgustar	*to displease*	to disgust	*repugnar, dar asco a*
disgusto	*displeasure*	disgust	*aversión,* †*asco*
†**divisar**	*to catch sight of*	to devise	†*inventar*
editar	*to publish*	to edit	*redactar (un artículo); corregir*
editor	*publisher*	editor	*redactor;* †*jefe,* †*director (head of paper)*
embarazada (ADJ f)	*pregnant*	embarrassed	*confuso*
embarazar	*to make pregnant; to obstruct, to hinder*	to embarrass	*desconcertar, turbar*

'Falso amigo'	English equivalent	English cognate	Spanish equivalent
encuesta	*enquiry, survey*	inquest	**encuesta judicial**
engrosar (intr)	*to get fat, to swell*	to engross (tr)	**absorber**
ermita	*hermitage*	hermit	**ermitaño**
escuálido	*weak, skinny*	squalid	†**sucio**, †**asqueroso**
eventual	*fortuitous, contingent, possible*	eventual	†**final**
†**éxito**	*success*	exit	**salida**
extenuar	*to weaken*	to extenuate	**atenuar, disminuir**
fábrica	*factory*	fabric (cloth)	**tela, tejido**
fastidioso	*annoying*	fastidious	**puntilloso, quisquilloso**
fracaso	*failure*	fracas	†**riña, gresca**
gala	*full, best dress; elegance, variety show*	gala	†**fiesta, verbena** *(celebration);* †**competición,** †**certamen** *(m)* *(contest)*
genial	*full of genius, inspired*	genial	**afable, cordial**
†**gracioso**	*funny*	gracious	**afable, cortés**
guerrilla	*guerrilla warfare; guerrilla band*	guerrilla (fighter)	**guerrillero**
†**hábil**	*skilful, clever; fit*	able	†**capaz**
†**honesto**	*decent, modest*	honest	**franco, sincero;** †**honrado**
hostal (m)	*simple hotel*	hostel	**residencia** *(for students),* **albergue** *(m)* **juvenil** *(youth hostel)*
†**ignorar**	*not to know, to be ignorant of*	to ignore	**no** †**hacer caso,** †**pasar por alto**
incidencia	*repercussion, consequence;* BUT = *incidence in a technical sense, eg* **ángulo de incidencia**	incidence	**frecuencia, ritmo**

'Falso amigo'	English equivalent	English cognate	Spanish equivalent
ingenuidad	*frankness*	ingenuity	*ingeniosidad*
injuria	*insult, outrage*	injury	*herida, lesión*
[†] **injuriar**	*to insult*	to injure	[†]*herir, lesionar*
instancia(s)	*legal process*	instance	[†]*ejemplo*
intoxicar	*to poison*	to intoxicate	*embriagar*
jubilación	*retirement, pension*	jubilation	*júbilo*
[†]**largo**	*long*	large	[†]*grande, extenso, amplio*
lectura	*reading*	lecture	[†]*conferencia (formal), clase (f) (gen in university, etc)*
librería	*bookshop*	library	*biblioteca*
librero	*bookseller*	librarian	*bibliotecario/a*
maniático	*peculiar, cranky*	maniac	*loco, demente, maníaco*
marrón	*brown*	maroon	*carmín*
[†]**miseria**	*poverty, squalor*	misery	*sufrimiento, pena, aflicción*
[†]**molestar**	*to trouble, to annoy*	to molest	*importunar*
moroso	*slow, sluggish; slow to pay*	morose	*hosco, malhumorado*
motorista (m/f)	*motorcyclist*	motorist	*conductor (de coche)*
muslo	*thigh*	muscle	*músculo*
notorio	*well known*	notorious	*de mala fama*
obsequioso	*obliging, helpful*	obsequious	*servil*
[†]**paisano/a**	*fellow countryman; civilian; BUT in Arg = peasant, farm worker*	peasant	*campesino/a*
parangón (m)	*comparison, similarity*	paragon	[†]*dechado*
pariente/a	*relation, relative*	parent	*padre or madre (must be specified)*
		parents	*padres*

'Falso amigo'	English equivalent	English cognate	Spanish equivalent
†**pasar un examen**	*to take an exam*	to pass an exam	†*aprobar un examen*, BUT *aprobar en (francés)*
patético	*moving (pathetic (lit))*	pathetic (in pejorative sense)	*horrible, malísimo*
petróleo	*petroleum oil; paraffin, kerosene*	Brit petrol US petrol	*gasolina nafta*
petulancia	*insolence, daring, vanity*	petulance	*malhumor (m), displicencia*
pinta	*look; stain; pint*	paint	*pintura*
predicamento	*prestige*	predicament	*apuro, situación difícil*
†**pretender que…; pretender hacer algo**	*to claim that . . .; to try to do sth*	to pretend	†*fingir, aparentar*
†**prevenir**	*to foresee; to warn*	to prevent	†*impedir,* †*evitar*
†**pupilo/a**	*lodger; ward (legal)*	pupil	*alumno/a*
†**querella**	*complaint, charge*	quarrel	*riña,* †*disputa*
†**quitar**	*to take away; to take off*	to quit	†*dejar, salir de*
†**realizar**	*to put into effect*	to realize	*darse cuenta de*
recolección	*act of harvesting, gathering*	recollection	*recuerdo*
reconvenir	*to reprimand*	to reconvene	*convocar de nuevo*
refrán (m)	*proverb, saying*	refrain	*estribillo*
reino	*kingdom*	reign	*reinado*
relevancia	*importance*	relevance	*pertinencia*
relevante	*outstanding; important*	relevant	*pertinente, relacionado con*
renta	*(unearned) income*	rent	*alquiler (m)*
reportar	*to check, to restrain; to bring (advantage or benefit)*	to report	*relatar; denunciar*

'Falso amigo'	**English equivalent**	**English cognate**	**Spanish equivalent**
resumir	*to sum up, to summarize, to abridge*	to resume	*reanudar*
[†]**sensible**	*sensitive*	sensible	[†]*sensato*
simpático	*nice*	sympathetic	*compasivo;* [†]*comprensivo*
stárter (m)	*choke*	starter	*botón (m) de arranque*
suburbios (pl)	*poor district of town, slum*	suburb	[†]*barrio (exterior),* [†]*afueras (pl)*
suceso	*event; accident, crime*	success	[†]*éxito*
[†]**tabla**	*plank, board*	table	*mesa*
transpirar	*to sweat*	to transpire	[†]*ocurrir,* [†]*suceder*
verso	*line of poetry*	verse (poetry) verse (= stanza)	*poesía estrofa*

1.2 Similar form – partly similar meaning

Sometimes the meaning of Spanish and English cognates does correspond in part, but either the Spanish or English word has additional meanings. These are called partial deceptive cognates.

Spanish	**English lookalike**	**Notes**
[†]**abandonar**	*to abandon*	ALSO = to leave in a more general sense, eg **abandonó la casa a las ocho**
[†]**abusar**	*to abuse (= to take advantage of)*	BUT to abuse (= to insult) = **insultar,** [†]**injuriar**

| [†] More information about these words or expressions may be found in other sections. Use the Spanish word index to find the page numbers. | R1* vulgar or indecent
R1 informal, colloquial
R2 neutral
R3 formal, written
See also p 3. | The gender of nouns is only given where it is not predictable from the principles given in ch. **16**. | Am Spanish-speaking Latin America
Arg Argentina
Mex Mexico
Pen Peninsular Spain
See also p 1. |

Spanish	English lookalike	Notes
†**acusar**	*to accuse*	ALSO = to reveal, to highlight
alterar	*to alter, to change*	ALSO = to upset
amasar	*to amass (fig) (amasar una fortuna = to amass a fortune)*	(i) BUT to amass (lit) = **amontonar** (ii) ALSO = to knead
aplicación	*application (= diligence; putting into practice)*	BUT application (for a job) = †**solicitud**
†**apostar**	*to post, to station*	ALSO = to bet
†**aprobar**	*to approve*	ALSO = to pass (an exam)
argüir	*to argue (= to present a case)*	BUT to argue (= to quarrel) = **discutir, reñir**
argumento	*argument (= plot of book, etc; line of reasoning)*	BUT argument (= quarrel) = †**debate** (m), **discusión**, †**riña**
armar	*to arm*	ALSO = to cause (quarrel, scandal, noise) (R1)
asesor	*assessor (= adviser)*	BUT assessor (= valuer) = **tasador, persona que valora, que aconseja**
†**asistir**	*to assist (R2–3)*	ALSO = to be present
atestar	*to attest*	ALSO = to pack, cram
audiencia	*audience (eg with Pope)*	(i) ALSO = lawcourt (ii) BUT audience (in theatre, etc) = **público, espectadores**
†**bárbaro**	*barbarous*	ALSO = tremendous (R1)
†**bomba**	*bomb*	ALSO = pump
†**cámara**	*room, chamber (R3)*	ALSO = camera; inner tube (tyre); cavity (medical)
†**camping** (m)	*camping (as in hacer camping = to go camping)*	ALSO = campsite
canciller (m)	*chancellor*	(i) BUT chancellor of a university = **rector**, Chancellor of the Exchequer = **Ministro de Hacienda**, Lord Chancellor = **Presidente (de la Cámara de los Lores)** (ii) BUT in Am = Foreign Minister (iii) ALSO = member of diplomatic staff

Spanish	English lookalike	Notes
†**carácter** (m)	*character (= characteristics; letter, etc)*	BUT character (in play, etc) = **personaje**
caramelo	*caramel*	ALSO = sweet (gen)
carta	*card (= playing card)*	ALSO = letter
†**cartel** (m)	*cartel (commercial)*	ALSO = poster
carrera	*career*	ALSO = race; course (education)
caución (R2–3)	*caution, wariness*	ALSO = deposit, security (for sth)
†**celebrar**	*to celebrate*	ALSO = to hold (**celebrar una reunión** = to hold a meeting)
cínico	*cynical*	ALSO = brazen, shameless
colegio	*college*	ALSO = school
colonia	*colony (gen)*	ALSO = estate (of houses)
†**competencia**	*competence*	ALSO = competition; competitiveness
†**competición**	*competition (sport, business)*	BUT gen sense of competitiveness = **rivalidad**, †**competencia**
compromiso	*compromise*	ALSO = engagement (gen commitment, and agreement to marriage); awkward situation
concentración	*concentration*	ALSO = camp, headquarters (for sports team)
†**conferencia**	*conference*	ALSO = lecture; long-distance call
†**consentir**	*to consent*	ALSO = to allow, to permit, to tolerate
controlar	*to control*	ALSO = to check, to verify
copia	*copy (of paper etc)*	BUT copy (of book) = **ejemplar** (m)
†**coraje** (m)	*courage*	ALSO = anger
†**corresponder**	*to correspond*	ALSO = **corresponder a uno** = to be incumbent upon sb
criatura	*creature*	ALSO = baby
curso	*course*	ALSO = year of school, university
charlatán (m)	*charlatan (N)*	ALSO as ADJ = talkative
defectivo	*defective (eg verb)*	BUT defective (gen) = **defectuoso**
†**demandar**	*to demand (R3 only)*	ALSO = to sue

Spanish	English lookalike	Notes
†**denuncia**	*denunciation*	ALSO = report (legal)
departamento	*department*	ALSO = compartment (train) ALSO in Am = flat, apartment
dependencia	*dependence*	ALSO = outbuilding
derivar	*to derive*	ALSO = to drift, to deviate
†**destino**	*destiny*	ALSO = destination
diario	*diary, appointment book*	ALSO = daily paper
diligencia	*diligence*	ALSO = piece of business; pl = formalities, enquiries
dirección	*direction*	ALSO = management (of firm); address
dormitorio	*dormitory*	ALSO = bedroom (gen)
duelo	*duel*	ALSO = grief
†**editorial** (m)	*editorial, lead article*	BUT (f) = publishing house
efectivamente	*effectively*	ALSO = indeed, sure enough
elemental	*elemental*	ALSO = elementary
emoción	*emotion*	ALSO = excitement
†**énfasis** (m)	*emphasis*	ALSO = bombast
†**equipo**	*equipment*	ALSO = team (sport), brigade (eg fire)
escenario	*scenario*	ALSO = stage (theatre), setting (gen)
escolar (m/f)	*pupil, student*	BUT scholar (= researcher, learned person) = **estudioso**
†**espacio**	*space*	ALSO = programme (on TV, radio)
estación	*station*	ALSO = season (of year)
estudio	*study (act of studying, written or composed study); studio*	BUT study (= room) = **despacho**, †**oficina**
evolucionar	*to evolve, to develop*	ALSO = to move around (fish in pool, cars on track, dancers in hall, etc)
expediente (m)	*expedient, device*	ALSO = proceedings (law), records of a case; pupil's record (school)
experimentar	*to experiment with, to try out, to test*	ALSO = to experience, to undergo

Spanish	English lookalike	Notes
explotar	*to exploit*	ALSO = to explode
extravagante	*extravagant*	ALSO = odd, strange
†**facilitar**	*to facilitate*	ALSO = to provide
†**falta**	*fault, error*	ALSO = lack, need
fallo	*failure, weakness*	ALSO = judgment, sentence
familiar	*familiar*	ALSO = pertaining to the family
figura	*figure (shape; person)*	(i) ALSO = face (ii) BUT figure (= number) = **cifra**, **número**
firma	*firm, small business*	ALSO = signature
fiscal	*fiscal (ADJ)*	ALSO as N = prosecutor, attorney
†**forma**	*form, shape*	ALSO = manner, way (of doing sth)
formación	*formation*	ALSO = training, education
formal	*formal, serious*	ALSO = reliable, earnest
†**frase** (f)	*phrase (restricted:* ***frase hecha** = set* *phrase)*	(i) ALSO = sentence (ii) BUT phrase (gen) = **locución**, **expresión**
†**historia**	*history*	ALSO = story
ilusión	*illusion*	ALSO = hope; excitement, thrill
†**importante**	*important*	ALSO = considerable (sum, loss)
inconsciente	*unconscious*	ALSO = thoughtless, careless
†**inquirir**	*to enquire (= to* *enquire into)*	BUT to enquire (gen) = †**preguntar**
instruir	*to instruct*	ALSO = to inform; to investigate (legal) (**instruir una causa** = to investigate a case)
integrar	*to integrate*	ALSO = to form, to make up
†**intervenir**	*to intervene*	ALSO = to take part; to operate on (medical); to freeze (assets)
invertir	*to invert*	ALSO = to invest
irracional	*irrational*	ALSO = incapable of reasoning (eg animals)
laguna	*lagoon, lake*	ALSO = gap, lacuna (in knowledge, etc)
licencia	*licence, permission,* *permit*	ALSO = leave (military)

Spanish	English lookalike	Notes
†**lima**	*lime (fruit); lime tree*	(i) ALSO = file (tool) (ii) BUT (quick)lime = †**cal** (f)
linterna	*lantern*	ALSO = (electric) torch, flashlight
localidad	*locality, location*	ALSO = seat, ticket (eg theatre, sport)
manifestación	*manifestation*	ALSO = demonstration (eg political)
marcha	*march (military)*	ALSO = speed (of vehicle); gear (mechanical); trend, course of events
†**metálico**	*metallic (ADJ)*	ALSO as N = cash
†**monte** (m)	*mountain*	ALSO = woodland
†**ocupar**	*to occupy*	ALSO = to confiscate (police, customs)
óleo	*oil (for painting; ecclesiastical)*	BUT oil (for cooking, machinery) = **aceite** (m)
oportunidad	*opportunity*	ALSO = opportuneness
†**oposición**	*opposition*	ALSO in pl = competitive examination
particular	*particular*	ALSO = private (secretary, house, etc)
†**partir**	*to depart (R3)*	ALSO = to split, to divide, to break
pensión	*pension, allowance*	ALSO = accommodation with meals
†**percibir**	*to perceive, to notice*	ALSO = to earn, to receive (money)
petición	*petition*	ALSO = request (gen)
pieza	*piece (cloth, chess, music, etc)*	ALSO = part (mechanical) (eg **pieza de recambio** = spare part); room (R2–3); play (theatre)
plausible	*plausible*	ALSO = praiseworthy
†**precioso**	*precious*	ALSO = pretty, lovely (esp R1)
preservativo	*preservative*	ALSO = contraceptive
pretencioso	*pretentious, presumptuous, showy (Pen)*	ALSO in Am = vain, boastful
primitivo	*primitive, uncivilized*	ALSO = original (test, state)
proceso	*process*	ALSO = lawsuit, trial
†**procurar**	*to procure, to get hold of*	ALSO = to try
propaganda	*propaganda*	ALSO = advertising

Spanish	English lookalike	Notes
reactor (m)	*reactor*	ALSO = jet (plane or engine)
†**real**	*real, authentic*	ALSO = royal
referir	*to refer (ie sth to sb)*	ALSO = to tell (a story) (R3)
†**registrar**	*to register, to record*	ALSO = to search, to inspect
regular	*regular, normal*	ALSO = OK, all right (R1)
relaciones (pl)	*relations (= links)*	BUT relations (= relatives) = **parientes**, **familiares**, **allegados** (R3)
†**restar**	*as intr = to remain, to be left (R3)*	ALSO as tr = to take away, to deduct
†**rudo**	*rude (= rough)*	BUT rude (= uncouth, obscene) = †**grosero**, **obsceno**
salvar	*to save, to rescue*	ALSO = to cross, to get over, to overcome (barrier, obstacle, etc)
sentencia	*sentence (legal)*	BUT sentence (language) = †**frase** (f)
†**solicitud**	*solicitude, care, concern*	ALSO = request, application (for post)
solvente	*solvent, free of debt*	ALSO = reliable (of source)
†**suceder**	*to succeed (= to follow)*	(i) ALSO = to happen (ii) BUT to succeed (= to be successful) = **tener éxito**
sujeto	*subject (grammar)*	BUT (school) subject = **asignatura**; subject (of country) = **súbdito** ALSO = bloke, guy, chap (R1)
superioridad	*superiority*	ALSO = (higher) authority
†**susceptible**	*susceptible, capable (of)*	ALSO = sensitive, touchy
suspender	*to suspend, to hang*	ALSO = to fail (a candidate); (intr) to fail (an exam) (R1)
†**temporal**	*temporal (ADJ)*	ALSO = temporary, also as N (m) = storm, rainy weather
término	*terminus*	ALSO = term (language); boundary (of land)
tra(n)scendencia NOTE: similarly **tra(n)scendente** and **tra(n)scendental**.	*transcendence*	ALSO = importance, significance

Spanish	English lookalike	Notes
†**tronco**	*trunk (of tree; of body)*	BUT trunk (of car) = **maletero**; trunk (for packing) = **baúl** (m); trunk (of elephant) = **trompa**
turismo	*tourism*	ALSO = (saloon, sedan) car
†**vago**	*vague*	ALSO = lazy, slack (of person), unused (of thing)
verificar	*to verify*	ALSO = to check
violento	*violent*	ALSO = awkward, embarrassing (of situation), embarrassed (of people)

1.3 Similar form – similar meaning

Pairs or sets of words in a language may be easily confused because they are similar in form. Such pairs or sets are known as paronyms. Sometimes these similar words are related in meaning and sometimes they are quite unrelated. The following sets of words are related in meaning or are formed from the same root.

†**abertura** hole, gap, orifice	**apertura** act of opening, opening in the sense of inauguration (eg theatre, **las Cortes**)	**obertura** overture (music)

accesible accessible (place), approachable (person)	**asequible** obtainable, reasonable (price), feasible. Also widely used in the sense of approachable (person), though purists insist that only **accesible** has this meaning.
acepción sense, meaning	**aceptación** acceptance, approval
aclarar to clarify, to shed light on; ALSO to rinse (clothes), to dilute (liquid)	**esclarecer** to clarify

---

† More information about these words or expressions may be found in other sections. Use the Spanish word index to find the page numbers.

R1* vulgar or indecent
R1 informal, colloquial
R2 neutral
R3 formal, written
See also p 3.

The gender of nouns is only given where it is not predictable from the principles given in ch. **16**.

Am Spanish-speaking Latin America
Arg Argentina
Mex Mexico
Pen Peninsular Spain
See also p 1.

acompañante (m/f)
sb who accompanies (escort or musician)

compañero/a
companion, often in general sense of friend;
comrade (political)

---

aderezar
to prepare, to embellish

enderezar
to straighten, to set upright

---

†**adjudicar (algo a uno)**
to award (sth to sb)

ajusticiar
to execute, to put to death

---

afrentar
to affront, to insult

†**afrontar**
to place (two things or persons) face to face;
to confront (danger, difficulties)

---

†**agrupación**
association, gathering (political, religious,
etc)

†**grupo**
group (gen)

---

ambiente (m)
atmosphere, milieu, environment

ámbito
compass, field, range

---

ametralladora
machine gun

metralleta
sub-machine gun

---

amortiguar
to deaden noise, to cushion blow, to absorb
shock (**amortiguador** = shock absorber)

amortizar
to pay off (debt, loan, mortgage)

---

animado
lively, merry, anything with life or
movement

†**animoso**
courageous, energetic

---

aparición
act of appearing, eg publication of book,
apparition

†**apariencia**
outer appearance, impression

---

atracción
act of attracting (physical and
psychological); entertainment

atractivo
attractive quality, appeal

---

autobús (m)
local bus serving town

autocar (m)
coach, long–distance bus

---

autónomo
autonomous (gen)

autonómico
relating to regional autonomy in Spain

---

†**avance** (m)
advance (military or financial)

avanzada
advance party

---

baja
drop, fall (esp in price,
temperature, economic
activity); casualty (military)

bajada
act of lowering; slope,
descent

†**rebaja**
reduction (in sale)

---

balance (m)
act of swinging or rocking, tossing (boat);
balance sheet; hesitation

balanza
weighing scales; also in phrases **balanza de
comercio, de pagos**

†barba	**barbilla**	
beard, chin	chin (more common than **barba**)	

bocado	**bocanada**	**bocadillo**
mouthful (gen)	mouthful in sense of contents of mouth being swallowed or ejected; a puff of smoke (from mouth)	sandwich

†bravío	**†bravo**
wild, abandoned (of persons or countryside); suggests greater aggressiveness than **bravo**	brave, tough

busca	**búsqueda**
search, often pejorative, eg in relation to women, but **en busca de** = in search of	search (gen)

calidad	**cualidad**
quality (abstract and gen): **un vino de calidad**	individual quality: **tiene buenas cualidades**

cálido	**caliente**	**caluroso**
hot (climate); warm (colour)	hot, warm (drink, food)	warm (welcome, day)

†cambiar	**canjear** (R3)
to change, to exchange, to swap	to exchange, esp **canjear notas diplomáticas, prisioneros de guerra**

campamento	**†camping** (m)
camp (military, or for organized group)	campsite

canción	**†cantar** (m)	**cante** (m)	**†canto**
song	ballad: **el Cantar de los Cantares** = the Song of Songs	singing (Andalusia), eg **cante flamenco**, **cante jondo**	art of singing; edge or border of a place; rock, piece of stone

captar	**capturar**	**cautivar**
to attract (attention, esteem, interest, etc); to grasp, to catch (understand); to collect (eg water from a spring); to receive (eg radio programme)	to capture, to apprehend	to attract, to captivate

carreta	**carrete** (m)	**carretilla**	**carro**
long, low cart with two wheels	spool, reel (photography, fishing, sewing) (but in Am this is **carretel, carretón**)	wheelbarrow, shopping trolley; in Am = jaw	cart, tank; in Am = car

†caza	**cacería**
act of hunting; animals which are the object of hunting, game	hunting party; total of animals killed in hunt

celeste pertaining to the sky, eg colour		**celestial** heavenly (with spiritual connotation)

cemento cement	**cimiento** foundation of building; premise, principle of idea

central (ADJ) central, main	**céntrico** in or near the centre of a town

†**cerco** enclosure; rim; siege	**circo** circus	†**círculo** circle

cintura (see also **cinta**, **cinto** on p 47) waist	**cinturón** (m) belt, safety belt, girdle

color (m) colour	**colorido** colouring, degree of intensity of colour	**colorado** (ADJ) red

competer a uno to be within the competence, to be under the jurisdiction of sb	**competir** to compete

complementar to complement, to complete	**cumplimentar** to pay one's respects to, to congratulate	†**cumplir** (also with **con**) to fulfil, to comply with; **cumplir x años** = to reach the age of x, to have one's xth birthday

comprensible understandable	†**comprensivo** comprehensive, all-embracing; understanding (of person)

concejo/concejal (m) council/councillor	**consejo/consejero** counsel, advice/adviser, consultant

†**confianza en uno** confidence, trust in sb	†**confidencia** secret, item of confidence

consumar/consumación to complete, to consummate/consummation	**consumir/consumición** to consume, to eat, to use up, to burn (fuel)/meal or drink in a bar, restaurant

costo cost of a large project	**coste** (m) cost, price (gen)	**costa** cost in set expressions: **a costa de** at the expense of, **a toda costa** at all costs; pl = legal costs; coast

NOTE: a distinction between **costo** and **coste** is drawn by purists; but for practical purposes the two are synonymous.

creador (as N) the Creator; (as ADJ) creative (R3)	**creativo** creative

dedicación
act of dedicating (eg church); devotion (to subject, etc)

dedicatoria
(written) dedication (in book, etc)

---

desértico
pertaining to desert

desierto (ADJ)
deserted (of area, building, road, etc)

---

desfiladero
pass, gorge

†desfile (m)
procession, (military) parade

---

efectivo
effective (eg remedy); real (cf **en efecto**, in fact)

eficaz (R2)
effective (more gen than **efectivo**); efficient

eficiente (R3)
efficient

---

ejercer
to exercise (power); to exert (influence); to practise (a career, profession)

ejercitar
to exercise (a member of the body, skills)

---

emocionante
exciting, thrilling

emotivo
emotional, related to emotions

---

encajar
to fit (one thing into another); to let in (a goal); to dish out or to receive (a blow) (R1)

encajonar
to put and keep in a box (eg eggs for transport); to squeeze into a tight place

---

energético
related to fuel, energy

†enérgico
energetic

---

especia
spice

especie (f)
species, kind, sort

---

felicidad
happiness, good fortune; pl = congratulations (R3)

felicitación
congratulation, pl = congratulations

---

fundación
act of founding (eg **la fundación de Roma**); foundation in sense of organization (eg **la Fundación March**)

fundamento
basis on which sth is built, both concrete and abstract

---

gobernador
governor, usu in official capacity

gobernante (m/f)
anyone who governs, ruler

---

guarda (m)
watchman (of factory, building site, etc)

†guardia (m and f)
m = guard, policeman
f = guard, police as a group; custody, care

guardián (m)
custodian, keeper (in museum, etc)

---

†hilo
thread

†hilera
line, row

hilandero/a
person who spins (cotton)

---

†historia
story, history

historial (m)
record, survey of performance (of business, club, etc)

historieta
anecdote; comic strip

†**honesto**	†**honrado**	**honroso**	**honorable**
decent, decorous, modest, chaste	honest, upright	respectable, highly esteemed	honourable

honor (m)		**honra**	**honradez** (f)
honour (gen)		personal honour, self-esteem, reputation	honesty, integrity

incluido	**inclusive**	**incluso**
included (eg **el desayuno está incluido**)	inclusive (eg **hasta el día dieciocho inclusive**)	even (eg **todo el mundo puede ir, incluso los franceses**)

información	**informe** (m)	**informática**
information	report (on sth that has happened)	information science, computing

interrogación	†**interrogatorio**
question (eg **punto de interrogación** = question mark)	interrogation, questioning in court

invento	**invención**
invention, invented thing	invention (R3); imagination, inventiveness (R2)

liberar	**libertar** (R3)	**librar**
to free from physical restraint; to free from obligation	to free from physical restraint	to free from obligation; to rescue from danger

lucido	†**lúcido**
splendid, brilliant	lucid, clear (person, mind)

lujo/lujoso	**lujuria/lujurioso**
luxury/luxurious	lust/lustful

llama	**llamada**	**llamamiento**	**llamarada**
flame, blaze, passion; llama (animal)	call, knock on door	call (to arms, to strike)	sudden, short-lived blaze; sudden flush to face

media	**promedio**	†**medio**
mean (maths); mid-field (soccer); stocking	average	middle; medium; means

medicamento	**medicina**
medicine (drug)	study of medicine; cure in abstract sense (eg **una medicina amarga**)

†**medio** (ADJ)	**mediano** (ADJ)
half	average (in pejorative sense)

montañés (ADJ)
native of **la Montaña** in Cantabria

montañero (N)
mountaineer

montañoso (ADJ)
mountainous

montés (ADJ)
mountain-dweller

montaraz (ADJ)
wild

montuno (ADJ)
pertaining to **monte**; in Am = rustic

montuoso (ADJ)
hilly

---

†**monte** (m)
mountain; woodland

montaña
mountain, mountainous area

---

†**moral** (f)
morality, ethics, morale

moraleja
moral (of a story, etc)

---

movedizo
movable; unstable, loose; inconstant (fig)

movible
movable

móvil
mobile

conmovedor
moving (in psychological sense), poignant

---

oferta
offer in a shop, gift, bargain; offer to do sth

ofrecimiento
offer to do sth

†**ofrenda**
offering (in religious sense)

---

oficial
official (ADJ); official, officer (N)

oficioso
meddlesome, interfering

---

oficio
trade, profession

†**oficina**
office (= room, agency)

---

papa (m)
Pope

papá (m)
Daddy

---

parada
stop (eg bus stop); parade (military)

paradero
whereabouts; in Am = bus stop; train station

parado
unemployed (ADJ and N); stationary (ADJ)

parador
hotel run by state agency (Pen)

paro
unemployment

---

†**parte** (m)
message, report (eg **parte meteorológico**)

†**parte** (f)
part, share

parto
childbirth

---

párroco
parish priest

parroquiano
parishioner; regular customer

parroquia
parish, parish church; clientele

---

perjuicio
damage, harm

prejuicio
prejudice

---

pesca
fishing

pescado
fish when caught

†**pez** (m)
fish when alive

†**pisar**
to walk on; to walk off with (sth that sb else was hoping to have) (R1)

†**pisotear**
to trample on, to stamp on

---

†**plan** (m) (see also **plana, plano** on p 49)
plan, scheme; basis, arrangement

†**plano**
plane, level; plan, map (of city)

---

plantar
to plant; to throw out (R1); to curb (R1)

plantear
to pose (problem)

---

†**plato** (n)
plate

plató
set (cinema)

---

poder
power, authority; physical strength (R3)

poderío
dominion, supremacy; physical strength (R3)

potencia
power (= country); power of motor, machine

---

policíaco
used in a restricted number of contexts, eg **novela policíaca** = thriller (novel), **expediente policíaco** = police file

policial
related to the police (gen), eg **medidas policiales** = police measures

---

polvo
dust, powder

pólvora
gunpowder

polvera
powder compact

polvareda
polvero (Am)
cloud of dust

---

preparación
act of preparing; preparedness

†**preparativos** (pl)
preparations, preliminaries

---

†**presenciar**
to be present at, to witness

†**presentar**
to present (gen), to introduce sb

---

prodigio
prodigy, eg **niño prodigio** = child prodigy

pródigo
prodigal, lavish, eg **el hijo pródigo** = the prodigal son

---

proposición
proposition, proposal

propósito
aim, purpose

---

recepción
act of receiving; reception as ceremony; desk in hotel, etc

recibimiento
reception in moral sense, welcome

recibo
receipt (written)

---

respecto
respect = relation; in phrases such as **con respecto a**

respeto
respect, deference

---

retiro
withdrawal (money); retirement; quiet spot; retreat (religious)

retirada
retreat (military)

---

rodar
to roll, to travel; to shoot (film)

rodear
to surround

romántico
related to
Romanticism;
sentimental;
generous

romance
N = Romance
(language);
Castilian; verse form
comparable with
ballad
ADJ = Romance (of
languages)

románico
Romanesque,
Norman
(architecture);
Romance (of
languages)

romano
Roman

rumano
Rumanian

romanista
versed in Roman law or Romance languages

seco
dry

reseco
very dry; skinny

secretaria
female secretary

secretaría
secretariat

secundar
to second, to support

segundar
to do sth again; to finish second

semilla
seed

semillero
nursery (for plants); den (of vice)

†**sensato**
sensible

†**sensible**
sensitive; noticeable (change, increase, etc)

significado
meaning

significación (R3)
meaning, significance

†**sostener**
to maintain, to hold (lit and fig)

sustentar
to maintain economically

sueño
dream, sleep

ensueño
dream, fantasy

sugerencia
suggestion (gen), idea, invitation

sugestión
act of suggesting; = suggestion in **las
sugestiones del diablo**, **la sugestión
hipnótica**

†**tabla**
plank, board (large); table
(in mathematics, etc)

†**tablero**
plank (small), slat; board
(for chess, etc)

tablado
plank floor, esp stage

tarta
tart, often as dessert

torta
pie, anything that has been
kneaded

tortilla
omelette (Pen); maize/corn
pancake (Mex)

†**tempestad**
storm (lit and fig)

temporada
season, period, spell

†**temporal** (m)
spell of rough weather,
usually at sea

terreno
piece of land, field; terrain

terruño
native soil, homeland

tierra
land (as opposed to sea),
soil, earth; country

tratamiento (see also **trata**, **trato** on p 49) treatment (medical, chemical, etc); style of address, eg **tratamiento de tú**	†**trato** relationship between people; behaviour	**tratado** treaty; treatise
válido valid; strong	**valioso** valuable; powerful	†**valeroso** brave, valiant
votación act of voting; number of votes cast	**voto** vote (political); vow (religious); pl = wishes	

1.4   Similar form – different meaning

The following sets of paronyms are similar in form but unrelated in meaning.

abrasar to burn up, to parch		**abrazar** to embrace (sb, a cause); to seize (opportunity)	
acantilado cliff	**alcantarilla** sewer	**cantera** quarry	**cántaro** pitcher
alegar to allege, to plead		**allegar** to gather, to bring together; to add, to state in addition	
legar to bequeath	**ligar** to bind; to court, to pick up (R1)	**liar** to tie, to wrap, to roll; to die (R1)	
amagar to threaten		**amargar** to make bitter (lit and fig)	
aparejar to get ready (tr)	**aparear** to match up (tr)	†**aparecer** to appear, to come into sight	

---

† More information about these words or expressions may be found in other sections. Use the Spanish word index to find the page numbers.

R1*   vulgar or indecent
R1   informal, colloquial
R2   neutral
R3   formal, written
See also p 3.

The gender of nouns is only given where it is not predictable from the principles given in ch. **16**.

apuntalar
to prop up

apuntar
to aim, to point (gun); to point out, to point at; to note down; to prompt (theatre)

---

aterrar
to frighten

aterrizar
to land

---

atracar
to hold up (eg bank); to moor, to bring alongside; to stuff, to cram with food

atrancar
to bar (eg door); to clog (eg pipe), to jam

---

averiguar
to find out (address, time of train, etc)

averiar
to damage

---

bandeja
tray

bandera
flag

---

bronco
rough (surface), gruff (voice), rude (manner)

ronco
hoarse

---

cacharro
earthenware pot; useless object, old car (R1)

cachorro
puppy

cachondo (ADJ)
sexy

---

calar
to soak, to drench, to permeate

colar
to filter, to strain off (eg water from vegetables); to slip sth through (eg customs); to bleach

†**callar**
to be quiet

---

campana
bell

campaña
countryside (esp Am); campaign (gen)

campiña
open country, flat stretch of farmland

---

†**cana**
white, grey hair (usu pl)

†**caña**
reed, stalk, cane (of sugar), rod (for fishing); tall wine-glass, beer-glass

---

canon (m)
canon (music, Bible, etc)

†**cañón** (m)
tube, pipe, barrel (gun), canyon

canónigo
canon (religious)

---

†**cima**
peak

sima
abyss

---

ciudad
city, town

†**cuidado**
care

---

coro
chorus, choir

corro
ring, circle (of people)

---

crear
to create

†**creer**
to believe, to think

criar
to produce (eg of the earth); to nurture, to raise, to bring up, to educate (R1–2)

---

crepitar to crackle		**increpar** to scold	

cuna cradle (lit and fig)	**cuña** wedge; influence, influential person (R1)

derrocar to throw down; to demolish (building); to overthrow (government)	†**derrochar** to squander (money)	†**derrotar** to destroy (house, furniture), to ruin (clothes, health); to defeat, to rout (army)

dividir to divide	†**divisar** to make out, to descry

enjugar to wipe	**enjuagar** to rinse

†**escándalo** scandal, uproar	**escandallo** lead for sounding depth; process of determining cost and sale price of goods (commerce)

expresar to express (words, actions, etc) NOTE: French *exprimer* = to express.	**exprimir** to squeeze out

feraz (R3) fertile (only with *tierra*)	†**feroz** fierce

fundar to found	†**fundir** to fuse, to melt	**hundir** to sink (tr) (to sink (intr) = **hundirse**); to confuse, to dumbfound	†**hender** to cleave, to make one's way through (a crowd)

grabadora tape-recorder	**grapadora** stapler

†**jugar** to play (game)	†**juzgar** to judge

mentar to mention	†**mentalizarse** to decide	**mentir** to lie

†**negar** to deny	**anegar** to flood

pana corduroy	**paño** cloth (gen); duster, rag

†**pelo** hair	**piel** (f) skin, peel, fur

picar	**pinchar**	**pizcar**
to sting (of insect), to bite (of fish); to itch (of eyes, skin, etc); to burn (of sun); to punch (holes in paper)	to prick, to puncture (tyre); to eat **pinchos** (= snacks)	to pinch, to nip

rallar	**rayar**
to grate, eg **pan rallado**, **queso rallado**	to make a line on, to cross (out); to border on, eg **raya en lo fantástico**

remedar	**remediar**	**remendar**
to copy, to imitate	to remedy, to make good	to mend (usu clothes), to repair

sabana	**sábana**
savannah	sheet (on bed)

sauce (m)	**saúco**
willow	elder

semanario	**seminario**
weekly (paper)	seminary, seminar

sotana	**sótano**
cassock	basement, (bank) vault

tope (m)	**topo**
limit, eg **fecha tope** = deadline; collision; snag	mole (animal)

valla	**valle** (m)
fence, barrier, hurdle (athletics)	valley

1.5 Similar verb stem

The sets of words in this section each have the same or a similar verb stem. Such sets are especially liable to confusion.

alumbrar	†**deslumbrar**	†**vislumbrar**
to light up, to shed light on (lit and fig)	to dazzle (lit and fig)	to catch a glimpse of (lit and fig)

avalar	**avalorar**	**evaluar** (R2–3), **avaluar**, **valorar**, **valorizar**
to support, to endorse, to guarantee	to estimate; to encourage	to value, to price; **valorar** is the most common

†**caer**	**decaer**	**recaer**
to fall (gen); **caer en algo** (R1) = to understand sth	to decay, to decline (health, fortune), to flag (effort)	to fall again; to have a relapse (health), to backslide (criminal); often fig as in responsibility or advantage falling to sb

†**coger**	**acoger**	†**escoger**	**recoger**
to take hold of, to catch, to seize, to pick (fruit)	to welcome	to choose	to gather, to pick up (sth fallen), to collect (things and people, eg from station)

†**cortar**	**acortar**	**recortar**
to cut (gen)	to shorten length or duration of	to cut away excess; to cut out (eg from newspaper)

†**correr**	**descorrer**	†**recorrer**
(intr) to run (of water, person), to pass quickly (of time); to travel quickly (of car) (tr) to cover (distance); to draw (bolt, curtain)	to pull back (eg bolt, curtain)	to travel through (a place, country)

†**gastar**	†**desgastar**	†**malgastar**	**engastar**
to spend (money, time), to waste	to wear out, to wear away, to waste	to waste, to squander	to set (eg stone in ring)

†**llevar**	**conllevar**	**sobrellevar**
to carry, to transport, to take; to wear; to spend (time) (see **20.8** and **24.6**)	to bear, to suffer (with patience), to put up with (sb who is difficult)	to put up with; to help (sb else); to help (sb) through a difficulty

mantener	†**sostener**
to maintain (gen of a conversation, interview, etc); to hold up	to hold up (lit): more frequent in this sense than **mantener**

matar	**rematar**
to kill (person, time)	to finish off, to polish off (work, etc)

†**mover**	**conmover**	**conmocionar**
to move (tr) (physical)	to move (tr) (emotional)	to shock, to upset, to trouble

NOTE: to move (intr) = **moverse**.

†**negar (algo a uno)**	**denegar (algo a uno)**	†**renegar de algo**
to deny (sb sth)	to refuse, to reject; to deny (sb sth)	to renounce, to deny sth

NOTE: **negarse a hacer algo** = to refuse to do sth.

†**poner**	**componer**	**descomponer**	**recomponer**
to put; to lay (egg); to plant (bomb); (refl) to put on (clothes, play, etc)	to compose; to fix, to repair	to decompose (tr); to upset (order, tranquillity)	to fix, to repair

†**probar**	†**aprobar**	**comprobar**	**reprobar**
to prove, to test, to taste, to try (food)	to approve of; to pass (exam)	to check, to verify	to blame, to condemn

reglar	**regir**	**arreglar**
to rule (line); to make rules for; to regulate, to adjust	to rule (country), to run (business, college); to govern (grammar)	to arrange; to repair; to tidy up
reglamentar	**regular**	
to make rules for	to regulate	

†**seguir**	†**conseguir**	**perseguir**	**proseguir**
to follow, to carry on	to get, to obtain	to chase, to hunt, to persecute	to carry on, to continue (R3)

†**volver**	**revolver**	**devolver**
(tr) to turn round, to turn over; to give back (R1); to turn, to make, eg **eso lo volvió feliz** (intr) to return	to stir, to mess up, to disturb	to give back; to vomit

1.6   Words distinguished by gender

Because of its distinctive gender endings, Spanish does not have many words with the same form but different meanings (true homonyms). However, there are many pairs of words distinguished only by the **–o** and **–a** (and sometimes also **–e**) endings which are easily confused. These are known as gender paronyms.

1.6.1   Different gender – similar meaning

See also **16.10**.

acta	**acto**
minutes, record (of proceedings), often pl	action, deed, act (in play)

† More information about these words or expressions may be found in other sections. Use the Spanish word index to find the page numbers.	**R1*** vulgar or indecent **R1** informal, colloquial **R2** neutral **R3** formal, written *See also p 3.*	The gender of nouns is only given where it is not predictable from the principles given in ch. **16**.	**Am** Spanish-speaking Latin America **Arg** Argentina **Mex** Mexico **Pen** Peninsular Spain *See also p 1.*

ánima soul, spirit (as religious concept)	**ánimo** energy, courage, spirit (as quality)
banca banking (as system)	**banco** bank (as individual establishment); bench
†**banda** band, gang; band (music); strip, ribbon	†**bando** faction, party; edict; pl = banns (ie announcement in church of impending marriage)
†**barca** small boat (rowing, fishing, etc)	†**barco** boat (gen), ship, vessel
bolsa bag (gen); purse; stock exchange NOTE ALSO: **bolsillo** = pocket.	**bolso** handbag, bag (more stylish than **bolsa**)
†**caña** reed, stalk, cane (of sugar), rod (for fishing); tall wine–glass, beer–glass	**caño** pipe, jet
carga load to be carried; duty; charge (military and explosive) NOTE ALSO: **cargamento** = act of loading; shipment, cargo.	**cargo** burden (fig), responsibility
cerca hedge, fence	†**cerco** ring, hoop, rim; siege (BUT in Am = fence)
cesta basket (for shopping, waste paper)	**cesto** basket, usu larger than **cesta**; bore (R1)
cinta band, strip, ribbon	**cinto** leather or silk sash for waist
conducta conduct, behaviour	**conducto** conduit
†**cuba** cask, barrel	**cubo** cube; bucket, bin (for rubbish)
cuenca basin (geographical)	**cuenco** earthenware bowl; hollow (of hand, etc)
†**cuenta** account, bill, calculation; report (of event)	**cuento** story, tale; pl = troubles, upsets, tales, silly things (R1)
derecha right hand, right side, right wing (political)	**derecho** right (rightful claim), justice, law
emisora radio station	**emisor** transmitter

escala scale; stop (on air journey)	**escalo** scaling (**robo con escalo** = burglary)
fosa grave; depression in sea or on land	**foso** pit, hole, ditch
fruta fruit (what is eaten, on the table), also fig, eg **fruta prohibida** NOTE ALSO: **frutos secos** = dried fruits.	**fruto** fruit (gen, of trees and plants, and fig, eg **fruto de su labor**)
gimnasia gymastics	**gimnasio** gymnasium
†**gira** tour, trip (eg theatrical)	**giro** gyration, turn; trend (in events)
gorra cap with peak	**gorro** cap with no peak (eg swimming)
grada step, stair	**grado** degree
grana seed (of flower)	**grano** grain (cereals); particle (eg sand); pimple (on face)
helada frost	**helado** ice-cream
jarra jug NOTE: there are regional differences.	**jarro** pitcher
labia (R1) talkativeness	**labio** lip (lit)
madera wood, plank	**madero** beam, log
manta blanket, large shawl	**manto** cloak, gown
moda fashion, style	**modo** way, method; mood (grammar)
muñeca wrist; female doll, tailor's dummy	**muñeco** male doll: **muñeco de nieve** = snowman
papelera container for rubbish, waste-paper basket; desk; paper mill	**papelero** paper manufacturer, owner of shop selling paper, pens, books, etc

†**partida**
departure (R3); register, certificate (eg birth); game (chess, cards); party (eg hunting)

partido
party (political); game, match; advantage (eg **sacar partido** (**de algo**) = benefit (by sth))

pesa
weight (physical object placed on scales or pendulum of clock)

peso
weight (measurement); weighing scales

pimienta
pepper for seasoning

pimiento
sweet pepper (vegetable)

plana
sheet (of paper)

†**plano**
plane, level; map (of city)

punta
point, sharp end; touch, tinge

†**punto**
dot, speck; point in scoring or in discussion or in time or place; stitch (sewing)

rama
branch, bough (from trunk)

ramo
(small) branch (from another branch); bunch (of flowers); BUT NOTE: **Domingo de Ramos** = Palm Sunday.

†**rebaja**
reduction (in sale)

rebajo
recess (lit)

resta
subtraction (in arithmetic)

†**resto**
remains, remainder

ría
estuary (north-west coast of Spain)

río
river

suela
sole (of shoe); sole (fish)

suelo
ground, surface, floor(ing) (of house)

†**tormenta**
storm (lit and fig)

tormento
torment, anguish

trata
trade (esp **de esclavos**, etc)

†**trato**
relationship between people; behaviour

1.6.2   Different gender – different meaning

acera
pavement

acero
steel

arca
chest, box

arco
arch(way); bow (violin, archery)

†**barra**
bar, rail

barro
mud

baza
trick (at cards)

bazo
spleen

NOTE: **bazo/a** as ADJ = fawn, brownish.

†bola	**bolo**
ball, often solid, as in bowls or billiards	skittle
†bomba	**bombo**
bomb; pump	bass drum; exaggerated praise (R1)
braza	**brazo**
stroke, style (swimming)	arm
casa	**†caso**
house, home, business firm	case, instance; case (grammar); notice (eg **hacer caso a** = to notice)
casca	**casco**
bark (used in tanning); grape skins (after being trampled)	helmet (soldier, motor-cyclist); area of city (eg **casco antiguo**)
cigarra	**cigarro**
cicada	cigarette, cigar
†copa	**copo**
glass, goblet, cup, trophy	flake (snowflake, cornflake); small bundle of wool, etc, ready to be woven; top (of a tree)
cota	**coto**
contour, level	reserve (game, fishing); in Am = goitre
†cuadra	**cuadro**
stable (for all animals); in Am = block (of flats, houses)	square; pane (of glass); frame, picture
foca	**foco**
seal (animal)	focus, focal point
fonda	**†fondo**
tavern, small restaurant	bottom, background; fund
gama	**gamo**
hind (female deer); scale, range	buck (male deer)
grupa	**†grupo**
rump (of horse)	group (gen)
libra	**libro**
pound (weight, money)	book
†loma	**†lomo**
small hill	back (of animal)
llanta	**llanto**
metal rim of wheel	weeping, crying
manga	**mango**
sleeve (coat, shirt)	handle
marca	**marco**
brand, trademark; record (sport)	frame, framework

pala shovel, spade	**†palo** stick, post, mast
pata foot, paw (of animal); leg (of animal, furniture)	**†pato** duck
†plata silver; in Am = money	**†plato** plate, dish, course (of meal)
plaza public square; place (eg in car-park); job; fortress, fortified town (as **plaza fuerte**)	**plazo** period of time, time limit; periodic payment (**a plazos** = on instalments)
puerta door, gate	**puerto** port; pass (in mountains)
puesta PP of **poner**, and used in many of the senses of this verb: **puesta en marcha** = starting (of engine), **puesta en escena** = staging (of play), etc	**†puesto** place, position; job, post; stall
†pupila pupil (of eye); ward (legal)	**†pupilo** lodger; ward (legal)
†rata rat NOTE ALSO: **ratón** (m) = mouse.	**rato** short time
raya line, streak (on paper, stone, sand, etc); boundary, limit; parting (hair); crease (in trousers)	**rayo** ray, beam of light; (flash of) lightning; thunderbolt
rodilla knee	**rodillo** roller, rolling pin
seta mushroom	**seto** fence, hedge
sigla symbol, abbreviation, acronym	**siglo** century
tira strip (of paper, cloth, etc)	**tiro** throw, shot (military, sport)
†trama woof (weaving); plot (literary), intrigue	**tramo** section, stretch (eg of road); flight of steps
traza layout (architecture); appearance (of person, often pejorative, eg **mala traza** = shabby appearance)	**†trazo** line, stroke; boundary

tuna	**†tuno**
student music group	member of a **tuna**; rascal (R1)
vela	**velo**
wakefulness, vigil; candle; sail; pl = snot (R1)	veil

2 Fields of meaning – vocabulary extension

This section looks at the vocabulary of a number of general fields of meaning. Choice of these fields has been motivated partly by the richness of Spanish vocabulary in certain areas of meaning, and partly by the rather different divisions of meaning which Spanish and English often make. The information is presented in diagrammatic form, with the most general Spanish word (if there is one) usually at the top of the diagram. This method of presentation reveals the structure of vocabulary within each field more clearly and more memorably than is possible in a traditional dictionary. The information in this section may be used in order to build up a wider and more finely tuned vocabulary. The material presented here may be approached either via the English title of each diagram (arranged for ease of reference in alphabetical order) or via the individual Spanish words, all of which are listed in the Spanish word index at the end of the book.

ACCIDENT

accidente (m)		
contratiempo (minor) mishap, unforeseen upset	**percance** (m) (minor) misfortune, more serious than *contratiempo*	**siniestro** (serious) accident, catastrophe (esp natural disaster)

minor ⟵————————————————————⟶ *serious*

† More information about these words or expressions may be found in other sections. Use the Spanish word index to find the page numbers.	R1★ vulgar or indecent R1 informal, colloquial R2 neutral R3 formal, written *See also p 3.*	The gender of nouns is only given where it is not predictable from the principles given in ch. **16**.

TO AGREE

		to agree with sb else (one person with another or two or more people together)	to agree, to tally (of things)
		estar †de acuerdo (con uno) to be in agreement (with sb)	**concordar (con algo)** **†corresponder (a algo)** to agree, to tally (with sth)
		ponerse †de acuerdo (con uno) **†acordarse (con uno) (R3)** **avenirse (con uno) (R3)** to come to an agreement (with sb)	
	to accept a suggestion		
followed by N	**†acceder a algo** **†aceptar algo** to agree to sth	**†acordar algo** **†avenirse en algo** **†convenir en algo** to agree on sth	
followed by infinitive	**†acceder a hacer algo** **aceptar hacer algo** **†consentir en hacer algo** **quedar en hacer algo** to agree to do sth	**†acordar hacer algo** **†avenirse a hacer algo** **†convenir en hacer algo** to agree to do sth	
followed by a clause	**†reconocer que . . .** to agree that . . .	**†concordar en que . . .** to agree that . . .	

TO GET ANGRY

†**enfadarse** (R1–3)			
cabrearse (R1★)	**ponerse †hecho una fiera** (R1) **ponerse negro** (R1)	**enojarse** (R2–3) †**irritarse** (R2–3) **enfurecerse** (R2–3) **airarse** (R3) **atufarse** (R1–2)	**molestarse** (R2–3) **disgustarse** (R3) **incomodarse** (R3)

strong   ⟵──────────────────────⟶   *weak*
lower register   *higher register*

to get furious   *to get upset*

TO ANNOY

†**fastidiar** (R2–3)		†**molestar**	
†**joder** (R1★) to mess sb around	**causar/dar** †**asco a**[io] (R1) **crispar** (R1–2) **fregar** (R1 Am) to annoy intensely	†**dar la lata a**[io] (R1) **jorobar** **incordiar** to be a nuisance to, to pester	**estorbar** (R2–3) to hinder, to disturb **incomodar** (R3) to inconvenience

strong   ⟵──────────────────────⟶   *weak*
lower register   *higher register*

TO APPEAR

†**aparecer** to come into view	**comparecer** to appear (legal), eg *comparecer ante un tribunal*	†**parecer** to seem

APPEARANCE

†**apariencia**	**aspecto**
bearing **porte** (m) (R3) **aire** (m) **presencia** (R2–3)	*face* †**semblante** (m) (R3) †**facha** (R1) looks

Adjectives
expressing
APPROVAL

†**estupendo** splendid		
sorprendente surprising	†**increíble** incredible	**admirable** admirable
portentoso **prodigioso** prodigious		**asombroso** **pasmoso** (R2–3) astonishing
†**cojonudo** (R1★) **de puta madre** (R1★) bloody amazing		†**bárbaro** (R1) **tremendo** (R1) tremendous, super

TO ASK

	as a question	*as a demand*
	†**preguntar algo a**^{IO} **uno** to ask sb sth	†**pedir algo a**^{IO} **uno/a**^{IO} **uno que** + subj †**rogar** (R2–3) (as **pedir**) to ask sb for sth/sb to do sth
		requerir a^{IO} **uno para que** + subj to ask sb to do sth
		†**solicitar** (as **pedir**) to request
	hacer (**una pregunta**) to ask (a question)	†**suplicar** (as **pedir**) to beg
		†**exigir** (as **pedir**) †**reclamar** (as **pedir**) to demand
		†**demandar** (R3) to demand

IO	**a**^{IO} introduces the indirect object
PERS	**a**^{PERS} denotes the Spanish personal **a**

BACK (N)

espalda(s) of a person		†lomo of an animal	
dorso of hand, document	revés (m) 'wrong' side of fabric	respaldo of chair; ALSO (fig) backing, support	
†fondo of room, stage		parte (f) posterior of house, etc	

BALL

general

†bola ball	esfera sphere	globo globe (*el globo* *terráqueo* = the globe); balloon	

for specific purposes

bola (billiard) ball; (snow)ball; ball–bearing; marble; football (R1)	balón (m) football	pelota pelotín (m) (R1) football; tennis ball	bala (cannon) ball; bullet
balita pellet	canica marble	ovillo ball (of wool)	

BEAUTIFUL

general (of people or things)	**hermoso** **bello** (R2–3) beautiful	*R1–2 general purpose words* **bonito** **lindo** (esp Am) †**precioso** nice

	of things	*of people only*
more distinctive alternatives (esp R2–3)	**encantador** charming	**guapo** good-looking, elegant, attractive
	maravilloso wonderful	**majo** pretty, attractive, flashy
	delicioso delightful	†**rico** sweet, cute, lovely (of children)

TO BECOME

with noun	**convertirse en** neutral: not as strong as Eng to be converted into, eg *se convirtió en (un) asesino* **transformarse en** stronger than *convertirse en*, eg *tomó una poción mágica y se transformó en un monstruo*	†**llegar a** implies progress or achievement, eg *llegó a diputado*	
with noun or adjective	**volverse** **tornarse** (R3) most neutral, eg *se volvió loca; su duda se tornó en admiración*	†**hacerse** implies a neutral or expected development, eg *se hizo ingeniero en tres años*	**llegar a ser** implies progress or achievement, eg *llegó a ser rey*
	†**quedar**(se) to be left, to begin to be (restricted to *huérfano, viuda*, etc)	†**caer** implies misfortune: with *enfermo, prisionero*, etc.	**venir a ser** implies casualness: to come to be, eg *viene a ser lo mismo*
with adjective	†**ponerse** used with adjectives that take *estar*, eg *se puso triste*		

Note also:

†**ser de**
to become of, eg *¿qué va a ser de ti?*

TO BEGIN

transitive	intransitive	with infinitive
†**empezar** †**comenzar** **iniciar** (R2–3)	†**empezar** †**comenzar** †**principiar**	†**empezar a hacer** **algo** †**comenzar a hacer** **algo** †**principiar a hacer** **algo** †**ponerse a hacer** **algo** †**echar(se) a hacer** **algo** to begin to do sth
†**emprender** to undertake		
Special uses with *certain objects:* **entablar (una** **conversación,** **negociaciones,** **un pleito)** to start (a con- versation, business, a lawsuit) (R3) **trabar (amistad, una** **conversación)** to start (a friendship, a conversation)		

BEHIND,
BACKSIDE
(anatomy)

R1*	R1	R2	R3
culo **pompis** (m) arse, ass	←———————	**trasero** ——————————————→ behind, backside	
		←———— **nalgas** (pl) ————→ buttocks	
			posaderas (pl) **asentaderas** (pl) posterior (euphemistic)

BOAT, SHIP

†barco			
†barca rowing boat, or small boat with motor **bote** (m) dinghy **lancha** inflatable boat with motor	**embarcación** craft, small vessel	**nave** (f) vessel, (sailing) ship (*nave espacial* = spaceship) **navío** sailing ship, naval ship (*navío de guerra* = warship, *capitán de navío* = naval captain)	**buque** (m) big ship with engine: merchant ship, warship (eg *buque de guerra*)

small ←——————————————————————————→ *large*

BOTTLE

general	*small* ←————————————————→ *large*	
	botellín (m) **botella** **botellón** (m)	

specific	*for water* **botijo, botija** earthenware pitcher (with spout and handle) **cantimplora** canteen	*for wine* **bota** (leather) wineskin **porrón** (m) (glass) jar (with long spout)
	for perfume or medicine **frasco**	*for babies' feed* **biberón** (m) **pezonera** (Arg)

BOY/GIRL

muchacho/a		†chico/a
nene (m)/†**nena** small baby	†**niño/a** baby, little boy/girl	**hijo/a** son/daughter
chaval/a (R1) **mozo/a** **joven** (m/f) boy/girl, young person		**zagal/a** (R2–3) country lad/lass

BRAVE

	†**bravo**	†**valeroso**	**valiente**
general			
specific	†**animoso** lively, spirited	**brioso** dashing	**arriesgado** †**osado** bold, daring
	intrépido fearless, intrepid		†**bizarro** (R3) **caballeroso** (R2–3) gallant, chivalrous

TO BREAK (tr)

	†**romper**	
to crack, to split	**quebrantar** (R2–3) to break, to crack, also fig (eg *la ley*, *una promesa*)	†**cascar** (R1–2) to split, to crunch
	†**partir** to divide, to crack	**fracturar** (R3) to fracture (eg bone)
to break into pieces	†**deshacer** to undo, to destroy	**desmenuzar** to crumble, to shred
	hacer pedazos to break, to crack into pieces	**descuajaringar** (R1) to smash to pieces

TO CLIMB

	corresponding to English transitive	*corresponding to English intransitive*
	†subir to go up, to ascend, eg *subir la escalera*	
	trepar involves contact with hands and feet; also used of plants. Always with a preposition, eg *trepar a un árbol, trepar por una pared*	**subir** **†elevarse** (R2–3) **ascender** (R3) to go up, to rise (also of prices, temperature, etc)
	escalar to scale	
	to mount, to climb on to **subir a** (**un caballo**) to mount (a horse) **†encaramarse a/en** (**un árbol**) (R3) to climb (a tree) **encarapitarse** (Am) **a** (**un árbol**)	*to go climbing* **hacer alpinismo** (Pen)/ **andinismo** (Am)

COARSE

general (also literal)	**basto** (R1–2) rude	**tosco** crude	**†rudo** rough	**burdo** (R2–3) rough
specific	**vulgar** **ordinario** common, vulgar	**†grosero** vulgar, indecent	**incivilizado** **inculto** uncultivated, uncivilized	**zafio** (R3) uncouth

COAT

jacket, short coat	three-quarter-length coat	full-length coat, overcoat
chaqueta **americana** **saco** (Am) **cazadora**, **campera** (Arg) casual, usu with zip	**tres cuartos** (m) **trenca** duffel coat	**abrigo** **gabán** (m) (R2–3) **sobretodo** (R3) **tapado** (Am)

	housecoat, overalls
gabardina **impermeable** (m) waterproof	**guardapolvo** for cleaning **bata** housecoat; schoolchild's overalls; doctor's white coat; dressing gown

COMPETITION

concrete   *abstract*

←——————— †**competición** ———————→	
concurso	†**competencia** competition (often commercial); competitiveness
†**certamen** (m) (R2–3) eg of music, literature, art	
†**oposición** competitive exam for a public job, usu in pl	

CORNER

general

ángulo	
rincón (m) inside angle, eg corner of room	**esquina** outside angle, eg corner of street

specific

curva bend, eg in road	**†pico** sharp corner, eg of a piece of furniture
rabillo corner of the eye	**comisura** corner of the mouth

CRIME, OFFENCE

crimen (m) **delito** serious crime	**†infracción** infringement	**†falta** offence; foul (in sport)
transgresión **pecado** transgression, sin (moral)	**reincidencia** second offence	

TO CUT

†cortar			
amputar to amputate, to cut off	**†hender** **†partir** to cleave, to split	**podar** to prune	**practicar** (**un** **agujero**) to cut (a hole)
reducir to cut down (fig), to reduce in quantity	**seccionar** (R3) to cut into sections	**suprimir** **tachar** to cut (out), to delete	**†talar** **cercenar** to cut (down), eg a tree
	tallar to carve	**truncar** to cut (short), to truncate	

TO DAMAGE, TO SPOIL

R1*	R1	R2	R3
	←———————— dañar ————————→		
	←———————— maltratar ————————→		
†joder	†estropear †fastidiar		†deteriorar

TO DECEIVE

engañar		
estafar algo a[IO] **uno** **timar algo a**[IO] **uno** (R1–2) to swindle sb out of sth **defraudar a**[PERS] **uno** to cheat, to swindle sb	†**burlar** (R2–3) **a**[PERS] **uno** to hoax sb	**engatusar a**[PERS] **uno** **para que haga** **algo** to inveigle, to coax sb into doing sth

TO DEFEAT, TO BEAT, TO WIN

†**derrotar** (R2–3) **vencer** to beat (an opponent) (gen)	**conquistar** to conquer, to overcome, to win (sb or sth)	**triunfar de/sobre** **algo/uno** (R2–3) to triumph over sth/sb
rendir (R3) **someter** (R2–3) **subyugar** (R3) **sojuzgar** (R3) to conquer, to overcome, to bring under one's control	†**ganar algo/a**[PERS] **uno** to earn, to win, to gain sth; to win sb over **ganar a**[PERS] **uno a** **un deporte** to beat sb at a game	**batir** to beat (to hit); to beat (person, team, record)

[IO]	**a**[IO] introduces the indirect object
[PERS]	**a**[PERS] denotes the Spanish personal **a**

TO DESTROY

	destruir	
to demolish	*to raze, to lay waste*	*to damage, to spoil*

desmantelar
to take down
 	
demoler (R2–3)
to pull down
 	
derribar
to knock down
 	
derrumbar
to knock down, to
  fling down
 	
derruir
to tear down
	devastar
	desolar
	to lay waste
	
	talar
	to lay waste, to fell
	  (tree)
	
	arrasar
	asolar
	to raze
		deshacer
		†**estropear**
		inutilizar (R3)

to smash, to break up	*to annihilate*	*to ruin*
desbaratar (ALSO to thwart) **destrozar**	**aniquilar** **arrollar** to crush (an enemy)	**arruinar**

DIRTY

general	†**sucio**			
more specific	**manchado** stained	**desaseado** soiled; messy, untidy		**mugriento** **tiznado** grimy
expressing disgust	**inmundo** (R3)	†**asqueroso** **sórdido**	**guarro** (R1) **cochambroso** (R1)	**marrano** (R1★) **puerco** (R1★) **merdoso** (R1★) **cochino** (R1★)

DISPUTE

	primarily associated with verbal dispute: 'argument'	*primarily associated with physical dispute: 'fight'*	*primarily associated with noise: 'row'*
	†**discusión** †**debate** (m) **controversia** †**disputa** †**querella** **altercado** (R2–3) **rencilla**(s) sg: argument pl: bickering	**contienda** (R2–3) †**riña** **porfía** (R3) †**lucha** **pelea** **reyerta** **pendencia** (R3) **camorra** (R1)	**pelotera** (R1) **trifulca** (R1) **bronca** (R1)

TO DIVE

literal	**tirarse** †**echarse** ⎬ **(de** **zambullirse** ⎭ **cabeza)** to dive from bank, etc.	†**echarse** †**arrojarse** **abalanzarse** †**lanzarse** to dive from a height	**sumergirse** to dive from surface of water (eg submarine, duck)
	saltar to practise high diving		**bucear** to swim underwater
figurative	†**precipitarse** to rush		**despeñarse** to throw oneself headlong

DRAWING, SKETCH, DESIGN

†**dibujo**		
esbozo **bosquejo** **apunte** (m) sketch, outline	**croquis** (m) sketch, plan (often to show where a place is)	†**trazo** outline **trazado** layout
†**diseño** design (technical); drawing (art)		**diagrama** (m) **esquema** (m) diagram

EDGE

†**borde** (m)				
†**orilla** water	**límite** (m) †**linde** (m) territory	†**margen** (m) page	†**canto** coin, book; vertical part of table top	**arista** cube, etc
†**corte** (m) **filo** sharp edge of knife, etc			†**canto** blunt edge of knife, etc; rim of glass	

TO ENJOY
ONESELF

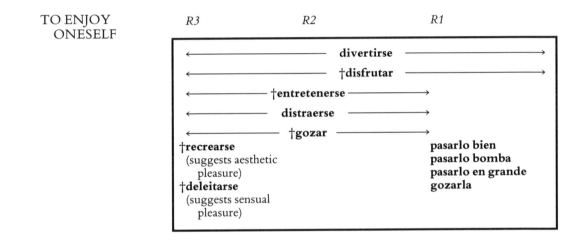

R3   R2   R1

←——————————— divertirse ——————————→
←——————————— †disfrutar ——————————→
←———————— †entretenerse ————————→
←———————— distraerse ————————→
←————————— †gozar ————————→

†**recrearse**
(suggests aesthetic
   pleasure)
†**deleitarse**
(suggests sensual
   pleasure)

pasarlo bien
pasarlo bomba
pasarlo en grande
gozarla

EVILDOER

malhechor/-ora **malvado/a** **maleante** (m only) wicked person	**criminal** (m/f) **delincuente** (m/f) criminal **gamberro/a** (R1) hooligan, juvenile delinquent	**pícaro/a** **pillo/a** **bribón/-ona** (R1–2) †**granuja** (m only) (R1–2) **tunante** (m/f) (R3) rogue, rascal
enredador/-ora troublemaker	**canalla** (m) (R1) (**canalla** (f) = riffraff) **sinvergüenza** (m/f) rogue, shameless person	†**tuno/a** **bellaco/a** **pillín/-ina** **pilluelo/a** (gen affectionate)

TO EXAMINE

general	**examinar**			
more specific types of examination	**inspeccionar** to inspect	†**registrar** to search	**escudriñar** (R3) **escrutar** (R3) to scrutinize	**indagar** **investigar** to investigate
specialized	**pesquisar** (R3) to inspect (usu of police)		†**reconocer** to examine (medical); to reconnoitre (military)	

FACE

physical part of body	*countenance, expression, appearance*	*surface*

←————————————————— †**cara** —————————————————→
also gen used in set expressions
and in all fig senses

←——————— †**semblante** (m) ———————→

| **faz** (f) (R3) **rostro** (R2–3) **jeta** (R1★–1) | | †**faz** (f) †**superficie** (f) |

TO FACE (tr)

	literal	*figurative*
	static (= to be facing) **estar enfrente de** gen †**dar a** of room, etc **mirar hacia** of person	†**enfrentar(se a/con)** †**encarar(se a)** **arrostrar** (R3) **dar la cara a** (R1) **hacer** (R2–3)/**plantar** (R2) **cara a** †**afrontar** to face (up to)
		arrostrarse con **hacer frente a** to stand up to
	movement (= to turn to face) **volver la cara hacia** **mirar hacia** **ponerse de cara a**	**confrontar a**PERS **uno con** **algo** to face sb with sth
		soportar **aguantar** to put up with

IO   **a**IO introduces the indirect object
PERS   **a**PERS denotes the Spanish personal **a**

FAT (of people)

general	†**gordo, grueso**			
of body	**corpulento** corpulent		**obeso** obese	

	regordete
	gordezuelo
	    (R1)
	gordinflón
	    (R1)
	plump, chubby
		rollizo
		chubby, usu
		    of babies
			rechoncho
			    (R1)
			thickset,
			    plump
				cerdo (R1★)
				fat, tubby

more specific	**mofletudo** of cheeks		**panzudo** (R1) **ventrudo** (R2–3) of belly	

TO FIND

†**encontrar**	**hallar** (R2–3)
†**dar con** †**tropezar con** **topar con** (R3) to come upon unexpectedly	†**descubrir** to discover

FIRE

fuego fire to heat or cook; gunfire	**incendio** fire which destroys property
lumbre (f) fire(light)	**estufa** heating appliance (electric, gas, etc)

**FORTUNE,
LUCK,
CHANCE**

suerte (f)	
bad luck **mala suerte** **mala ventura** **(suerte) negra** (R1) **mala pata** (R1)	*good luck* **buena suerte** **(buena) fortuna** **ventura** (R3)
azar (m) **casualidad** **ventura** chance	†**destino** **sino** (R3) **hado** (R3) **fortuna** fate, destiny

FULL

general

lleno

degrees of fullness

concrete	abstract
relleno full up (stronger than **lleno**) **completo** full to capacity in numbers (eg a bus) **repleto** full to capacity in volume (eg with food) †**harto** full to or beyond sufficiency	**pleno** eg *a plena vista* = in full view **completo** finished, complete (eg *un estudio completo* = a full study)

specific types of fullness

abarrotado **atestado** packed, crammed	**atascado** jammed, clogged up	**atiborrado** stuffed, packed	**colmado** full to brim
henchido filled up, swollen	**rebosante** brimming, overflowing	**ahíto** gorged (with food)	

FUNNY

humorous	*strange*
†**gracioso** †**divertido** amusing	†**raro** †**extraño** odd
†**cómico** comical	
salado **chistoso** **ingenioso** witty	

GIFT

	present, gift	*natural gift*
	regalo †**presente** (m) **don** (m) (R2–3) **obsequio** (R3)	
	donación **donativo** endowment, donation, bequest	**talento** **don** (m) †**dote** (f)
	†**ofrenda** offering (in church)	

TO GIVE

dar			

entregar
to deliver,
   to hand in,
   to hand over
	†**facilitar**
	proporcionar
	  (R3)
	to provide
		abastecer de
		suministrar
		to supply
		  with (eg
		  food, gas,
		  water)
			donar
			to donate

dotar
to endow
	regalar
	to give as a
	  present
		conceder (R3)
		†**otorgar** (R3)
		to grant, to
		  bestow
		  (eg prize,
		  honour)
			deparar (R3)
			to offer, to
			  afford

GLASS

substance	**vidrio** gen	**†cristal** (m) pane of glass; covering of glass (eg on watch); type of glass (eg *cristal ahumado*); crystal, quality glass

for drinking	**vaso**	**†copa** with stem	**copita** (sherry) glass

for looking through	**gafas** **anteojos** (pl) (Am) glasses	**prismáticos** (pl) **gemelos** (pl) binoculars, (field) glasses	**lupa** (magnifying) glass

GROUP (of people)

†grupo					
†agrupación formal association	**camarilla** lobby, pressure group	**corrillo** group of people standing talking	**†equipo** team	**conjunto** gen, or musical	**†partida** party (eg hunting)
†panda gang	**†banda** pack, throng	**†bando** faction, side	**pandilla** gang, clique	**cuadrilla** small group with a specific task, eg in bullfighting	

TO GROW (intr)

general	**crecer** as natural process, and gen in size	
more abstract	**acrecentarse** (R2–3) **acrecer** to increase (in size)	**aumentar** **incrementarse** to increase (in quantity)
more specific	**ampliarse** **extenderse** to expand, to extend	**alargarse** **prolongarse** to increase in length
	engrandecerse **agrandarse** to get bigger	**†elevarse** to increase in height
figurative	**desarrollarse** **desenvolverse** to develop	**medrar** (R3) to prosper

GUN

arma (de fuego) weapon, (fire)arm		
revólver (m) revolver	**pistola** pistol	**fusil** (m) rifle (military) **rifle** (m) rifle (smaller, eg for hunting)
escopeta shotgun	**†cañón** (m) large gun	**artillería** artillery, guns

HAIR

†pelo **pelos** (pl) (suggests disorder) **cabellos** (pl) (R3) **cabellera** head of hair	**pelo** **cabello** (R3) individual hair	**†cana(s)** white/grey hair

TO HAPPEN, TO TAKE PLACE

general	†ocurrir †pasar †suceder **acontecer** (R2–3) **acaecer** (R3)	*of event* **tener lugar** **celebrarse** (more formal, eg of ceremony, meeting, etc)

specific	**realizarse** to be fulfilled, accomplished (esp plans, hopes)	**producirse** to come about (esp accident)	**surgir** **sobrevenir** to happen unexpectedly	**verificarse** to come true; also gen to take place

HAPPY

general	**feliz**	**estar †contento** to be pleased

specific	**dichoso** fortunate, lucky	**jovial** jovial, cheerful	**alegre** cheerful
	estar alborozado to be overjoyed	**estar regocijado** (R3) to be merry, joyous	

HEEL

talón (m) part of foot	**tacón** (m) part of shoe

TO HELP

†ayudar		
auxiliar (R3) **socorrer** (R3) suggests difficulty or danger	†**apoyar** to support	†**asistir** to assist (R3); to attend (medical) (R2)
coadyuvar (R3) suggests contribution towards obtaining sth	†**echar una mano a** (R1) **echar un cable a** (R1) to give a hand to	

HILL

	hill as a whole		*slope*
			cuesta eg on road
	†**monte** (m) ALSO woodland	*large* ↑	**repecho** short, steep slope
	cerro steep hill		†**pendiente** (f) †**vertiente** (f) †**declive** (m) gradient
	colina **montículo**		
	otero †**loma**		†**ladera** hillside
	altozano ALSO high part of a town		
	collado ALSO pass	*small* ↓	**ribazo** embankment

TO HIT

to strike with blows

pegar to hit, to smack, to slap		**golpear** to strike, to punch, to beat	
abofetear to slap (in face)	**apalear** to beat, to thrash	**aporrear** (R1) to beat up	**azotar** to lash
sacudir (R1) to wallop	**vapulear** (R1) to give a beating	**zurrar** (R1) to thump, to belt	
asestar **dar** } a^{IO} uno un golpe **pegar** to strike sb a blow			

other meanings

to hit with whole body †**dar en** of person **chocar con/contra** of vehicle	**dar en** (**un blanco**) to hit (a target)	†**alcanzar** to hit (of shots)

IO	a^{IO} introduces the indirect object
PERS	a^{PERS} denotes the Spanish personal **a**

TO GET HOLD OF

general	†**coger** (Pen) (R1–3) †**agarrar** (Am) †**tomar** (Am)	**pillar** (R1) **atrapar** (R1)
specific	†**tomar** to adopt (eg *malas* *costumbres*)	†**agarrar(se a)** to grip, to hold on to (R2–3) to get hold of (R1)
	†**asir(se de)** (R3) to seize	**empuñar** to take a firm hold of

NOTE: in some parts of Latin America, **coger** = *to screw* (R1★), and is
therefore avoided, **agarrar** or **tomar** being used instead.

HOLE

†**abertura** opening	**agujero** hole through sth; hole in a wall	**hoyo** hole in ground	**cavidad** cavity
hueco hollow, gap	**brecha** gap (in fence or wall)	**boquete** (m) large, irregular- shaped hole	**bache** (m) pothole (in road)

HOLIDAYS

vacaciones (pl) long, usu involving absence	†**fiesta** **día** (m) **festivo** **festividad** single day (public) holiday	**fiestas** (pl) (public) holiday over period of days	†**permiso** (soldier's) leave

TO HURRY

†**apresurarse** †**darse prisa** †**apurarse** (Am) } (R1–3)		**menearse** **espabilarse** **aligerarse** } (R1)

IMPROVEMENT

general	**mejoría** gen, esp of state of health (and by extension to economy, performance, etc)	**mejora** gen, though not normally used of health. May refer to sth concrete (eg home improvement)	**†mejoramiento** (R3) gen
specific	**adelantos** (pl) advances (eg in science)	**†progresos** (pl) progress (eg in economy, performance, etc)	

TO INFORM

general	**†informar**	**enterar** (R2–3)
specific	**avisar** **notificar** (R3) to notify	**anunciar** to announce
	†indicar **comunicar** **†manifestar** to communicate	**†prevenir** **advertir** **amonestar** to warn

INTELLIGENT

general	**†listo**	**inteligente**
specific	**†astuto** **perspicaz** (R2–3) **sagaz** (R2–3) shrewd, bright	**†lúcido** **clarividente** clear-sighted
	†despejado (R1) **avispado** (R1) **despierto** (R1–2) **despabilado** wide-awake, bright	**agudo** **penetrante** sharp, keen (stresses quality of mind)

JOURNEY

viaje (m)		
recorrido **periplo** (R3) tour	**trayecto** short ride (eg on a bus route in town)	**excursión** †**gira** **vuelta** trip

KIND

amable **amistoso** friendly	*gentle* **benévolo** (R3) of people **benigno**	**cariñoso** **entrañable** **afectuoso** affectionate
†**bueno** **bondadoso** **bonachón** (R1) good-natured	**bienintencionado** well-meaning	**generoso** **filantrópico** (R2–3) generous

TO KNOW

†**saber** to have knowledge of sth, eg *Sabe francés* He knows French to know how to do sth, eg *Sabe tocar el violín* He knows how to play the violin	**conocer** to be acquainted with, eg *Conozco el país* I know the country

LANGUAGE

lengua			
lenguaje (m) type of language	**idioma** (m) language (eg Spanish, French, etc)	**habla** speech	**jerga** **jerigonza** **argot** (m) jargon, slang

LAZY, IDLE

perezoso		
indolente (R2–3) **ocioso** **poltrón** (R3)	**holgazán** **haragán**	†**vago** **gandul** (R1) **perro** (R1)

weaker ⟵   ⟶ *stronger*

LEADER, BOSS

†**jefe** (m) leader, chief	**caudillo** political leader (Franco's title)	**cacique** (m) local boss, petty tyrant (used of landowners)	**cabecilla** (m) leader (pej)
líder (m) leader who has following, as in politics, church	†**patrón** (m) boss, chief (often in industry)	**señor** (m) **dueño** owner, master	†**responsable** (m/f) person in charge

TO LEAVE

transitive	†**dejar**	†**abandonar** not necessarily as definitive as Eng to abandon	
intransitive	†**salir**	†**partir** usu with idea of destination (**para**)	**zarpar** of a ship
	irse to go away †**marcharse** to go away (suggests for a long time, or for ever)	**apartarse de** wander from, eg a path	**largarse** (R1) **pirarse**, †**pirárselas** (R1) †**abrirse** (R1) to leave, to clear off

MONEY

dinero †**plata** (Am)		
†**capital** (m) capital	**moneda** coin (individual); coinage, currency	**divisas** (pl) foreign currency

†**metálico**
(hard) cash; coin
  (collective)
†**pasta** (R1)
dosh, cash
	†**fondo(s)**
	fund(s)
		fortuna
		dineral (m)
		caudal (m)
		fortune, lots of
		  money

NAME

†**nombre** (m) gen and first name		
nombre de pila Christian name	**apellido** surname	**apodo** **sobrenombre** (m) **mote** (m) nickname

NATIVE
(N and ADJ)

of people (N and ADJ)	*of country (ADJ)*

nativo
 	
†**natural**
oriundo (R2–3)
coming from
 	
indígeno
usu of cultures and peoples
  outside Europe
 	
aborigen
primitive native (not restricted,
  as Eng aborigine, to Australia)
	natal

of things, cultures, art, etc (ADJ)	*of language (ADJ)*
indígeno **autóctono** (R3)	**materno** **nativo**

NOISES OF
ANIMALS

animal	*verb*	*noun*
asno	rebuznar	rebuzno
caballo	relinchar	relincho
cuervo	graznar	graznido
culebra	sisear	siseo
gallina	cacarear	cacareo
gallo	†cantar	†canto
gato	maullar	maullido
oveja	balar	balido
pájaro	†cantar to sing trinar to trill piar to chirp	†canto song trino trilling pío chirping
†pato	graznar	graznido
†perro	ladrar	ladrido
vaca	mugir	mugido

OLD

†viejo			
anciano mayor of people: 　more polite 　than *viejo*	†antiguo ancient, 　pertaining to 　antiquity; 　antique	vetusto (R3) ancient 　(= very old)	antiguo former
añejo of wine	usado of clothes		

OUTSKIRTS
(of town)

†**barrio** district (any)	**arrabal** (m) outer district	**periferia** areas on edge	†**afueras** (pl) suburb on edge of town or area just outside
alrededores (pl) **cercanías** (pl) **contornos** (pl) **inmediaciones** (pl) (R2–3) **aledaños** (pl) (R3)		wider area outside town, including neighbouring towns	

PATTERN

	model	*form*
general	†**modelo** model	†**forma** form
	†**ejemplo** example	**pauta** guideline(s)
	†**dechado** perfect model, paragon	
specific	**muestra** part, sample of whole	†**dibujo** drawn pattern
	†**patrón** (m) pattern for dressmaking	**estampado** pattern printed on cloth
	escantillón (m) **plantilla** template, stencil	**diseño** design (eg pattern on china)

PAY

sueldo salary	**salario** wage	**paga** (R2) pay (usu weekly)
pago payment (instalment or act of paying)	†**honorarios** (pl) (professional) fee, emoluments; salary (R1)	**jornal** (m) day's pay **mensualidad** month's pay

POOL, POND

general	*natural* **charca**		*artificial* **estanque** (m) **balsa**
special senses	**pozo** pool in a river	**poza** **pozo** (Am) **charco** (eg *un charco* *de sangre*) large puddle	**piscina** **pileta** (Am) (swimming) pool

POOR

needy	*unfortunate*	*poor in quality*
†**pobre** **necesitado** **indigente** **menesteroso** (R2–3) **desvalido** (R2–3)	†**pobre** **desgraciado**	**malo**
	desamparado alone, helpless	

TO TAKE POSSESSION OF

general	**adueñarse de** (R3) **†posesionarse de** (R3)	**†apoderarse de**	**†echar mano a**
specific	**†quitar algo a uno** **†ocupar algo a uno** (R3) to take sth from sb	**hacerse con** (R1) **†apropiarse de** (R2–3) to get hold of, to appropriate	**usurpar** (R3) to usurp

POSTER, NOTICE

letrero sign	**†cartel** (m) poster	**anuncio** advertisement, placard
pancarta banner, placard (eg at political meetings)	**póster** (m) poster (colourful and artistic, as an embellishment)	

PROUD

general	**orgulloso** may have a 'positive' meaning: *estar orgulloso de* = to be proud of	
specific and pejorative	**arrogante** **soberbio** **altivo** (R2–3) **altanero** (R2–3) haughty, arrogant	**presuntuoso** presumptuous
	engreído **vanidoso** **fatuo** (R2–3) vain, conceited	**jactoso** (R3) **jactancioso** (R3) **presumido** boastful

TO PUT

†poner	
meter **introducir** to put in, to insert	**colocar** **situar** (R2–3) **emplazar** (R3) **ubicar** (Am) to place, to situate
†disponer to lay out, to arrange	**†apostar** to station, to post (eg soldier, policeman)

NOTE: **ubicar** has the meaning of *to be situated* in Peninsular Spanish.

TO RAISE

†levantar		
elevar to raise, to erect (implies to high point)	**alzar** (R2–3) to raise, to lift up; to put vertical (eg hand)	**†subir** to put up (eg blind); to take up (eg suitcases)

TO REBEL

rebelarse		
alzarse **sublevarse** (R2–3) **insurreccionarse** (R3) to revolt	**indisciplinarse** to be insubordinate	**amotinarse** to riot, to mutiny

RICH

†**rico**	
†**ricacho** (R1) **ricachón** (R1) **acaudalado** (R2–3) **adinerado** (R2–3) very rich	**acomodado** **pudiente** (R2–3) well-off, well-to-do

TO RIDE

to ride a horse	*to ride (eg a bicycle)*	*to ride (eg on a bus)*
montar a caballo **cabalgar** (R2–3)	**montar (en** **bicicleta)**	†**ir (en autobús)** **viajar (en autobús)**

RING

general

concrete		*abstract*
†**anillo** **arete** (m)	**aro** ALSO hoop **argolla** usu metal	†**círculo**
small ⟷ *large*		

specific

for finger			
anillo gen	**sortija** ring with stones	**alianza** **anillo de** **boda/** **matrimonio** **argolla** (Am) wedding ring	**sello** signet ring
llavero keyring	**anilla** for curtains; for birds; in gymnastics	**servilletero** napkin-ring	†**pendiente** (m) **arete** (m) (Am) **aro** (Am) earring

ROCK, STONE

roca rock in geological sense; an individual piece of rock *in situ* or collected	
peña individual rock *in situ*	**†piedra** type of or individual stone
peñasco large rock, crag	**guijarro** pebble; cobblestone **china** pebble **guija** small stone
el Peñón (ALSO **la Roca**) the Rock (of Gibraltar)	**guijo** **grava** gravel

ROOM

room in a building	**cuarto** gen	**habitación** gen; (bed)room in a hotel, etc
	sala large room; public hall	**aposento** (R3) room(s), lodging
spacing, place	**sitio** space to occupy	**†espacio** (empty) space

SAD

	of people	*of things*
	←————————— †**triste** —————————→	
	†**descontento** (opposite of *contento*) unhappy, discontented	**doloroso** painful, distressing
	pesimista (m/f) **tristón** (R1) sad, gloomy (inherent)	
	melancólico (R2–3) melancholy	
	desconsolado (R2–3) **afligido** (R2–3) disconsolate, woebegone	
	†**abatido** **deprimido** depressed	**lamentable** deplorable
	en baja forma (R1) out of sorts, depressed	
	atribulado (R3) **apenado** (R2–3) **apesadumbrado** (R2–3) deeply unhappy	

TO SAY, TO SPEAK, TO TALK

†**decir** to say (tr); sometimes = *hablar* (Am)		†**hablar** to speak (intr); to speak (tr) (a language)	
charlar †**departir** (R3) **platicar** (R3) **conversar** (R2–3) to chat, to converse		**cotorrear** (R1) **parlotear** (R1) †**cascar** (R1) to chatter away	
expresarse to express oneself	**pronunciarse sobre algo** to make a statement on	**pronunciar un discurso** to give a speech	†**tomar la palabra** to contribute in a meeting

TO SEE

	to see	*to look at*
general	†**ver**	†**mirar**
specific	**observar** **notar** to observe	
	guipar (R1) **descubrir** †**percibir** †**reparar en** to spot, to notice	**ojear** **fijar la vista en** to stare at
	columbrar †**vislumbrar** †**divisar** **atisbar** (R2–3) to see from a distance	
	†**presenciar** to witness	**echar una vista/ojeada a** **dar/echar un vistazo a** (R1–2) to glance at
	otear to scan, to survey	

TO SEND

†**mandar**		**enviar**	
despachar to dispatch (goods or people)	**destinar** to post (sb), to assign	**expedir** (R2–3) to dispatch (commercial)	**remitir** (R3) to remit, to consign (eg money)

TO SHINE

	literal				*figurative*
constant	⟵————————— **brillar** —————————⟶ ⟵————————— **lucir** —————————⟶				
	resplandecer to shine, to blaze		†**deslumbrar** to dazzle		**sobresalir** to be brilliant
intermittent	**relucir** **relumbrar**	**espejear** (R3) to glint	**rutilar** (R3) to sparkle	**centellear** to sparkle, to flash, to twinkle	
		refulgir to glitter	**destellar** to flash, to sparkle, to glitter	**fulgurar** (R3) to shine very brightly, to flash	†**lucirse** to excel

TO SHOOT

	to fire (a weapon)	to shoot (sb)	to shoot (game)
associated with weapons	**disparar**	**†herir** to shoot and wound **matar de un tiro** shoot and kill **tirar a** **pegar un tiro a** **disparar contra** to shoot at **fusilar** **abalear** (Am) to execute by shooting	**cazar** **ir de caza** to go shooting

	to kick (a ball)	to throw
general	**†tirar** gen **chutar** in football	**†lanzar** **tirar** **†arrojar**

SHOP, STORE

tienda (small) shop	**almacén** (m) large store (but in Am often = grocer's shop)	

negocio
comercio
business
	comercios (pl)
	shops, stores,
	  shopping facilities
		supermercado
		hipermercado
		supermarket,
		  hypermarket

TO SHOW

†enseñar		mostrar
señalar **†indicar** to point out, to indicate	**demostrar** to demonstrate	**exponer** **exhibir** **†presentar** to exhibit, to present
ostentar to show off, to make a show		**desplegar** to display, to deploy, to unfold

SIDE

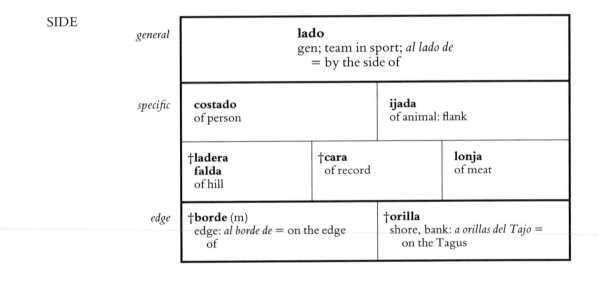

general	**lado** gen; team in sport; *al lado de* = by the side of	
specific	**costado** of person	**ijada** of animal: flank
	†ladera **falda** of hill	**†cara** of record
		lonja of meat
edge	**†borde** (m) edge: *al borde de* = on the edge of	**†orilla** shore, bank: *a orillas del Tajo* = on the Tagus

SLICE

rodaja of sausage, salami, lemon: has idea of roundness	**rebanada** of bread
loncha **lonja** of ham	**tajada** of meat, cheese, melon: has idea of cutting
raja of most things except bread, ham and meat in general	**trozo** irregular slice or chunk, esp of meat

TO SQUEAK

chirriar of brakes, hinges, locks; ALSO to cheep, to chirp (of birds)	**chillar** of animals; ALSO to squeal
crujir of shoes; ALSO to creak, to crunch	**rechinar** of machinery; ALSO to grate, to grind

TO STEAL

R3	*R2*	*R1*

←————————————————— †**robar** —————————————————→
←———————————— †**hurtar** ————————————→
†**sustraer**   **birlar**
                                                       afanar
                                                       limpiar
                                                       mangar

STICK

†**palo** gen; stick to hold sth with (eg of broom, lollipop)	†**vara** pole, rod	**bastón** (m) walking stick **báculo** (R3) staff
porra truncheon	**garrote** (m) **tranca** cudgel, club	**batuta** baton (music)
estaca stake in ground	†**barra** stick of candy, etc	**astillas** (pl) sticks for fire

STORM

†**tormenta** thunderstorm	**borrasca** high wind, squall	†**temporal** (m) †**tempestad** storm at sea
nevada snowstorm	**granizada** hailstorm	

STRING

literal (for tying or threading)

cuerda rope	**cordón** (m) (shoe) lace	**guita** twine	**†hilo** thread, yarn
cordel (m) thin rope, cord		**bramante** (m) string, twine	

thick ⟵————————————————⟶ *thin*

special purposes

sarta (of onions, etc)	**ristra** (esp of garlic)

figurative

general	*things or people going by*	*abstract*

fila
row
†hilera
row, line
	†desfile (m)
	procession,
	  march–past
	caravana
	caravan (of camels);
	  also of cars
	reata
	of horses
		serie (f)
		gen
		retahíla
		(of insults)
		sarta
		(of lies, etc)

STRONG (of people)

†fuerte		
recio **robusto** (R2–3) tough, solid	**poderoso** powerful	**forzudo** tough, brawny
fornido hefty	**bragado** (R1★–1) tough	**vigoroso** **†enérgico** vigorous

STUBBORN

obstinado (R2–3)	**testarudo** (R2–3)		**terco**

persistente
porfiado (R3)
pertinaz (R3)
persistent
	tenaz
	tenacious
		contumaz
		(R3)
		stubborn in
		  error,
		  incorrigible
			cabezudo
			(R1)
			pig-headed

STUPID

estúpido	tonto
necio (R3) **bobo** (R1) silly	**lerdo** (R2–3) **torpe** slow of understanding
idiota (R1) **imbécil** **cretino** (R1) idiot, imbecile	**ser un(a) jilí** (R1★) **ser un(a) jilipolla(s)** (R1★) to be really stupid

TO TAKE

†**llevar** to carry †**llevarse** to take away; to steal	**conducir** to drive	**guiar** to lead, to guide	**transportar** to transport **trasladar** (R3 with person as object) to transport, to transfer
†**coger** (see note on p. 79) to pick up, to seize, to catch (bus, etc)	†**tomar** to take (medicine, food, notes etc)	†**sacar** to take (photograph, copy, ticket, etc)	

NOTE: †**llevar** (= to take from the place the subject is at) and †**traer** (= to bring from the place the subject is at) are rigorously distinguished in Spanish, though in English *bring* is often used in the sense of **llevar**:

Si te quedas allí te lo llevaré

If you stay there I'll bring it to you

A similar rigorous distinction is made in Spanish between †**ir** and †**venir**:

Está llamando alguien a la puerta. ¡Ya voy!

Someone's knocking at the door. I'm coming!

Cuando llegues a Barcelona, dímelo e iré a verte

When you get to Barcelona, tell me and I'll come and see you.

TEACHER

profesor/a profe (m/f) (R1) gen and more specifically secondary/high school teacher; teacher in university/college		

maestro/a
primary/elementary
  school teacher;
  also gen in sense
  of expert
 	
señorita (R1)
female primary/
  elementary school
  teacher
 	
enseñante (m/f)
  (R2–3)
teacher
	†catedrático/a
	(university)
	  professor; head of
	  department in
	  school
		†director/a
		headmaster/
		  mistress,
		  principal

THIN (of people)

flaco		delgado	

esbelto
slim
  (suggesting
  elegance)
	huesudo
	bony
		descarnado
		thin (in the
		  face)
			enjuto (R3)
			lean, skinny

esquelético skeletal, extremely thin	**famélico** (R2–3) skinny, starving	**desmedrado** (R3) **enclenque** (R3) **esmirriado** (R1–2) **escuchimizado** (R1) skinny, emaciated, puny	

⟫⟫→

TO THINK

pensar (tr and intr)		
to think that . . .	*to imagine sth*	*to think (intr and with prep)*
†**pensar que** . . . †**creer que** . . . †**parecer a uno que** . . . to think †**figurarse que** . . . †**imaginarse que** . . . to imagine **opinar que** . . . to be of the opinion that . . .	**imaginar idear concebir** to imagine, to conceive †**inventar** to invent, to think up	**reflexionar sobre** to reflect on †**cavilar sobre discurrir en** to brood over **meditar en, sobre** to meditate on

TO THROW

†**tirar** gen; ALSO: to throw away			
†**lanzar** to throw (R3), to launch (R2) (suggests aim, precision)	†**echar** to cast, to put	†**arrojar** to hurl	†**proyectar** to project

TOOTH

diente (m) gen; of saw		**muela** gen: often used in referring to teeth in plural, as in *dolor de muelas*	
muela molar	**canino** (R3) **colmillo** canine tooth	**colmillo** fang; tusk	**púa** of comb

TOP

la parte superior **la parte de arriba** **la parte de encima** gen	**lo alto** the high part (eg of stairs)

†**pico** **cumbre** (f) †**cima** **cresta** of hill, mountain	†**copa** of tree	†**tablero** of table	**remate** (m) of building
principio of list	†**final** (m) of street	†**superficie** (f) of liquid	**techo** of bus, house

TRICK

†**engaño** **truco** **treta** act of deception	**estafa** swindle	
	trampa **ardid** (m) †**estratagema** (f) ruse	**truco** **triquiñuela** (R1) knack, skill, trick
travesura act of mischief	**burla** **mala pasada** †**faena** (R1) **jugarreta** (R1) **trastada** (R1) hoax, dirty trick	

TO TRY

with verb	†**intentar hacer algo** †**tratar de hacer algo** †**probar hacer algo** (R3) to try to do sth	
	†**procurar hacer algo** (R2–3) to endeavour to do sth	†**esforzarse por/en hacer algo** to strive to do sth	†**esmerarse por/en hacer algo** to try one's hardest to do sth
with noun	†**intentar algo** to attempt sth	†**probar algo** to try, to taste sth	**ensayar algo** to test, to try out sth

WALL

pared (f) interior wall of building	**muro** exterior wall of building; large free-standing wall	†**tapia** small free-standing wall (eg of garden, field)
muralla wall, usu fortified, of city, castle, etc	**tabique** (m) (thin) partition wall	**barrera** barrier, wall in fig sense

TO WASTE

†**malgastar**		
desperdiciar (food, time) †**perder** (time, opportunity)	**despilfarrar** †**derrochar** to squander (eg money, resources)	†**tirar** to throw away

TO WEAR

†**ponerse**
  to put on
	†**llevar**
	  vestir
	  usar (gafas)
	†**echarse** (Am)
	  to wear
		tener/traer puesto
		  to be wearing

†**lucir**
  to sport
	†**estrenar**
	  to wear for first time	

†**(des)gastar** to wear out		

WILD

salvaje (of animals or primitive culture)		**silvestre** (of plants)	

†**bravo**
†**bravío**
  fierce (of
    person or
    animal);
  rough (of
    landscape)
	bruto
	brutal
	brutish, brutal
		†**feroz**
		ferocious
			agresivo
			aggressive

WIND

viento			
ráfaga gust of wind			
brisa breeze, gentle wind	**vendaval** (m) gale	**huracán** (m) hurricane	**torbellino** **remolino** whirlwind

WINDOW

ventana in house	†ventanilla in train, car; office counter	escaparate (m) vitrina (Am) shop/store window
vidriera stained–glass window	†cristal (m) windowpane	taquilla booking-office window

NOTE: in Peninsular Spanish **vitrina** = *glass showcase*.

WORK

trabajo		
empleo †puesto situación ocupación chamba (Mex) post, position, job	tarea †faena (R1) labor (f) (R3) task	obra piece of work
	tajo (R1) job	

3 Complex verbal expressions

It often happens that a simple verb in English has only a 'complex' paraphrase equivalent, with an essentially different syntax, in Spanish, or vice versa. Some very common and useful verbal ideas fall into this category, and a selection of these is given in the following sections.

3.1 A complex expression in Spanish corresponding to a single verb in English

to blame sb	**echar/achacar la culpa a uno**
to borrow sth from sb	†**pedir algo prestado a uno** (= to ask to borrow)
· I borrowed two books from him	· **Le pedí prestados dos libros**
	tomar algo prestado a uno (= to take sth on loan) NOTE: **prestar** sometimes = to borrow ☐! in Am.
to compete with sb	**hacer la competencia a uno**
to discharge sb · The doctor discharged us the same day	**dar de alta a uno** · **El médico nos dio de alta el mismo día**
to dismiss sb	**dar de baja a uno**
to drop sth	**dejar caer algo**
to ignore sth/sb	†**pasar algo/a**PERS **uno por alto**
to insist on sth	**hacer hincapié en algo**
to jilt sb	**dejar plantado a**PERS **uno**
to miss sth/sb	**echar de menos algo/a**PERS **uno** (Pen) (= †**extrañar** in Am)
to notice sth/sb	†**hacer caso a/de algo/uno**
to welcome sb	**dar la bienvenida a**IO **uno**
to wind up (a watch)	**dar cuerda (a un reloj)**

IO **a**IO introduces the indirect object
PERS **a**PERS denotes the Spanish personal **a**

R1* vulgar or indecent
R1 informal, colloquial
R2 neutral
R3 formal, written
See also p 3.

† More information about these words or expressions may be found in other sections. Use the Spanish word index to find the page numbers.

3.2 A single verb in Spanish corresponding to a complex expression in English

amanecer (R3) · **Cogió el tren en Madrid y amaneció en Córdoba**	to be in a place at daybreak · He caught the train in Madrid and arrived in Córdoba at dawn
†**despedirse de uno**	to take one's leave of sb
destacar(se) · **Destacan tres posibilidades** · **Este alumno se destaca de todos los otros/destaca sobre los demás**	to stand out · There are three obvious possibilities · This student stands out from all the others
†**no dignarse hacer algo** · **No se dignó contestar**	not so much as to do sth · He didn't even reply
distar de algo · **Mi casa no dista mucho de la tuya** · **Dista mucho de ser inteligente**	to be a long way from sth (lit and fig) · My house isn't far from yours · He's a long way from being bright
†**entrevistarse con uno**	to have an interview, talks with sb
†**estrenar algo** · **Estrenaron sus vestidos para la ópera**	to use sth for the first time · They wore their new clothes for the opera
golear (a^{PERS} **un equipo**) (R1) · **El Real (Madrid) goleó al Barcelona**	to score a lot of goals (against a team) · Real Madrid scored a hatful against Barcelona
guardarse (bien) de hacer algo · **Yo me guardaré bien de salir**	to be (very) careful not to do sth · I'll take care not to go out
independizarse	to become independent
limitarse a hacer algo · **Se limitó a decir que...**	only to do sth · He just said that . . .
†**llevar x años a uno** · **Mi hermana me lleva dos años**	to be older than sb by x years · My sister is two years older than me

meterse de (eg **peluquero**)	to take on a job as (eg a hairdresser)
[†]**profundizar en algo**	to go deeply into sth
[†]**regatear algo**	to haggle over sth, to be stingy with sth
repercutir en algo	to have repercussions on/throughout sth
· **El cambio repercutió en todo el departamento**	· The change had repercussions throughout the whole department
responsabilizar a[PERS] **uno de algo**	to lay responsibility for sth on sb
· **El diputado comunista responsabilizó al gobierno del paro**	· The communist deputy laid the responsibility for unemployment on the government
[†]**soler hacer algo**	to be accustomed to doing sth, usually to do sth
· **Suelo levantarme a las siete**	· I usually get up at seven
[†]**tardar (tiempo**, eg **cinco horas) en hacer algo**	to take (time, eg five hours) to do sth
· **El barco tarda cinco horas en llegar**	· It takes the boat five hours to get there (The boat takes five hours to get there)
tratarse de algo	to be a question of sth
[†]**volver a hacer algo**	to do sth again
· **Volvió a ver la película**	· She saw the film again

3.3 Common complex expressions in Spanish corresponding to complex expressions in English

sacar adelante	to bring up (eg a child); to produce, to turn out (eg a student); to go on with (eg business)
· **Trabajó mucho para sacar adelante la empresa**	· He worked hard to make the business prosper
salir adelante	to make progress, to get on
tener [†]**afición a algo**	to be enthusiastic about sth

tener a bien hacer algo (R2–3) · **Le pedí que tuviera a bien venir hoy**	to be kind enough to do sth · I asked her to be kind enough to come today
dejar constancia de algo	to place sth on record, give evidence of sth
tener algo en cuenta	to take sth into account
llevarse bien/mal con uno	get on well/badly with sb
ponerse de parte de uno · **Me puse de parte de mi amigo**	to take sb's side · I took my friend's side
†**pasarse sin algo**	to do without sth
salir al paso a¹⁰ uno · **Me salió al paso**	to go and meet sb · He came out to meet me
echarse a perder (intr) · **Se me ha echado a perder la chaqueta**	to get ruined/spoiled · My jacket's got ruined
no poder menos de hacer algo · **No pudo menos de sonreír**	not to be able to avoid doing sth · He could not help smiling
tener algo presente	to bear sth in mind
entrar en razón **meter/poner/hacer entrar en razón a uno**	to see reason to make sb see reason
pasar revista a algo/uno · **La señorita pasó revista a su guardarropa** · **El primer ministro pasó revista a las tropas**	to go through sth; to review sb (eg troops) · The girl went through her wardrobe · The prime minister reviewed the troops
†**dar la vuelta a algo** · **Dieron la vuelta a la plaza**	to go round sth · They went round the square

3.4 Spanish impersonal verbs

The usage of impersonal verbs in Spanish (see also **20.1.1**) can cause problems, and the English equivalents are not always obvious.

†**antojarse a¹⁰ uno hacer algo** · **Se le antojó ir al parque**	to occur to sb to do sth · It occurred to her to go to the park

†**bastar**	to be sufficient
· **Basta ⟨con⟩ decir que sí**	· It's enough to say so
· **Bastan cinco**	· Five's enough
†**caber**	to be contained
· **No cabe aquí**	· There's not enough room for it here
· **Al ministro le caben dos posibilidades**	· The minister has two possibilities
· **Cabe recordar que...**	· It is useful to remember that . . .
escasear (R3)	to be in short supply
· **Escasea el azúcar**	· Sugar is in short supply
†**faltar**	to be lacking
· **Faltan diez minutos para llegar a Londres**	· We'll be arriving in London in ten minutes
· **Faltan cinco minutos para que llegue mi tía**	· My aunt will be here in five minutes
†**importar**	to be important, to matter
· **Importa saberlo**	· It is important to know
· **Me importa que vengas**	· It's important for me that you come
· **¿Le importa si cierro la ventana?**	· Do you mind if I shut the window?
menudear (R3)	to be frequent, numerous
· **Menudean los problemas en esta empresa**	· There are many problems in this firm
†**quedar**	to be remaining
· **Le quedan a ella pocos amigos**	· She has few friends left
†**sobrar**	to be in excess, to be left (over)
· **Me sobran dos kilos de patatas**	· I've got two kilos of potatoes too many left
†**urgir** (R3)	to be urgent, imperative
· **Me urge saber la verdad**	· It is imperative I know the truth
valer	to be worth (lit)
· **Su libro le valió un gran premio**	· His book brought him a big prize

3.5 Reflexive verbs + **la** or **las**

There are a number of verbal expressions in Spanish which involve a reflexive verb + **la** or **las**. They have little in common apart from this but the commonest are grouped here together for convenience.

apañárselas · **No te preocupes: me las apãnaré**	to manage, to get by · Don't worry: I'll manage
arreglárselas · **Me las arreglo solo en la cocina**	to manage, get by · I get by on my own in the kitchen
cargársela (R1) (Pen)	to get into trouble
dárselas de (listo)	to give oneself the appearance of being (clever)
echárselas de ADJ/N · **Se las echa de héroe**	to make a show of being ADJ/a(n) N · He's playing the hero/He's making a show of being a hero
habérselas con uno (R1) · **Se las tendrá que haber con la directora**	to deal with, to face sb · She'll have to face the principal
pegársela a uno	to deceive sb
†**pirárselas** (R1★–1)	to go away, to get out
sabérselas todas (R1)	to be a know-all
traérselas (R1)	to be shocking, difficult (of people)
vérselas con uno · **Tendrá que vérselas con su padre**	to give an account of oneself to sb · He'll have to explain it to his father

4 Affective suffixes

One of the characteristic richnesses of Spanish, especially in R1, is its use of suffixes which can express a wide range of affective notions (size, affection, disapproval, irony, etc). Some stems and suffixes are so firmly associated that they form words in their own right, eg: **bolita** = *berry*, **telón** = *(theatre) curtain*, **parrilla** = *grill*, **camarín** (m) = *dressing room*, **caballete** (m) = *easel*, **hoyuelo** = *dimple*.

Affective suffixes are used most often with nouns and adjectives, although the use of **–ito/a** extends to past participles used adjectivally and even to adverbs:

> **Está completamente dormidito**
> He's sound asleep
> **Hay que hablar bajito**
> You must speak really quietly
> **Lo haré en seguidita**
> I'll do it right away
> †**¡Ahorita!** (used regularly in the sense of Pen **ahora** in Central America)

NOTE: the attachment of some suffixes (the main ones are **–ín**, **–ete**, **–ón** and **-azo**) to noun stems may lead to a change in gender from feminine to masculine, eg **novela** (f), but **novelón** (m).

-ito/a (also -(e)cito/a)

This is one of the commonest suffixes, especially in Latin America. Its predominant meaning is diminutive:

> **Tengo alquilado un cochecito**
> I've hired a small car
> **Hernani es un pueblecito en el País Vasco**
> Hernani is a small village in the Basque Country

It also indicates affection, and is particularly associated with language used to and by children:

> **Dale un besito a Papá**
> Give Daddy a kiss
> **¡Oye, niño, deja al caballito!**
> Hey, leave the horse alone!
> **Le duele el dientecito al pequeño**
> The child's tooth hurts

It can also have an intensifying meaning:

> **Hace un poco fresquito, ¿no?**
> It's pretty chilly, isn't it?
> **Allí tienes un café calentito**
> There's a nice hot coffee
> **¡Ay, el pobrecito!**
> Poor old thing!

⟫⟩→

-ico/a and *-ín* are similar to *-ito/a*, though by no means as common: *-ico/a* is particularly associated with Aragón and with some areas of Latin America; *-ín* is particularly associated with north–west Spain.

-illo/a (also -(e)cillo/a)

This is a diminutive suffix which often has a pejorative overtone; in Latin America it is almost exclusively pejorative.

No me gusta este tonillo de superioridad
I don't like this (nasty) superior tone
Había en la tienda un hombrecillo que se quedaba callado
In the shop was a(n insignificant) little man who said nothing
Me parece un poco complicadillo
It seems a bit (unpleasantly) complicated
Es una novela fuertecilla
It's a heavy novel

However, *-illo/a* in 'established' words (see above) is not usually pejorative: **una †ventanilla** = *a train window*, **un cursillo** = *a short course*.

NOTE also the non–pejorative use in the following example:
Soplaba un airecillo/vientecillo muy agradable
A very pleasant light breeze was blowing

-uelo/a (also -(e)juelo/a, -(e)zuelo/a and -chuelo/a) and -ete (also -(e)cete)

These are diminutive and pejorative: **plazuela** = *(miserable) little square*, **riachuelo** = *(trickle of a) stream*, **pequeñuelo** = *little child*; **lugarete** = *insignificant little place*.

-ón/-ona

This suffix has a number of values. It may be simply augmentative, as in **hombretón** = *well-built fellow*, **sillón** = *easy chair*. As an augmentative, it most frequently has a pejorative overtone, since largeness or excess is often thought of as being bad, eg **solterón/ona** = *confirmed bachelor/spinster*, **†cabrón** (R1★) = *bastard*, **dulzón** = *over-sweet*. However, where excess could be construed as good, there is no pejorative overtone, eg **fiestón** = *great party*.

-ón can also form pejorative adjectives from nouns (**cabezón** = *stubborn*) and pejorative nouns from verbs (**empollón** = *hard-working student, swot*, **llorón** = *cry-baby*).

-ón also indicates the result of an action, eg **bofetón** = *blow*.

NOTE: in American Spanish, **-ón** often has the meaning *fairly*, eg **pobretón** = *rather poor*.

-azo

This is similar to **-ón**, but is less common, eg **bigotazo** = *big moustache* (neutral), **acentazo** = *bad accent*, but **exitazo** = *great success*. **-azo** also has the meaning of *a blow with*, eg **codazo** = *nudge, blow with the elbow*.

-ote/a

This is augmentative and pejorative, eg **librote** = *dull book*, **palabrota** = *dirty word*, **cabezota** (m or f) = *real bighead*, **brutote** = *rough, clumsy, slow-witted*, **francote** = *very easy-going*.

NOTE, however, **amigote** = *buddy, mate*, which is familiar rather than pejorative.

-ucho/a, -acho/a and *-uco/a*

These are pejorative:
   Vive en una casucha aislada en el campo
   She lives in an isolated hovel in the country
   un cuartucho asqueroso
   a disgustingly squalid room
   el populacho
   the common herd
   esos capitalistas †ricachos
   those stinking rich capitalists
   un frailuco
   an insignificant little monk
   una mujeruca
   an old woman

NOTE, however, **picachos** = *fierce-looking peaks*.

R1* vulgar or indecent
R1 informal, colloquial
R2 neutral
R3 formal, written
See also p 3.

† More information about these words or expressions may be found in other sections. Use the Spanish word index to find the page numbers.

5 Idioms, similes and proverbs

Language in all registers can be made more lively and interesting by the judicious use of idiomatic expressions. The following expressions are a small selection from the wealth of such material in Spanish. They are all in common use, and may be employed with confidence by learners.

5.1 Idioms

tener (muchas) agallas	to be courageous
hacer su agosto	to make one's pile, to make hay while the sun shines
estar con el agua/la soga al cuello	to be in great difficulties
caerse el alma a los pies	to be down in the dumps
· **Se me cayó el alma a los pies**	· I was down in the dumps
estar con el alma en un hilo/en vilo	to be in suspense
consultar con la almohada	to sleep on it
tener ángel/mal ángel	to be charming/to lack charm
armarse un ruido/un escándalo/la de Dios/un follón (R1)/**una gresca** (R1)/ **la de San Quintín**	to cause a row
estar/tener aᴾᴱᴿˢ **uno en ascuas**	to be/to keep sb on tenterhooks
todo bicho viviente (R1)	every living soul

NOTE: **bicho** is avoided in Caribbean and Chilean Spanish, where it has the meaning of *penis* in R1.

estar/quedarse sin blanca (Pen)/**sin un centavo** (Am) (R1–2)	not to have a bean
no importar un bledo/ comino/pepino (R1)	not to matter two hoots
a pedir de boca	perfectly
hacerse la boca agua aᴵᴼ **uno**	to make sb's mouth water
meterse en la boca del lobo	to enter the lion's den
quedar boquiabierto/ quedarse lelo	to be left gaping (in bewilderment)
echar la bronca aᴵᴼ **uno**	to give sb a real dressing down
no caber en sí/su piel	to be beside oneself (with joy, anger); to be presumptuous
caer bien/mal	to be well-timed/ill-timed
pasar las de Caín (R1)	to have a bad time
dar calabazas aᴵᴼ **uno** (R1)	to jilt; to fail sb (in exam)

ᴵᴼ **a**ᴵᴼ introduces the indirect object
ᴾᴱᴿˢ **a**ᴾᴱᴿˢ denotes the Spanish personal **a**

meterse en un callejón sin salida	to get into a jam
ponérsele a[IO] uno la carne de gallina	to get goose pimples
dar carta blanca a[IO] uno	to give sb a free hand, carte blanche
no saber a qué carta quedarse	to be uncertain
ser un cero a la izquierda (R1)	to be of no value, count for nothing (of person)
charlar por los codos	to talk incessantly
†estar en condiciones (de hacer algo)	to be in good shape, to be able (to do sth)
llevar la contraria	to take an opposite point of view
marchar/nadar/ir contra la corriente	to go against the current, to swim against the tide
ser un cuco	to be cunning
ajustar las cuentas a[IO] uno (R1–2)	to settle accounts with sb, to sort sb out
venir a cuento	to be appropriate, fitting
llevarse un chasco	to be disappointed
echar/arrojar/lanzar chispas	to get angry
está chupado (commoner with younger people)/tirado (commoner with older people) (R1)	it's a piece of cake
un lío, ruido, etc de todos los demonios (R1–2)	a hell of a problem, noise, etc
tomar el desquite (de algo) (R3)	to get revenge, to get one's own back (for sth)
todo el santo día (R1–2)	the whole blessed day
mandar a[PERS] uno al diablo/a paseo (R1)	to send sb packing
Dios mediante (R3)	God willing
hacer época (R2–3)	to be sensational, to attract much public attention
mandar a[PERS] uno a freír espárragos (R1)	to send sb packing
dar el esquinazo a[IO] uno	to give sb the slip
tener buena/mala estrella	to be lucky/unlucky
ser la flor y nata	to be the cream
estar entre dos fuegos	to be caught in the crossfire
estar fuera de sí	to be beside oneself (emotionally, both positive and negative)
ser la gallina de los huevos de oro (R1–2)	to be the goose that lays the golden eggs
hay gato encerrado	there's sth fishy
buscar tres pies al gato	to split hairs, to make things more complicated than they are
dar el golpe de gracia a[IO] uno	to finish sb off
ir al grano	to go straight to the point
†Ni hablar (R1–2)	Nothing doing

hablar en cristiano	to talk plainly, clearly
hacer de las suyas	to be up to one's old tricks
ser harina de otro costal	to be another kettle of fish
†**estar hecho una fiera**	to get furious
estar hecho una pena	to be in a sorry state
estar hecho polvo	to get worn out
estar hecho una sopa	
estar calado/mojado hasta los huesos	to get soaked to the skin
estar hecho un mar de lágrimas	to weep floods of tears
entrar/poner en juego	to be/to put at stake
tirar (R1)/**irse** (R2) **cada uno por su lado**	each to go his/her separate way
†**dar la lata a**[IO] **uno** (R1)	to get on sb's nerves
ser una lata (R1)	to be annoying
dormirse en/sobre los laureles	to rest on one's laurels
tener mala leche (R1*)/**mal café** (R1)	to be a nasty type
levantar la liebre	to spill the beans
tener líos/un lío (R1–2)	to have difficulties
estar loco de atar/de remate (R1–2)	to be completely mad
entre dos luces (R3)	in the evening
estar en la luna	to have one's head in the clouds
salir/sacar a luz	to be published/to publish (eg a book)
dar a luz un niño	to give birth to a child
¡toca madera!	touch wood!
estar en mangas de camisa	to be in one's shirt-sleeves
†**echar mano a**	to take hold of
†**echar una mano a**[IO] **uno**	to give sb a hand
tener buena/mala mano para algo	to be expert/clumsy at sth
un libro de segunda mano	a second-hand book
irse/venir/llegar a las manos/los puños	to come to blows
estar de más/de sobra	to be in excess
sin más ni más	without further hesitation
como el que más	more than anyone
hacer mella en/a[IO] **uno**	to make an impression on sb
meterse en barullos/ berenjenales/líos (R1)	to get into a real mess
meterse en donde no le llaman	to snoop around
hacer (buenas) migas con uno	to hit it off with sb
ser de mírame y no me toques	to be finicky, delicate
ser un mirlo blanco	to be an exceptional thing, an impossible dream
ser moneda corriente (R3)	to be a common occurrence
ser de poca monta	to be of little value
Hay moros en la costa	Careful, people are listening

[IO] **a**[IO] introduces the indirect object
[PERS] **a**[PERS] denotes the Spanish personal **a**

picarle a^{PERS} uno la mosca (R1–2)	to get upset, irritated
desde que el mundo es el mundo	since time began
¡Nada de eso!	Nothing doing!
como si nada/tal	as if nothing had happened
no saber nada de nada	to be totally ignorant
meter la nariz/las narices en algo (R1)	to snoop around in sth
hinchársele a^{IO} uno las narices	to lose patience, to get irritated
pasar las noches en blanco	to have sleepless nights
llamar a las cosas por su nombre	} to call a spade a spade
llamar al pan pan y al vino vino	
estar en las nubes	to be up in the clouds
hacer oídos sordos	to turn a deaf ear
ser todos oídos	to be all ears
tener ojeriza a algo	to take a dislike to sth
¡(Mucho) ojo (con algo)!	Careful (with sth)!
andar con ojo	to go carefully
ser el ojo/ojito derecho de uno	to be sb's pet
no pegar ojo/los ojos en toda la noche	not to sleep a wink all night
en un abrir y cerrar de ojos	in the twinkling of an eye
saltar a los ojos/la vista	to be patently obvious
enseñar la oreja	to show one's true character/intentions, to give oneself away
con las orejas gachas (R1)	depressed
matar dos pájaros de un tiro	to kill two birds with one stone
tener/[†]tomar la palabra	to have/to take the floor
tener palabra/no tener palabra	to keep one's word/to be unreliable
ser pan comido (R1)	to be as easy as pie
estar/vivir a pan y agua	to live in poverty
perder hasta los pantalones/la camisa	to lose everything
meter la pata	to put one's foot in it
peces gordos	big shots, important people
estar/moverse/sentirse como pez en el agua	to be in one's element
como Pedro por su casa	freely, easily, without obstacle
ser de película	to be magnificent
tomar el pelo a^{IO} uno	to pull sb's leg, to kid sb
no vérsele el pelo a^{IO} uno	
· No se le ve el pelo	· He's made himself scarce
llevarse como el perro y el gato	to be always squabbling
¡A otro perro con ese hueso!	Nonsense!, Tell me another!
caer en picado	to dive (of plane)
cerrar el pico	to shut up, to keep quiet

no dejar piedra por mover remover Roma con Santiago }	to leave no stone unturned
No se tiene de pie	It doesn't hold water (of argument)
dormir a pierna suelta	to sleep soundly
no tener ni pies ni cabeza	to be pointless (of argument), to have no meaning
dorar la píldora	to sugar the pill, to make sth easier to swallow
tragarse la píldora	to swallow the whole story
estar entre Pinto y Valdemoro	to be undecided
irse a pique	to sink (of ship), to be ruined (of family, etc)
pisar fuerte	to show resolve
poner los puntos sobre las íes	to dot the i's and cross the t's
predicar en el desierto	to preach/to talk to deaf ears
no soltar prenda	not to divulge a secret, to keep mum
por el qué dirán	because of what the neighbours will say
sacar de quicio a^{PERS} uno	to get on sb's nerves
andarse por las ramas	to beat about the bush
mantener a raya a^{PERS} uno	to keep sb in check/at bay
dar la razón a^{IO} uno	to say that sb is right
dar rienda suelta a^{IO} uno	to give sb a free rein
costar un riñón (R1)	to cost the earth/an arm and a leg
pegársele a uno las sábanas	to get up later than necessary
sacar en claro/en limpio	to make clear
a lo que salga	come what may, however it turns out
salirse con la suya	to get one's own way
calentársele/encendérsele la sangre a^{IO} uno	to get angry/impatient
no saber a qué santo encomendarse	not to know where to turn
tomar en serio	to take seriously
saltarse los sesos	to blow one's brains out
ir a la suya/a lo suyo	to go one's own way
hacer de las suyas	to be up to one's old tricks
sobre el terreno	on the job, where the work actually takes place
andando el tiempo	as time goes/went by
ir tirando	to get by
Le salió el tiro por la culata	In the end the joke was on him
faltarle a^{IO} uno un tornillo	to have a screw loose
dar al traste con	to ruin, to spoil (eg plans)
irse al traste	to be ruined
rasgarse la túnica/las vestiduras (R2–3)	to rend one's clothes/to tear one's hair (with frustration, anger)

tomar a[PERS] uno por cabeza de turco (R2–3)	to use sb as a scapegoat
estar en las últimas (R1)	to be about to die; to be down and out
valer un dineral/un mundo/un ojo de la cara/un Potosí	to be worth a fortune
verlo todo color de rosa	to see life through rose-tinted glasses, to take an unduly cheerful view of things
verlo todo negro/nublado	to be pessimistic
tener siete vidas	to have nine lives (as a cat)
contra viento y marea	against all the odds
hacer(se) (de (Am)) la vista gorda	to turn a blind eye
hacer su santa voluntad	to do just what one likes
volver en sí	to regain consciousness
dar una vuelta	to go for a walk
†dar la vuelta	to go back
dar vueltas a algo	to think sth over
ir/quedar a la zaga (R2–3)	to go/drag behind
ponerle zancadillas a[IO] uno	to catch sb out

5.2 Similes based on adjectives

más †astuto que la zorra	as cunning as a fox
más blanco que la nieve	as white as snow
†bueno como un ángel	as good as gold
más †bueno que el pan	goodness itself
tan claro como el agua	as clear as crystal
más †contento que unas Pascuas	as happy as a lark
más duro que un mendrugo/una †piedra	as tough as nails
más feo que Picio	as ugly as sin
más frío que el hielo/un témpano	as cold as ice
†fuerte como un roble	as strong as an ox
tan negro/oscuro como boca de lobo	as black as pitch
más †pobre que una †rata	as poor as a church mouse
más sordo que una †tapia	as deaf as a post
†viejo como el mundo	as old as the hills

NOTE: the patterns más ADJ que and (tan) ADJ como are interchangeable.

5.3 Similes based on verbs

†aburrirse como una ostra/almeja	to be bored to tears
bailar como una peonza	to spin like a top
beber como una †cuba	to drink like a fish
†caer/venir como †anillo al dedo	to fit like a glove
†cantar como un jilguero	to sing like a canary
†comer como una †lima	to eat like a horse
†correr como un galgo	to run like a greyhound
†dormir como un lirón/una †piedra/un †tronco/un leño	to sleep like a log
fumar como un carretero	to smoke like a chimney
†hablar como un loro	to talk like a parrot
†llorar como un †niño/una Magdalena	to cry like a baby
nadar como un †pez	to swim like a fish
venderse como churros/pan bendito	to sell like hot cakes

5.4 Proverbs and proverbial expressions

En casa del ahorcado no se ha de nombrar la soga	*lit* You shouldn't mention the rope in the house of a hanged man, ie *Avoid talking about things that may cause embarrassment*
Arrancada de caballo y parada de asno	*lit* starting like a horse and stopping like an ass, ie *If you set off too quickly you get tired*
Uno piensa el bayo, y otro el que lo ensilla	*lit* The bay horse thinks one thing, and the person who saddles him thinks another, ie *Everyone sees things from their own point of view*
Quien mala cama hace, en ella se yace	*You made your bed, now lie in it!*
A mal tiempo buena cara	*lit* a good face to bad weather, ie *Grin and bear it*
Empezar la casa por el tejado	*lit* to begin the house with the roof, ie *to put the cart before the horse*
Antes que te cases, mira lo que haces	*lit* Before you marry, look what you are doing, ie *Marry in haste, repent at leisure*, or *Look before you leap*

Eso es el cuento de la lechera	*counting one's chickens before they are hatched* (refers to the story of the milkmaid who planned what to do with the money she would get for her milk, but dropped the pitcher on the way to market)
Del dicho al hecho hay gran trecho	*There's many a slip 'twixt cup and lip*
Los dineros del sacristán, cantando se vienen y cantando se van	*Easy come, easy go*
Poderoso caballero es don Dinero	*Money talks*
Dios aprieta pero no ahoga	*lit* God squeezes but he doesn't stifle, ie *Keep calm, all will come right in the end*
Dios los cría y ellos se juntan	*Birds of a feather flock together*
A Dios rogando y con el mazo dando	*lit* asking God and wielding the mallet, ie *God helps those who help themselves*
Gato escaldado del agua fría huye	*lit* A scalded cat avoids cold water (as well), ie *Once bitten, twice shy*
A lo hecho, pecho	*It's no use crying over spilt milk*
A quien madruga, Dios le ayuda	*lit* God helps the early riser, ie *The early bird catches the worm.* The answer often given to this is **No por mucho madrugar amanece más temprano** = *It doesn't dawn any earlier because you get up earlier*
Ojos que no ven, corazón que no siente	*Out of sight, out of mind*
Más vale pájaro en mano que cien volando	*A bird in the hand is worth two in the bush*
De tal palo, tal astilla	*a chip off the old block*
Las paredes oyen	*Walls have ears*
El que quiere peces que se moje el culo (R1)	*lit* He who wants fish must get his bottom wet, ie *If you want to be successful you must take risks*

El que se pica ajos come	*lit* He who is cross eats garlic, ie *If the shoe fits, wear it*
El puchero dijo a la sartén: 'Apártate de mí que me tiznas'	*the pot calling the kettle black*
A cada puerco llega su San Martín	*lit* To every pig comes his Martinmas (the day on which the pig is killed), ie *There is a day of reckoning for everyone*
No se puede repicar y andar en la procesión	*lit* You cannot ring the bells and walk in the procession, ie *You cannot do two things at once*
Al río revuelto ganancias de pescadores	*lit* Fishermen gain from a turbulent river, ie *It's an ill wind that blows nobody any good*
Cuando el río suena agua lleva	*lit* When the river makes a noise there's a lot of water, ie *There's no smoke without fire*
Cuando a Roma fueres/Allí donde fueres, haz como vieres	*When in Rome, do as the Romans do*
El sapo a la sapa tiénela por muy guapa	*lit* The male toad considers the female toad very pretty, ie *Beauty is in the eye of the beholder*
Ir a vendimia y llevar uvas de postre	*lit* to go to the grape harvest and take grapes as a dessert, ie *to take coals to Newcastle*
En una hora no se ganó Zamora	*Rome wasn't built in a day*
Mucho sabe la zorra pero más el que la toma	*lit* The vixen is clever, but the one who catches her is cleverer

R1★	vulgar or indecent
R1	informal, colloquial
R2	neutral
R3	formal, written
See also p 3.	

† More information about these words or expressions may be found in other sections. Use the Spanish word index to find the page numbers.

6 Proper names

Wherever a Spanish equivalent for a foreign name exists, Spanish uses it. Christian names are regularly adapted. For example, Queen Elizabeth and Prince Charles are always **la Reina Isabel** and **el Príncipe Carlos** in the Spanish press. Spanish has in the course of history hispanized a number of foreign personal and place names, many of which survive in current usage. The following lists, though long, are by no means exhaustive; they include the commonest of such names and those which are not immediately recognizable, together with the English equivalent (which is frequently an anglicized name). It should be stressed that Spanish speakers expect these forms to be used: for example, it would be odd to refer to New York as anything other than **Nueva York** in a Spanish-speaking context.

NOTE: English has anglicized some Spanish names, eg Corunna (**La Coruña**), Havana (**La Habana**), Majorca (**Mallorca**), Minorca (**Menorca**), Biscay (**Vizcaya**), Saragossa (**Zaragoza**).

6.1 Names of people

The Ancient Greek world	Alejandro	Alexander
	Aquiles	Achilles
	Ariana	Ariadne
	Aristófanes	Aristophanes
	Aristóteles	Aristotle
	Arquímedes	Archimedes
	Edipo	Oedipus
	Esopo	Aesop
	Esquilo	Aeschylus
	Euclides	Euclid
	Eurípides	Euripides
	Febo	Phoebus
	Homero	Homer
	Ilíada	Iliad
	Odisea	Odyssey
	Jenofonte	Xenophon
	Jerjes	Xerxes
	Leandro	Leander
	Pitágoras	Pythagoras
	Platón	Plato
The Ancient Roman world	Adriano	Hadrian
	Aníbal	Hannibal
	Augusto	Augustus
	Boecio	Boethius
	Cartago	Carthage

	Catón	*Cato*
	(Julio) César	*(Julius) Caesar*
	Cicerón	*Cicero*
	Escipión	*Scipio*
	Horacio	*Horace*
	Marco Antonio	*Mark Antony*
	Nerón	*Nero*
	Ovidio	*Ovid*
	Plinio	*Pliny*
	Tito Livio	*Livy*
The Bible: Old Testament	Adán	*Adam*
	Baltasar	*Belshazzar*
	Dalila	*Delilah*
	Isaías	*Isaiah*
	Jehová	*Jehovah*
	Jonás	*Jonah*
	Josué	*Joshua*
	Judá	*Judah*
	Matusalén	*Methuselah*
	Moisés	*Moses*
	Nabucodonosor	*Nebuchadnezzar*
	Noé	*Noah*
	Rut	*Ruth*
	Saba	*Sheba*
	Saúl	*Saul*

NOTE: the New Testament Saul (later Paul) = **Saulo**.

The Bible: New Testament	Andrés	*Andrew*
	Herodes	*Herod*
	Jesucristo/Jesús	*Jesus Christ/Jesus*
	José	*Joseph*
	Juan Bautista	*John the Baptist*
	Lucas	*Luke*
	Magdalena	*Mary Magdalene*
	Marcos (cf Marco Antonio, above)	*Mark*
	el Mesías	*the Messiah*
	Poncio Pilato	*Pontius Pilate*
	Satanás	*Satan*

NOTE ALSO the place names **Belén**, *Bethlehem*; **Jerusalén**, *Jerusalem*; **Nazaret**, *Nazareth*; **Sión**, *Zion*.

People in the medieval and Renaissance world	Colón	*Columbus*
	Durero	*Dürer*
	Lutero	*Luther*
	Magallanes	*Magellan*
	Mahoma	*Mohammed*
	Maquiavelo	*Machiavelli*
	Miguel-Ángel	*Michelangelo*
	Petrarca	*Petrarch*
	Ticiano OR Tiziano	*Titian*

6.2 Names of places

Europe

Amberes	*Antwerp*
Aquisgrán	*Aachen/Aix-la-Chapelle*
Atenas	*Athens*
Aviñón	*Avignon*
Basilea	*Basle*
Baviera	*Bavaria*
Berna	*Berne*
Borgoña	*Burgundy*
Brujas	*Bruges*
Bruselas	*Brussels*
Burdeos	*Bordeaux*
Cerdeña	*Sardinia*

NOTE: do not confuse with **Cerdaña**, an eastern Pyrenean valley.

Colonia	*Cologne*
Copenhague	*Copenhagen*
Córcega	*Corsica*
Cornualles	*Cornwall*
Cracovia	*Cracow*
Dresde	*Dresden*
Edimburgo	*Edinburgh*
Estambul	*Istanbul*
Estocolmo	*Stockholm*
Flandes	*Flanders*
Florencia	*Florence*
Francfort (del Meno)	*Frankfurt (am Main)*
Friburgo	*Freiburg*
Gante	*Ghent*
Gascuña	*Gascony*
Génova	*Genoa*
Ginebra	*Geneva*
Gotinga	*Göttingen*
La Haya	*The Hague*

NOTE: **La** is the article, despite the normal rule that **el** precedes nouns beginning with a stressed **a-** or **ha-**.

Liorna	*Livorno*
Lisboa	*Lisbon*
Londres	*London*
Lovaina	*Louvain/Leuven*
Madera	*Madeira*
Maguncia	*Mainz*
Malinas	*Mechlin/Mechelen/Malines*
Mantua	*Mantua/Mantova*
Marsella	*Marseilles*
Micenas	*Mycenae*
Milán	*Milan/Milano*
Moscú	*Moscow*
Munich	*Munich/München*
Nápoles	*Naples*
Nicosia	*Nicosia*

NOTE the difference in stress

Islas Orcadas	*Orkneys*

Padua	*Padua/Padova*
París	*Paris*
Provenza	*Provence*
Ratisbona *also* Regensburgo	*Regensburg*
Rodas	*Rhodes*
Roma	*Rome*
Rosellón	*Roussillon*
Ruán	*Rouen*
Saboya	*Savoy*
Sajonia	*Saxony*
el Sarre	*The Saar*
Tesalónica	*Thessalonica*
Tolosa	*Toulouse*
Tréveris	*Trier*
Turín	*Turin/Torino*
La Valeta	*(La) Valletta*
Varsovia	*Warsaw*
Venecia	*Venice*
Versalles	*Versailles*
Viena	*Vienna*

Asia

Antioquía	*Antioch*

NOTE: do not confuse with **Antioquia** in Colombia.

La Meca	*Mecca*
Pekín	*Beijing*
Seúl	*Seoul*
Singapur	*Singapore*

Africa

Addis–Abeba	*Addis Ababa*
Alejandría	*Alexandria*
Argel	*Algiers*
el Cairo	*Cairo*
Ciudad del Cabo	*Cape Town*

NOTE: **en la Ciudad del Cabo**.

(el) Sáhara	*Sahara (desert and state)*
Tánger	*Tangier*
Túnez	*Tunis/Tunisia*

North America

Carolina del Norte/del Sur	*North/South Carolina*
Columbia Británica	*British Columbia*
Filadelfia	*Philadelphia*
La Guadalupe	*Guadeloupe*
Islas Lucayas *also* Bahamas	*Bahamas*
Luisiana	*Louisiana*
La Martinica	*Martinique*
Nueva Brunswick	*New Brunswick*
Nueva Escocia	*Nova Scotia*
Nuevo Méjico/México	*New Mexico*
Nueva Orleáns	*New Orleans*
Nueva York	*New York*
Pensilvania	*Pennsylvania*
Tejas	*Texas*
Terranova	*Newfoundland*

South America

Islas Malvinas	*Falkland Islands*

6.3   Names of rivers

Amazonas (m)	*Amazon*
Misisipí (m)	*Mississippi*
Misuri (m)	*Missouri*
Nilo	*Nile*
Rin (m)	*Rhine*
Ródano	*Rhone*
Sena (m)	*Seine*
Tajo	*Tagus*
Támesis (m)	*Thames*

6.4   Names of mountains and volcanoes

Alpes (m pl)	*Alps*
Apalaches (m pl)	*Appalachians*
Apeninos	*Apennines*
Himalaya (m)	*Himalayas*
Las Montañas Rocosas	*The Rockie Mountains*
Pirineos	*Pyrenees*
Vesubio	*Vesuvius*

The gender of nouns is only given where it is not predictable from the principles given in ch. **16**.

7 Adjectives pertaining to countries and towns

Spanish has a wealth of special adjectives for inhabitants of countries and towns. By contrast with similar adjectives in English (Mancunian, Liverpudlian, etc), the Spanish ones are in extremely common use. It is difficult to predict which of the several suffixes available will combine with a particular name, and sometimes the adjective will be unrelated to the name, or derive from an older name.

The following list includes the commoner of these adjectives, and those which are not immediately recognizable.

7.1 España→ **español** OR **hispano** (R3)

NOTE the use of **hispano-** in compounds, eg **hispanoárabe**.
NOTE: Spain is frequently referred to as **la Península** (*peninsular*), especially when distinguishing between the mainland and **Baleares** and **Canarias**.

Regions

Andalucía→ **andaluz**
Aragón→ **aragonés** OR **maño/mañico** (R1)
(las Islas) Baleares→ **balear**
(las Islas) Canarias→ **canario** OR **guanche**
  NOTE: the Canaries are also referred to as simply as **Las Islas**.
Cantabria→ **cántabro**
  NOTE: la Cordillera Cantábrica, el Mar Cantábrico.
Castilla→ **castellano**
Cataluña→ **catalán**
Extremadura→ **extremeño**
Galicia→ **gallego**
el País Vasco→ **vasco** OR **euskadi** (invariable), the latter preferred by Basques
  NOTE: **vascongado** is used chiefly in the expression **las Provincias Vascongadas**. **Vascuence** is used for the Basque language (also **euskera**).

Towns

Alcalá de Henares→ **complutense**
  NOTE: **complutense** is also used of the Madrid University which was transferred from Alcalá.
Ávila→ **abulense**
Barcelona→ **barcelonés**
  NOTE: Barcelona is also frequently referred to, especially in journalistic R3, as **la Ciudad Condal**.
Burgos→ **burgalés**
Cádiz→ **gaditano**
Córdoba→ **cordobés**
Elche→ **ilicitano**
Granada→ **granadino**
Huelva→ **onubense**

Huesca→ **oscense**
Jaén→ **jaenés** OR **jienense**
Madrid→ **madrileño**
Málaga→ **malagueño**
Oviedo→ **ovetense**
Salamanca→ **salmantino**
San Sebastián→ **donostiarra**
Santander→ **santanderino**
> NOTE: Santander (Colombia) has the adjective **santandereano**.

Santiago de Compostela→ **compostelano** OR **santiagués**
> NOTE: the Santiagos of Latin America all have different adjectives:
> see the Latin American list.

Sevilla→ **sevillano**
Tarragona→ **tarraconense**
Valencia→ **valenciano**
Valladolid→ **vallisoletano**
Zaragoza→ **zaragozano**

Islands

Ibiza→ **ibicenco**
Mallorca→ **mallorquín**
Menorca→ **menorquín**
Tenerife→ **tinerfeño**

7.2 América Latina / Latinoamérica→ (latino)americano

The following names should be distinguished:

América Latina/Latinoamérica→ **latinoamericano** = Spanish-
and Portuguese-speaking America
América del Sur/Sudamérica→ **sudamericano** = South America
(ie from isthmus of Panama south)
América Central/Centroamérica→ **centroamericano** = Central
America (ie Panama to Mexico)
Hispanoamérica→ **hispanoamericano** = Spanish-speaking
America (ie not including Brazil, etc)
Iberoamérica→ **iberoamericano** = América Latina

NOTE: the adjective **americano** may correspond to English *Latin
American*; English *American*, which usually refers to North America,
is often **norteamericano**.

NOTE: **el hemisferio**, a term often used in journalistic American
Spanish, refers to the entire American continent.

(la) Argentina→ argentino

Buenos Aires→ **porteño** OR **bonaerense**
> NOTE: **porteño** is used of other ports as well, notably of Valparaíso
> (Chile).

Patagonia→ **patagón**
Santa Fe→ **santafecino**
Santiago del Estero→ **santiagueño**
Tierra del Fuego→ **fueguino**

Bolivia→ **boliviano**

La Paz→ **paceño**
Potosí→ **potosino**
Sucre→ **sucrense**

Colombia→ **colombiano**

Bogotá→ **bogotano**
Medellín→ **medellinense**

Costa Rica→ **costarriqueño** OR **costarricense**

San José→ **josefino**

Cuba→ **cubano**

La Habana→ **habanero**
Santiago→ **santiaguero**

Chile (m)→ **chileno**

Concepción→ **penquisto** OR **pencón**
Santiago→ **santiaguino**
Valparaíso→ **porteño**

(el) Ecuador (m)→ **ecuatoriano**

Quito→ **quiteño**

Guatemala→ **guatemalteco**

Honduras→ **hondureño**

Tegucigalpa→ **tegucigalpense**

México (Am)/Méjico (Pen)→ **mexicano** (Am)/**mejicano** (Pen)

Guadalajara→ **guadalajarense**
   NOTE: Guadalajara (Spain) has the adjective **guadalajareño**.
Mérida→ **meridano**
   NOTE: Mérida (Spain and Venezuela) has the adjective **merideño**.

Nicaragua→ **nicaragüense**

Managua→ **managüense**

Panamá (m)→ **panameño**

(el) Paraguay (m)→ **paraguayo**

Asunción→ **asunceno**

(el) Perú (m)→ **peruano**

Callao→ **chalaco**
(el) Cuzco→ **cuzqueño**
Lima→ **limeño**

Puerto Rico→ **puertorriqueño** OR **portorriqueño**

El Salvador (m)→ **salvadoreño**

(el) Uruguay (m)→ **uruguayo**

Montevideo→ **montevideano**

Venezuela→ **venezolano**

Caracas→ **caraqueño**
Maracaibo→ **maracaibero**

7.3 Europa→ **europeo**

Albania→ **albanés**
Alemania→ **alemán**
  Berlín→ **berlinés**
  Hamburgo→ **hamburgués**
Andorra→ **andorrano**
Austria→ **austríaco** OR **austriaco**
Bélgica→ **belga**
Bulgaria→ **búlgaro**
Cerdeña→ **sardo**
Córcega→ **corso**
Creta→ **cretense**
Checoslovaquia→ **checo(slovaco)**
Chipre (f)→ **chipriota**
Dinamarca→ **danés** OR **dinamarqués** (R3)
Escocia→ **escocés** (but see **Gran Bretaña** below)
Finlandia→ **finlandés**
Francia→ **francés** OR **galo** (R3)
  NOTE the use of **franco** in compounds, eg **franco-belga**.
  París→ **parisiense** OR **parisino** ⚡
Gales (m)→ **galés**
Gran Bretaña/(el) Reino Unido→ **británico**
  NOTE: Spanish-speaking people often use **inglés** for any inhabitant
    of the British Isles.
  Londres→ **londinense**
Grecia→ **griego**
  NOTE: the now obsolete adjective **greco** is still used in compounds,
    eg **grecolatino**, and in the name of the painter **El Greco**.
  Atenas→ **ateniense**
Holanda/los Países Bajos→ **holandés**
Hungría→ **húngaro**

Inglaterra→ **inglés**
Irlanda del Norte/el Úlster→ **irlandés** (but see **Gran Bretaña** above)
Irlanda del Sur/República de Irlanda→ **irlandés** (but see **Gran Bretaña** above)
Italia→ **italiano**
Luxemburgo→ **luxemburgués**
Malta→ **maltés**
Noruega→ **noruego**
Polonia→ **polaco**
Portugal (m)→ **portugués** OR **lusitano** (R3)
 NOTE the use of **luso–** in compounds, eg **luso–hispano** (R3).
 Lisboa→ **lisboeta**
Romanía/Rumania→ **rumano**
Rusia/la URSS (see **8.3**)/la Unión Soviética→ **ruso** OR **soviético**
 Moscú→ **moscovita**
Suecia→ **sueco**
Suiza→ **suizo**
Turquía→ **turco**
Yugoslavia→ **yugoslavo**

7.4 África→ **africano**

África del Sur/Sudáfrica/Suráfrica→ **sudafricano** OR **surafricano**
 NOTE: África Meridional = Southern Africa.
Angola→ **angoleño**
Argelia→ **argelino**
Benín (m)→ **beninés**
Burkina Faso (m)→ **burkinés**
(el) Camerún→ **camerunense** OR **camerunés**
Costa de Marfil→ **(costa)marfileño**
Chad (m)→ **chadiense**
Egipto→ **egipcio**
Etiopía→ **etíope**
Gabón (m)→ **gabonés**
Ghana→ **ganés**
Guinea→ **guineo**
Kenia→ **kenyata** OR **keniano**
Liberia→ **liberiano**
Libia→ **libio**
Madagascar (m)→ **malgache**
Malawi (m)→ **malawi**
Mali (m)→ **malagués**
Marruecos (m sg)→ **marroquí**
Mauritania→ **mauritano**
Mozambique (m)→ **mozambiqueño** OR **mozambicano**
Namibia→ **namibiano** OR **namibio**
Níger (m)→ **nigerino**
Nigeria→ **nigeriano**
(la) República Centroafricana→ **centroafricano**
(el) Senegal→ **senegalés**
Sierra Leone→ **sierraleonés**

Somalia→ **somalí**
(el) Sudán→ **sudanés**
Tanzania→ **tanzano**
Togo (m)→ **togolés**
Túnez (m)→ **tunecino**
Uganda→ **ugandés**
Zaire (m)→ **zaireño**
Zambia→ **zambiano**
Zimbabwe/Zimbabue (m)→ **zimbabuo** OR **cimbabués**

7.5   Asia→ **asiático** y Australia→ **australiano**

Afganistán (m)→ **afgano**
Bangladés/Bangla Desh (m)→ **bengalí**
Birmania→ **birmanés**
Corea del Norte→ **norte-coreano**
Corea del Sur→ **surcoreano**
(la) China→ **chino**
(las) Filipinas→ **filipino**
la India→ **indio**
Indonesia→ **indonesio**
(el) Japón→ **japonés** OR **nipón** (R3)
Kampuchea→ **camboyano** OR **kampucheano**
Laos (m)→ **laosiano**
Malasia→ **malayo**
(el) Nepal→ **nepalés**
Nueva Caledonia→ **neocaledoniano**
Nueva Zelanda→ **neozelandés** OR **neocelandés**
(el) Pakistán→ **pakistaní**
Sri Lanka (m)→ **srilanqués**
Tailandia→ **tailandés**
(el) Tibet→ **tibetano**
(el) Vietnam→ **vietnamita**

7.6   Oriente Medio

Arabia Saudita→ **arabesaudí** OR **saudí**
(el) Irak→ **iraquí**
(el) Irán→ **iraní**
Israel (m)→ **israelí**

7.7   América del Norte→ **norteamericano**

(el) Canadá→ **canadiense**
(los) Estados Unidos→ **(norte)americano** OR **estadounidense** ALSO
   yanqui, **gringo** (R1–2 Am)
   NOTE: Estados Unidos used without the article is generally treated
      as singular, eg **Estados Unidos suspendió sus garantías**
      defensivas hacia Nueva Zelanda, a las que está
      comprometido…
Nueva York→ **neoyorquino**

8 Abbreviations

Abbreviations and acronyms (*siglas*) abound in the Spanish–speaking world, and it is beyond the scope of this book to provide a comprehensive survey. In practice, many abbreviations relating to political parties and commercial organizations are not recognized outside their immediate area of relevance, and they tend to be shortlived; when they are used in the press, for instance, they are usually explained when they first appear. A selection of the more important of these is given in the third list below. The majority of the abbreviations given here, however, are those which, unless stated otherwise, are used throughout the Hispanic world, and which are frequently used without explanation.

A more comprehensive list of abbreviations used in the Spanish-speaking world may be found in the *Diccionario de siglas y abreviaturas*, edited by M. Alvar and A. Miró (Alhambra, Madrid, 1983).

NOTE: the pronunciation of an abbreviation which is pronounced as if it were a word in its own right is given in conventional spelling in brackets, eg **SEAT** (séat). An abbreviation pronounced letter by letter is marked with an asterisk. In all other instances the words to which the abbreviation relates are spoken in full.

8.1 Abbreviations of titles and common words

Apdo.	apartado (de correos)	*(post office) box*
Arz.	arzobispo	*Archbishop: Abp*
Av(da).	avenida	*avenue (street name): Ave*
c/	calle	*street (street name): St*
cap. **capº.**	capítulo	*chapter: Ch.*
c/c	cuenta corriente	*current account: c/a*
c/d	casa de	*care of (address): c/o*
cfr.	confróntese	*compare: cf*
Cía.	compañía	*company: Co.*
cta.	cuenta	*account: a/c*
cte.	corriente	*instant (month): inst.*
D.	Don (title)	
Dª.	Doña (title)	
dcha.	derecha	*right-hand (apartment)*
dupdo.	duplicado	*copy*
E	este	*east: E*
e.p.d.	en paz descanse	*rest in peace: RIP*

NOTE: **★RIP** (= *requiescat in pace*) is also used

Exc.	Excelencia (title)	*Excellency*
Excmo.	Excelentísimo (title)	*Most Excellent*

FC	ferrocarril	*railway*
Fr.	Fray	*Brother (religious): Br*
Hnos.	hermanos	*brothers: Bros*
íd.	ídem	*ditto: do*
Ilmo.	Ilustrísimo (title)	*Most Illustrious*
izq(da).	izquierda	*left-hand (apartment)*
a. de J.C.	antes de Jesucristo	*before Christ: BC*
d. de J.C.	después de Jesucristo	*after Christ: AD*
Lic.	licenciatura	*equivalent of bachelor's degree: cf BA, BSc, BS, etc*
S.M., SS.MM.	Su Majestad, Sus Majestades	*Your/His/Her Majesty, Their/Your Majesties: HM*
Mons.	Monseñor	*Monsignor: Mgr*
N	norte	*north: N*
N.A.	nota del autor	*author's note*
N. (de la) R.	nota de la redacción	*editor's note: Ed.*
N.ª, S.ª	Nuestra Señora	*Our Lady*
N.S.	Nuestro Señor	*Our Lord*
N.T.	nota del traductor	*translator's note*
n.º, núm.	número	*number: no.*
O	oeste	*west: W*
P.	Padre	*Father (religious): Fr*
p.ª	para	*for*
pág(s).	página(s)	*page(s): p, pp*
P.D.	postdata	*postscript: PS*
pdo.	pasado	*last (month): ult.*
p.ej.	por ejemplo	*for example: eg*
pmo.	próximo	*next (month): prox.*
P.º	paseo	*(street name)*
rte.	remite/remitente	*sender (put on back of envelope)*
S	sur	*south: S*
S., Sta., Sto.	San, Santa, Santo	*Saint: St*
s/n	sin número	*unnumbered (address)*
Sr.	Señor	*Mr*
Sra.	Señora	*Mrs*
Srta.	Señorita	*Miss*

NOTE: there appears to be as yet no Spanish equivalent for English *Ms*.

SS	Santos	*Saints: SS*
tel., teléf.	teléfono	*telephone: tel.*
Ud., Uds. **Vd., Vds.** **V., VV.**	usted, ustedes	*you*
V.(º), B.(º)	visto bueno	*approved: OK*
v.gr.	verbigracia	*namely: viz*

8.2 Abbreviations of weights and measures (see also ch. **15**)

cm²	centímetro(s) cuadrado(s)	*square centimetre(s): sq cm* OR *cm²*
cm³	centímetro(s) cúbico(s)	*cubic centimetre(s): cc* OR *cm³*
cs	centavos	*centavos*
★C.V.	caballos de vapor	*horse power: hp*
gr.	gramo(s)	*gram(s): g*
h.	horas	*o'clock; hours*
Ha.	hectárea(s)	*hectare(s): ha*
kg.	kilogramo(s)	*kilogram(s)*
km.	kilómetro(s)	*kilometre(s)*
km/h.	kilómetros por hora	*kilometres per hour: cf mph*
kv. OR **kW.**	kilovatio(s)	*kilowatt(s)*
m.	metro(s)	*metre(s)*
m²	metro(s) cuadrado(s)	*square metre(s): sq m* OR *m²*
m³	metro(s) cúbico(s)	*cubic metre(s): cu m* OR *m³*
$	Used not only for American dollars but also for **pesos** in many Latin American countries (see **15.7**).	
T.m.	tonelada(s) métrica(s)	*metric ton(s): t*

8.3 Abbreviations of major national and international organizations

ALA...	*used in many siglas, standing for* Asociación latinoamericana de...
ALADI (aladi)	Asociación latinoamericana de integración
ALASEI (alasei)	Agencia latinoamericana de servicios de información
BID (bid)	Banco interamericano para el Desarrollo
★CD	Cuerpo diplomático
★CEE	Comunidad Económica Europea: *EEC*
★CELAM (celam)	Consejo episcopal latinoamericano
CEPAL (cepal)	Comité Económico para América Latina
CF	Club de Fútbol
EE.UU.	Estados Unidos
FAR...	*used in many siglas, standing for* Fuerzas armadas revolucionarias...
FMI	Fondo Monetario Internacional: *IMF*
FRE...	*used in many siglas, standing for* Frente...
ODECA (odeca)	Organización de estados centroamericanos
★OEA	Organización de estados americanos: *OAS*
★OLP	Organización para la liberación de Palestina: *PLO*

★ These abbreviations are pronounced letter by letter.

OMS (oms)	Organización Mundial de la Salud: *WHO*
ONU (onu)	Organización de las Naciones Unidas: *UNO*
OPEP (opep)	Organización de los Países Exportadores de Petróleo: *OPEC*
OTAN (otan)	Organización del Tratado del Atlántico Norte: *NATO*
★OUA	Organización de la Unidad Africana: *OAU*
★PNB	Producto nacional bruto: *GNP*
RAE	Real Academia Española
★SA	Sociedad Anónima *(cf Ltd, PLC, Inc.)*
...SA	*used in many siglas, with the above meaning*
SELA (sela)	Sistema económico latinoamericano
URSS (urs)	Unión de Repúblicas Socialistas Soviéticas: *USSR*

8.4 Other abbreviations from Spanish-speaking countries

Here is a selection of other abbreviations currently in use in Spanish-speaking countries:

★AA	Aerolíneas argentinas
ANAPO (anapo)	Alianza Nacional Popular *(Colombia)*
AVENSA (avensa)	Aerovías venezolanas
Av. Pte.	Avenida Presidente *(Arg)*
BANAMEX (banamex)	Banco Nacional de México
BANPAIS (banpaís)	Banco del País *(Mex)*
BANXICO (banjico)	Banco de México
Bs. As.	Buenos Aires
BUP (bup)	Bachillerato unificado y polivalente *(Pen)*: *corresponds to British GCSE (taken at 16 years of age)*
Cap. Fed.	Capital Federal *(Arg)*
CONACYT (conacit)	Consejo Nacional de Ciencia y Tecnología *(Mex)*
COU (cou)	Curso de orientación universitaria *(Pen)*: *corresponds to British A Level/high school degree*
★CVG	Corporación venezolana de Guayana
★D.F.	Distrito Federal *(Mex)*
★DNI	Documento nacional de identidad *(Pen)*
★EGB	Educación general básica *(Pen)*
FAS (fas)	Fuerzas armadas *(Pen)*
★FDR	Frente Democrático Revolucionario *(El Salvador)*
★FNM/FF.NN.	Ferrocarriles Nacionales de México *(also referred to as* Ferronales*)*
GEO (geo)	Grupo especial de operaciones *(Pen)*: *anti-terrorist squad*

ICETEX (icetex)	Instituto colombiano de especialización técnica en el exterior
IVA (iva)	Impuesto sobre el valor añadido *(Pen)*: *VAT (value added tax)*
LAN (lan)	Línea aérea nacional *(Chile)*
la N uno, etc	la carretera nacional número uno, etc *(Pen)*: *the Spanish classification of main roads*
OVNI (ovni)	objeto volante no identificado: *UFO*
PEMEX (pémex)	Petróleos mexicanos
PETROVEN (petroven)	Petróleos de Venezuela
★**PM**	Policía militar *(Pen)*
PRI (pri)	Partido Revolucionario Institucional *(Mex)*
PVP	precio de venta al público *(Pen)*
PYMES (pimes)	pequeñas y medianas (empresas) *(Pen)*
RENFE (renfe)	Red Nacional de Ferrocarriles Españoles *(Pen)*
★**RNE**	Radio Nacional de España
★**RTVE**	Radio Televisión Española
SEAT (séat)	Sociedad Española de Automóviles de Turismo
SECTUR (sectur)	Secretaría de Turismo *(Mex)*
SENA (sena)	Servicio nacional de aprendizaje *(Colombia)*
SIDA (sida)	síndrome (m) de inmunodeficiencia adquirida: *AIDS*
SIDERMEX (sidermex)	*Mexican steel corporation (appears never to have had a full name)*
SIDOR (sidor)	Siderurgia del Orinoco *(Venezuela)*
★**S.S.**	Seguridad Social
TELMEX (telmex)	Teléfonos de México
UNAM (unam)	Universidad Nacional Autónoma *(Mex)*
VIASA (viasa)	Venezolana Internacional de Aviación
el día X	*red-letter day*

9 Latin expressions

There are a number of Latin expressions in common use in modern Spanish, particularly in educated R2 speech and in R3.

R3

ad hoc	a propósito: un argumento ad hoc	*for the purpose,* ad hoc
ex aequo	con igual mérito: tres ex aequo	*equals*
modus vivendi	arreglo entre dos o varias personas	*arrangement, compromise,* modus vivendi
persona non grata	persona indeseable	*undesirable, unwelcome person,* persona non grata
in extremis	en caso extremo	*in an extreme case,* in extremis
non plus ultra (N)	el no va más, el tope	*the absolute limit, the* ne plus ultra
a fortiori	con mayor razón	*with all the more reason,* a fortiori
sine qua non	imprescindible: una condición sine qua non	*essential condition* NOTE: *in English,* sine qua non *is used as a noun.*

R2 (and R3)

a posteriori	después: un juicio a posteriori	*after the event,* a posteriori
a priori	antes: un juicio a priori	*before the event,* a priori
exabrupto (N)	brusquedad: contestar con un exabrupto	*abrupt remark, outburst*
ex cáthedra	en tono magisterial: hablar ex cáthedra	*authoritatively,* ex cathedra
ex profeso	expresamente	*deliberately, expressly*
ex voto (N)	ofrenda dedicada a Dios	*offering*
ipso facto	inmediatamente; por el mismo hecho	*immediately; by the very fact* NOTE: *English* ipso facto *is used only in the second sense.*
statu quo (N)	el estado en que se hallan las cosas	*status quo*
ultra (N) (m)	extremista	*extremist*

vice versa	al revés	*the opposite way, vice versa*
(a) grosso modo	de forma general	in a general way
vía crucis (N) (m)	camino de la cruz, calvario	*way of the Cross (a path laid out with the stations of the Cross)*

NOTE: **vía crucis** is masculine, although **vía** is feminine.

All registers

etcétera (etc)	y lo demás	*and the others, et cetera*

10 Grammatical terms

In talking about the Spanish language, you will find the following terms, which are in common use among educated Spanish speakers, useful.

Grammatical terms   **términos gramaticales**

el acento (ortográfico)	*(written) accent*
tónico (ADJ)	*stressed*
átono (ADJ)	*unstressed*
palabra aguda	*word stressed on final syllable, eg* **hablar**
palabra llana *or* grave	*word stressed on next to last syllable, eg* **sale**
palabra esdrújula	*word stressed on antepenultimate syllable, eg* **clínico**
la consonante	*consonant*
la †sílaba	*syllable*
la †vocal	*vowel*
el adjetivo	*adjective*
el adverbio	*adverb*
el complemento	*object*
la conjunción	*conjunction*
la †frase, la oración	*sentence*
el género	*gender*
masculino (ADJ)	*masculine*
femenino (ADJ)	*feminine*
el †nombre, el sustantivo	*noun*
la ortografía	*spelling*
el participio	*participle*
el pronombre	*pronoun*
posesivo (ADJ)	*possessive*
demostrativo (ADJ)	*demonstrative*
relativo (ADJ)	*relative*
el sufijo	*suffix*
diminutivo (ADJ)	*diminutive*
despectivo (ADJ)	*pejorative*
aumentativo (ADJ)	*augmentative*
superlativo (ADJ)	*superlative*
el verbo	*verb*
el tiempo	*tense*
los tiempos †simples/compuestos	*simple/compound tenses*
†presente	*present* (**hablo**)
futuro	*future* (**hablaré**)
pretérito (*also* pretérito indefinido)	*preterite* (**hablé**)

imperfecto	*imperfect* (**hablaba**)
pretérito anterior	*past anterior* (**hube hablado**)
futuro	*future* (**hablaré**)
futuro perfecto	*future perfect* (**habré hablado**)
condicional	*conditional* (**hablaría**)
condicional perfecto	*conditional perfect* (**habría hablado**)
(pretérito) pluscuamperfecto	*pluperfect* (**había hablado**)
el subjuntivo	*subjunctive*
el indicativo	*indicative*
el imperativo	*imperative*) **¡habla!**, **¡hablad!**)
el infinitivo	*infinitive* (**hablar**)
el gerundio	*gerund* (**hablando**)
el participio pasado	*past participle* (**hablado**)

Punctuation marks **signos de puntuación**

el aparte	*new paragraph*	
el asterisco	*asterisk*	*
la †coma	*comma*	,
las comillas	*quotation marks*	« »
las comillas simples	*single quotation marks*	' '
los corchetes	*square brackets*	[ ]
la diéresis	*diaeresis*	¨
la exclamación	*exclamation mark*	¡ !
el guión	*hyphen*	–
la interrogación	*question mark*	¿ ?
las (letras) mayúsculas	*capital letters*	
las (letras) minúsculas	*small letters*	
el †paréntesis	*brackets*	( )
el párrafo	*paragraph*	
el punto	*full stop, dot* (see ch. **14**)	.
el punto y coma	*semicolon*	;
los dos puntos	*colon*	:
los puntos suspensivos	*suspension marks*	…
la †raya	*dash*	—
la tilde	*mark above* **ñ**; *the written accent*	˜ or '

11 Interjections

Interjections are typical of the spoken language, and are most common in the 'lower' registers. In the following table, the interjections most frequently used in modern Spanish are listed according to general meaning, with an indication of their register value. Particular attention should be paid to those marked as R1★: these are generally considered indecent, and should only be used with great care. Of course, the use of such expressions, in Spanish-speaking countries as in English-speaking countries, varies with personality and environment.

	R2	R1	R1★
Admiration	†¡estupendo! ¡hombre! ¡qué maravilla! ¡qué barbaridad! ¡(muy) bien! ¡bien bien! ¡extraordinario! ¡madre mía!	¡chachi! ¡olé! ¡de narices! †¡jo! ¡jolín!/¡jolines! ¡demasiado! ¡ostras!	†¡cojonudo! †¡coño! ¡de pelotas! †¡joder! ¡de puta madre! ¡hostia(s)! ¡de cojones!
Agreement	†¡de acuerdo! ¡muy bien! ¡perfecto!	¡OK! (oké) ¡por qué no!	¡de puta madre!
Annoyance	¡maldito sea!	¡qué asco! ¡por Dios! ¡qué caramba! ¡a la porra! ¡mecachis!	¡mierda! †¡coño! †¡joder! ¡me cago en Dios! ¡hijo de puta! ¡cojones! ¡(a) la mierda!
Disbelief	†¡imposible! †¡increíble! ¡qué va! ¡no me digas! †¡ni hablar!	¡de narices! ¡ca! ¡ja! †¡venga (venga)! ¡no trago! ¡anda ya! ¡no cuela! ¡vamos, hombre!	

⟫→

	R2	R1	R1★
Joy	¡(qué) caramba! ¡qué bien! ¡qué alegría! †¡hombre! NOTE: **¡hombre!** is used to both men and women. †¡mujer!	¡demasiado! ¡como enrolla! ¡qué pasada! ¡pipudo! ¡qué marcha!	¡de puta madre! †¡coño! †¡joder!
Objection	¡que no! ¡qué caramba! ¡para nada!	†¡nada, nada!	
Surprise	¡Dios mío! ¡caramba! ¡cielos!	†¡huy! ¡porras! ¡mecachis! ¡qué pasa! ¡ostras!	¡hostia(s)!
Warning	†¡cuidado! ¡atención!	¡ojo! ¡tate! ¡al loro!	

12 Fillers

In conversation, speakers often need time to formulate what they are going to say, and therefore make use of a range of introductory 'hesitation formulae' or 'fillers'. While overuse of such words can be annoying, their judicious use adds authenticity to a foreigner's speech – as well as giving time to think! The following are the most common such expressions in Spanish. English equivalents are suggested, but really their 'meaning' is minimal.

- **al fin y al cabo** *in the end, when all is said and done*
  Al fin y al cabo tuvo algo de razón

- **†bueno** *well*
  Used almost automatically when answering a question; also to call attention, eg:
  ¿Cuándo piensas volver? – Bueno, no sé …
  Bueno, ¿estás listo?

- **¿cómo se diría?** *how shall I put it?*
  Pues (¿cómo se diría?), es como una fruta

- **digamos** *let's say*
  Digamos que, al fin y al cabo, todo tiene relación

- **digámoslo así** *as it were*
  El alcohol es otra manera de escaparse, digámoslo así

- **en fin** *so, there it is*
  Often used in isolation to conclude a point.
  En fin, no sé qué decirte

- **entonces** *then*
  Frequently with **pues** (see below).
  Pues entonces, le daremos un aprobado

- **es que** *the thing is, was*
  Es que estaba enferma mi madre

- **esto** *er*
  Signifies deliberation.
  Esto … bueno, ya veremos

- **†hombre** *goodness, really*
  Hombre, pues cuesta mucho

- **†mira/mire** *look here*
  Mira, no tengo ni idea

- **no sé** *I don't know*
  No sé, digamos que vendrá mañana

- **o sea**   *or, that is*
  Also used as a general hesitation.
    Se puede hacer esta tarde, o sea, si vienes después del almuerzo
    Bueno, es que…o sea, no te puedo decir nada

- **podríamos decir**   *as one might say*
    Podríamos decir, es un mamífero

- **por decirlo así**   *so to speak*

- **†pues**   *well, then*
  The most frequent filler in Spanish, it is used meaninglessly at the beginning of any sentence and before other fillers.
    Pues tienes que pagar
    ¡Vámonos, pues!

  NOTE: **pues** corresponds to English *then* only in the 'weak' logical sense; it should not be used for *then* as a time adverb, which corresponds to Spanish **entonces**, **después**, etc.

- **vamos a ver**   *let me see, let's see*
    Vamos a ver, si contesto a la pregunta

13 Transition words

It is most useful to be familiar with the following words in speaking or writing Spanish, particularly in those registers where longer sentences are used and arguments sustained. They express a 'logical' relation between one proposition and another, and although frequently used, they are not simply 'fillers' as are the expressions in ch. **12**.

- †**a pesar de** N, **a pesar de que...**   *in spite of*
  Comimos, a pesar de que no teníamos ganas

- **ahora bien**   (i) *but*   (ii) *now*
  (i)   Te puedes llevar el coche; ahora bien, a las diez lo necesito
  (ii) Ahora bien, volvió su padre, y le dijo lo contrario

- †**al/por el contrario**   *on the contrary*
  No está claro; al/por el contrario está confuso

- **así**   *and*
  Quedamos aquí, así luego iremos al cine

- **así mismo**   *also*
  La paella es plato típicamente español; así mismo lo es la fabada

- †**aunque**   *although, even though*
  Está bien, aunque se podrá superar

- **claro que**   *of course*
  Sucedió así; claro que las consecuencias fueron inesperadas

- **de cualquier manera**   *anyway*
  Te puede resultar difícil; de cualquier manera, hay que hacerlo.

- †**dado que** (R2–3)   *since, given that*
  Dado que se sentía mal, no era de extrañar que suspendiese el examen

- **de modo/manera/forma que**   *so* (see p 256)
  Llegaremos a las ocho, de modo que nos tendrán que esperar

- **de tal modo que**   *in such a way that, so*
  Arregló el coche de tal modo que no tuvimos problemas después

- **empero** (R3)   *however*
  Baroja escribe muy bien; empero, se encuentran en sus novelas faltas gramaticales

- **en efecto/en (la) realidad**   *indeed, in fact*
  Tiene razón; en efecto/en realidad es como dice

- †**en resumen**   *in short*
  La conferencia fue agradable; en resumen, estuvo acertada

- **es decir**   *that is, that means*
  Hace calor, es decir, se puede salir sin abrigo

R1* vulgar or indecent
R1 informal, colloquial
R2 neutral
R3 formal, written
See also p 3.

† More information about these words or expressions may be found in other sections. Use the Spanish word index to find the page numbers.

- **no obstante/sin embargo** *nevertheless*
  Pensábamos ir; no obstante/sin embargo, si llueve nos quedamos

- **(o)... o bien/o...o.../bien...bien...**(R3) *either . . . or . . .*
  (O) vas a Madrid o bien vas a Santander
  O lo lees ahora o lo lees más tarde

- **ora...ora...**(R3) *now . . . now . . .*
  Ora sonríe, ora llora

- **pero** *but*
  Hay que correr, pero con precaución

- **†por consiguiente/†en consecuencia/por lo cual/por lo que** *so, consequently*
  No ganó mucho dinero, por lo cual no puede irse de vacaciones

- **†por lo tanto** *so, therefore*
  Tenemos un problema, por lo tanto hay que resolverlo

- **†por una parte... por otra (parte).../†por un lado...por otro (lado)...** *on the one hand . . . on the other . . .*
  Por una parte creo que está bien, por otra (parte) creo que está mal

- **porque** *because*
  No puedo venir porque me he roto el brazo

- **sino** *but* (contrastive: what follows **sino** must deny what precedes)
  No es así sino al contrario

- **tanto...como...** *both . . . and . . .*
  Tanto los ingleses como los italianos se opusieron al proyecto

- **ya que** *since*
  Ya que estás aquí, vamos a tomar algo

14 Numerals

Spanish uses a comma (**coma**) where English uses the decimal point, and a dot where English uses a comma in partitioning thousands. Thus Spanish **29,107** (**veintinueve coma uno cero siete**) = English 29.107 (twenty-nine point one zero seven), and Spanish **7.654.321** (**siete millones, seiscientos cincuenta y cuatro mil, trescientos veintiuno**) = English 7,654,321 (seven million, six hundred and fifty-four thousand, three hundred and twenty-one).

Spanish practice with telephone numbers is to pair the digits off as far as possible: 412568 is often written 41 25 68 or 41.25.68 and read **cuarenta y uno, veinticinco, sesenta y ocho**. When there is an odd number of digits in the number, the first is given in isolation: eg 369 47 11 is **tres sesenta y nueve, cuarenta y siete, once**. Alternatively, the digits may be read one by one, as in English (**cuatro, uno, dos, cinco, seis, ocho** and **tres, seis, nueve**, etc).

NOTE: numbers in English text below are given with the English decimal point; thousands are partitioned by a comma.

15 Measurements

Even though the metric system is gradually being accepted in the English-speaking world, the imperial system is entrenched in the minds of many English speakers. The Spanish-speaking world uses the metric system exclusively, at least officially, although older units of measurement may survive locally (see **15.8**). It is important to realize that although Spanish equivalents of some English terms do exist (eg **yarda**, **pie**), they are not generally understood, and measurements must be converted. While precise mathematical calculation will be necessary in some cases (eg height on a passport, a baby's birth-weight), for everyday purposes round numbers and rough equivalents are adequate. In translation it is particularly important to imitate such rounding up (or down): *200 yards away* is not to be rendered as **a 182,88 metros** but rather as **a (unos) 200 metros**.

The following sections give the standard equivalences to facilitate calculation, but also give typical rough equivalences for everyday use.

15.1 Length

Standard equivalences	
1 in (**pulgada**) = 2.54 cm	1 cm = 0.3937 in
1 ft (**pie**) = 30.48 cm	1 m = 3.28084 ft
1 yd (**yarda**) = 0.9144 m	1 km = 0.62137 miles
1 mile (**milla**) = 1.6093 km	(very nearly $\frac{5}{8}$ mile)

NOTE: **milla** in a purely Spanish context is a nautical mile (1,852 km or 6,076 ft).

Rough equivalences	
10 cm – 4 in	1 km – $\frac{1}{2}$ mile
50 cm – 1$\frac{1}{2}$ ft	100 km – 60 miles
1 m – 1 yd	
100 m – 100 yds	

Examples

una niña de noventa centímetros
a child 3 feet tall
un hombre de un metro ochenta
a man 6 feet tall
cien kilómetros por hora
60 miles an hour

Expressing length

Note the following ways of expressing measurements of length, etc:

Esta carretera tiene dos kilómetros de longitud (R3)/de †largo: Es una carretera de dos kilómetros de longitud/de largo

La casa tiene cinco metros de altura (R3)/de alto: Es una casa de cinco metros de altura/de alto

Este pozo tiene diez metros de profundidad (R3)/de profundo: Es un pozo de diez metros de profundidad/de profundo

La autopista tiene treinta metros de anchura (R3)/de ancho: Es una autopista de treinta metros de anchura/de ancho

Este acero tiene diez centímetros de espesor (R3)/de grueso: Este acero es de diez centímetros de espesor

15.2 Weight

Standard equivalences

1 oz (**onza**) = 28.35 g	1 g = 0.03527 oz
1 lb (**libra**) = 0.4536 kg	1 kg = 2.20462 lbs
1 stone/14 lbs = 6.35 kg	1 metric ton/tonne =
1 cwt = 50.8 kg	1000 kg = 0.9842 tons
1 ton (**tonelada**) = 1016.05 kg	

NOTE: in a Spanish context, **tonelada** would normally mean a metric ton or tonne.

Rough equivalences

$\frac{1}{4}$ kilo – $\frac{1}{2}$ lb
$\frac{1}{2}$ kilo – 1 lb
1 kilo – 2 lbs

Examples

un hombre de sesenta kilos
a 10–stone man

un hombre de ochenta kilos
a 13–stone man

15.3 Area

Standard equivalences

1 sq in = 6.4516 cm^2 1 cm^2 = 0.155 sq in
1 sq ft = 0.0929 m^2 1 m^2 = 10.764 sq ft
1 sq yd = 0.8361 m^2 1 km^2 = 0.3861 sq miles
1 sq mile = 2.589 km^2 or 258.9 ha   1 ha (= 10,000 m^2) = 2.471 acres
1 acre = 4,046.72 m^2 or 0.405 ha

Rough equivalences

6 cm^2 – 1 sq in   1 ha – 2½ acres
1 m^2 – 1 sq yd   50 ha – 125 acres
1,000 m^2 – ¼ acre   250 ha – 1 sq mile

Example

una finca de cuarenta hectáreas
a 100–acre estate

15.4 Volume

Standard equivalences

1 pint = 0.5682 litres (UK)/   1 litro = 1.759 pints (UK)/
           0.47 litres (US)   2.128 pints (US)
1 quart = 1.1364 litres (UK)/
            0.946 litres (US)
1 gallon = 4.546 litres (UK)/
            3.785 litres (US)

Rough equivalences

1 litro – 2 pints
4 litros – 1 gallon
16 litros – 4 gallons
24 litros – 5 gallons

Examples

Mi coche gasta/consume seis litros a los cien (kilómetros)
My car does 50 (miles) to the gallon
once litros a los cien
25 to the gallon
medio litro de cerveza
a pint of beer

15.5 Temperature

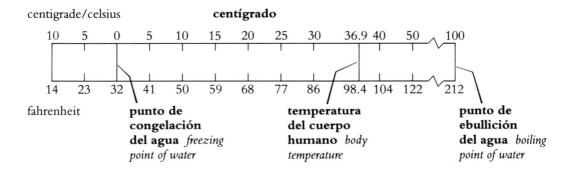

centigrade/celsius   **centígrado**

punto de congelación del agua *freezing point of water*

temperatura del cuerpo humano *body temperature*

punto de ebullición del agua *boiling point of water*

15.6 Time

The 24-hour system is used for official business, timetables, radio, etc, although more informally the 12-hour system is used, as in English. In Peninsular Spanish **de la madrugada**, **de la mañana**, **de la tarde**, **de la noche** are often used to resolve any resulting ambiguity; in Latin America, **am** and **pm** may also be used, as in English.

15.7 Currencies

Argentina	**austral** (m) (formerly **peso**)
Bolivia	**peso**
Colombia	**peso**
Costa Rica	**colón** (m)
Cuba	**peso**
Chile	**peso**
Ecuador	**sucre** (m)
El Salvador	**colón** (m)
Guatemala	**quetzal** (m)
Honduras	**lempira** (m)
México	**peso**
Nicaragua	**córdoba** (m)
Panamá	**balboa** (m)
Paraguay	**guaraní** (m)
Perú	**sol** (m)
Puerto Rico	**dólar** (= US $) (m)
República Dominicana	**peso**
Spain	**peseta** (**pela** (R1))
Uruguay	(**nuevo**) **peso**
Venezuela	**bolívar** (m)

15.8 Traditional measurements

Some traditional measurements are still used in some rural areas and persist in some expressions. The most common of these are the **arroba** (about $11\frac{1}{2}$ kg, and also used as a measure of capacity), the †**cuadra** (a measure of length; in Latin America it also means 'a block of houses' and is frequently used as an informal measure of distance in this sense, eg **vive a tres cuadras de aquí**), the **fanega** (just over $\frac{1}{2}$ ha as a measure of area, or about 50 litres as a measure of capacity), the **legua** (= English *league*, about 4–5 km or 3 miles), the **quintal** (formerly 100 lbs, now about 45 kg) and the †**vara** (just under 1 m).

Grammar

16 Gender

NOTE: in this book, the gender of nouns is indicated *only* when it is not predictable from the principles given in this section.

    Spanish nouns all belong to one of two genders, masculine or feminine, and articles and adjectives agree in gender with the noun to which they refer. It is sometimes said that Spanish has a neuter gender (see **16.9** below), but no noun belongs to this.

    Feminine nouns beginning in stressed **a-** or **ha-** (eg **alma**, **hambre**) take the article **el**. In R1, however, such nouns are often treated as masculine; eg: **mucho** $\boxed{!}$ **hambre, hambre epidémico** $\boxed{!}$.

16.1 Gender and sex

Nouns referring to people and animals of the male sex are usually masculine. Nouns referring to people and animals of the female sex are usually feminine.

Exceptions

Where the names of animals do not have distinct masculine and feminine forms, †**macho** and **hembra** (invariable) are used to make the distinction, but the gender of the noun does not change:

> **las ardillas macho**
> male squirrels
> **el ratón hembra**
> female mouse

la víctima (*victim*) and **la estrella** (*film-star*) are always feminine.
el desnudo (*picture of a*) *nude* is always masculine.

> † More information about these words or expressions may be found in other sections. Use the Spanish word index to find the page numbers.

16.2 Gender associated with types of noun

Masculine

Rivers	el Ebro, el Guadiana, el Amazonas, el Paraná
Months	(el) enero *January*, (el) abril *April*
Mountains and volcanoes	el Etna, el Mulhacén, el Aconcagua
Cars	el Mercedes, el Seat, el Ford
Watches	el Seiko, el Longines
Ships	el Reina Isabel
Planes	el Concorde, el Boeing

Languages	el guaraní, el vascuence *Basque*
Metals	el hierro *iron*, el cobre *copper*
Many trees	el olmo *elm*, el fresno *ash*, el roble *oak* BUT NOTE: el haya (f) *beech*, la encina *holm oak*, la higuera *fig tree*.
Musical notes	fa sostenido *F sharp*

Feminine

Islands	la apacible Barbados
Letters of the alphabet	la i, la b NOTE ALSO: la consonante *consonant*, la †vocal *vowel*.
Firms	la Ford

16.3 Gender associated with noun ending

Masculine

-o	*Most common exceptions*
	• Some masculine nouns which do not change their endings when they denote females: la soprano *soprano*, la modelo *model*, la testigo *witness*, la miembro *member*
	• Abbreviations of feminine nouns: la moto(cicleta) *motor bike*, la foto(grafía) *photograph*, la porno(grafía) (R1), la †radio(difusión) (but **radio** is usually masculine in Am) *radio*
	• Where a feminine noun is implied or understood: la Gestapo (policía), la UNESCO (organización)
	• Other: la mano, la dínamo (but **dínamo** is often masculine in Am)
-or	Denoting agent: el autor *author*, el conductor *driver*
-or	Not denoting agent: el calor *heat*, el licor *liquor*, el valor *value* *Exception* la labor *work*
-aje	el viaje *journey*, el linaje *lineage*, el andamiaje *scaffolding*
-men	el certamen *contest*, el volumen *volume*, el régimen *régime*

-gen	el origen *origin*

Most common exceptions

la imagen *image*, la †margen *margin* (see **16.5**)

Feminine

-a	*Exceptions*

- Nouns denoting males (see above):
  el cura *priest*, el artista *artist*, el guardia *guard*, el jesuita *Jesuit*

- Abstract nouns ending in **-ma**:
  el carisma *charisma*, el cisma *schism*, el clima *climate*, el prisma *prism*, el problema *problem*, el síntoma *symptom*, el reuma *rheumatism*
  Contrast:
  la crema *cream*, la diadema *diadem*, la yema *egg yolk*
  NOTE:
  el asma (f) *asthma*, †la estratagema *stratagem*, †la trama *plot*

- Other:
  el día *day*, el mapa *map*, el planeta *planet*, el tranvía *tram*, el †cometa *comet*, el †pijama *pyjamas*, el delta *delta (river)*

-ad	la verdad *truth*, la enfermedad *illness*, la majestad *majesty*
-ud	la virtud *virtue*, la longitud *length*

Exceptions

el ataúd *coffin*, el laúd *lute*

-ed	la merced *mercy*

Exceptions

el césped *lawn*, el huésped *guest*

-ión	Denoting abstraction: la ración *ration, portion*, la región *region*

Contrast
el gorrión *sparrow*, el avión *aeroplane*, el sarampión *measles*, el camión *truck*, etc.

-umbre	la certidumbre *certainty*, la costumbre *custom*
-ie	la serie *series*, la planicie *plain*
-sis	la síntesis *synthesis*, la metamorfosis *metamorphosis*

Exceptions

el análisis *analysis*, el apocalipsis *apocalypse*, el énfasis *emphasis*, el éxtasis *ecstasy*, el paréntesis *parenthesis*

16.4   Gender of compound nouns

Noun + noun combinations are usually feminine when both nouns are feminine, eg:

> la bocacalle *street entrance, turn*, la maniobra *manoeuvre*, la madreselva *honeysuckle*, la plumafuente *fountain pen*

BUT

> el/la purasangre *thoroughbred (horse, etc)*

NOTE ALSO:

> la enhorabuena *congratulations*, la sinrazón *outrage*

Otherwise, compound nouns formed with other parts of speech are usually masculine:

> el terremoto *earthquake*, el abrelatas *can opener*, el paraguas *umbrella*, el aguardiente *brandy*, el altavoz *loudspeaker* (altoparlante (Am)), el rompecabezas *teaser*

16.5   Words of varying gender

arte	Masculine in its meaning of *individual art* (**el arte precolombiano, los artes de dibujar y de escribir**) but feminine in its collective plural *the Arts* (**las bellas artes**).
dote	Masculine or feminine (usually feminine) in singular *dowry*, but always feminine in plural *gifts* (**las dotes intelectuales**).
mar	Masculine in general (**el Mar Mediterráneo**), but sometimes feminine in R3, and always feminine in some set phrases, eg: la mar de + ADJ = *very* ADJ (R1), alta mar *high seas*, mar gruesa *heavy sea*, hacerse a la mar *put to sea*, mar llena *high tide*
margen	Masculine in R1–2 but sometimes feminine in R3. In its meaning of *river bank* it is feminine.
masacre	Now generally feminine, though until recently it was often found as masculine.

Both masculine and feminine

The following words are currently found as both masculine and feminine in all registers:

> cas(s)et(t)e *cassette*, interrogante *question*, lente *lens*, †linde *boundary*, maratón *marathon*, monzón *monsoon*, terminal *terminal*

16.6 Names of towns

Usually the gender is suggested by the form of the name:
en el Oviedo moderno
en la Roma antigua

but all towns can be thought of as feminine, since **ciudad** is feminine:
Madrid es bella
la maravillosa Estambul

However, **un**, **medio**, **todo** and **mismo** may be used in the masculine even with apparently 'feminine' towns:
todo Málaga
el mismo Valencia

NOTE: **el Barcelona**, **el Málaga**, etc, are the names of the towns' respective football teams.

16.7 Formation of masculine/feminine pairs

The commonest masculine/feminine pairs in Spanish are:

–o/–a	el †tío/la †tía	*uncle/aunt*
–e/–a	el monje/la monja	*monk/nun*
–or/–ora	el autor/la autora	*author/authoress*

There are also one or two less common distinctive feminine endings, eg:

–esa	el abad/la abadesa	*abbott/abbess*
–isa	el profeta/la profetisa	*prophet/prophetess*
–riz	el actor/la actriz	*actor/actress*

However, not all masculines have corresponding feminine forms:
el/la hereje *heretic*
el/la mártir *martyr*
el/la testigo *witness*
el/la cómplice *accomplice*
el/la reo *convict*
all nouns in **–ista**, eg: el/la violinista *violinist*

Problems occur in the following situations:

(a) when the feminine form is already in use with a distinct meaning:
el físico *physicist*/la física *physics*
el alcalde *mayor*/la alcaldesa *wife of the mayor*
el policía *policeman*/la policía *police*

(b) when there was no feminine form in existence:
ministro (*now also* ministra) *minister*
presidente (*now also* presidenta) *president*
cónsul (la cónsul *now used*) *consul*
agente (la agente *now used*) *agent*

As women take on new rôles in society, Spanish has to find new feminines, and many of these are by no means firmly established. The feminine form of professional nouns is now regularly used to denote women working in those professions. For example, *médica* means *woman doctor* and not *doctor's wife* (though **la médico** is still preferred); **alcaldesa** means *woman mayor* and not exclusively *mayor's wife*; **abogada** means *woman lawyer* and not *lawyer's wife*; and **la policía** is now regularly used to mean *the policewoman* as well as *the police*. But there is hesitation, particularly in R3. Margaret Thatcher was both **la primer ministro** and **la primera ministra** in the press (mainly the latter). Difficulties in category (a) above can be resolved by reinforcements, eg: **una mujer policía** *policewoman*; and this may extend to other categories too, eg **una (mujer) candidata**.

The following are now accepted as female forms of the noun given, ie in the sense of 'female X':

> alcaldesa *mayor*, árbitra *referee*, cacica *local boss*, candidata *candidate*, †catedrática *professor*, clienta *client*, diputada *deputy*, jefa *head*, reportera *reporter*, senadora *senator*, sirvienta *servant*

In reverse, **el modisto** enjoyed some popularity as the masculine of **la modista**, *fashion designer*, but **el modista** now seems to be preferred.

16.8 Family relations and titles

With nouns denoting titles and family relations, a masculine plural in Spanish may correspond to a masculine and feminine pair, or to a 'genderless' plural in English:

¿Cuántos hijos tienes?
How many children (= sons *and* daughters) have you got?

los duques de Alba
the Duke and Duchess of Alba

los Reyes Católicos
the Catholic Monarchs (= Queen Isabel and King Fernando)

16.9 The neuter

The demonstratives and the third-person pronoun have a distinctive 'neuter' form: **esto, eso, aquello; ello, lo.** They are *always* used to refer to a proposition or general idea, *never* to a noun. Contrast:

Un pacto social resulta casi imprescindible. Por ello,...
A social compact is almost essential. Because of this . . .
BUT
Lo he hecho por él
I've done it for him

Eso de no tener dinero me sorprendió
That business of not having any money surprised me
BUT
Nuestra idea es ésa
That is our idea

† More information about these words or expressions may be found in other sections. Use the Spanish word index to find the page numbers.

The definite article also has a 'neuter' form which is used *with adjectives only*, similarly to denote a general idea. Contrast:

Lo más difícil fue escapar
The most difficult thing was to escape

BUT

El último ejemplo fue el más difícil
The last example was the most difficult

16.10   Homonyms distinguished by gender

A number of Spanish nouns are both masculine and feminine, but have a different, though usually related, meaning according to gender.

(a)   The feminine noun is collective, the masculine individual:

	f	m
batería	battery (of guns); set (of lights); footlights; percussion section of orchestra; kitchen utensils	drummer (in band)
centinela	guard, watch (body)	sentry (individual)
defensa	defence (gen)	(full)back (football)
escolta	escort (body)	escort (individual)
†**guardia**	guard (body), custody	guard (individual), policeman
policía	police	policeman (but see **16.7**)

(b)   The feminine noun is concrete, the masculine noun is a person or thing with an associated metaphorical function:

	f	m
bestia	beast; uncouth woman (R1)	uncouth man, brute (R1)
cabeza	head	head of organization, leader
calavera	skull	madcap; good for nothing
†**cámara**	camera	cameraman
caza	hunt	fighter plane
cura	cure	minister (having 'cure' of souls)
espada	sword	swordsman, matador
†**facha**	appearance, look (R1–2)	fascist (term of abuse) (R1)
génesis	origin	Book of Genesis
guía	guidebook	guide (person)
mañana	morning	future

	f	**m**
meta	goal (= objective)	goalkeeper
pareja	couple (of people); female partner	male partner
recluta	recruitment	recruit
vigía	watchtower	watchman

(c)   Others:

	f	**m**
canal	pipe	canal; channel
capital	capital city (national or provincial)	financial capital
†**central**	head office; (telephone) exchange; **central hidroeléctrica/nuclear** = hydroelectric/nuclear power station	centre forward, central defender (football)
cólera	anger (R3)	cholera
coma	comma	coma
cometa	kite	comet
corte	(royal) court: **la Corte madrileña** = Madrid; **las Cortes** = Spanish parliament	cut (gen), (power) cut
corriente	flow, current, draught, course	current month
editorial	publishing house	lead article
fantasma	bogey	ghost
†**final**	final (match)	end (of street, etc)
frente	forehead	front, front part; (battle, political) front
granuja	grape seed	urchin, rogue
hincha	ill-will, grudge	supporter (sport)
†**moral**	ethics; morale	mulbery tree
†**orden**	order, command; military/religious order, eg **la Orden de Calatrava**	order, arrangement (eg **orden alfabético** alphabetical order); (civil) order (eg **las fuerzas del orden** the forces of law and order); field, style (eg **el orden dórico** Doric order)
ordenanza	ordinance, decree	office boy

	f	m
†**panda**	gang	panda
†**parte**	part	report (eg **el parte meteorológico** the weather forecast)
†**pendiente**	slope	earring
†**pez**	pitch, tar	fish (alive)
†**radio**	radio	radius, spoke (of wheel); radium
	NOTE: **radio** = radio is usually masculine in Am.	
†**vocal**	vowel	member of committee

16.11   Problem genders

The gender of the following words is especially liable to confusion.

● **Words ending in -e**

m		f	
el auge	climax, boom	**la base**	base, basis
†**el avance**	advance	**la catástrofe**	catastrophe
el cauce	(river) bed, course	**la gripe**	flu
†**el declive**	slope, incline	**la higiene**	hygiene
el enchufe	plug; contacts, influence	**la índole**	disposition
		la mole	mass, bulk
el fraude	fraud	**la pirámide**	pyramid
el peine	comb	**la sede**	seat (of government), see (ecclesiastical)
el timbre	bell; stamp, seal		

● **Words ending in -al**

m		f	
el cereal	cereal	†**la cal**	lime
el zarzal	bramble, thicket	†**la central**	power station; (telephone) exchange
		la espiral	spiral
		la multinacional	multinational company
		la postal	postcard
		la sal	salt
		la señal	sign
		la sucursal	branch (office)

● Words ending in **-ante** and **-ente**

m		f	
el componente	component	**la constante**	constant
el paciente	patient	**la mente**	mind
		la patente	patent
		la simiente	seed
		†**la vertiente**	slope

● Words ending in **-z**

m		f	
el aprendiz	apprentice	†**la faz**	face, surface
el cáliz	chalice; calyx	**la hoz**	sickle; gorge
el lápiz	pencil	**la lombriz**	worm
el matiz	hue, shade	**la perdiz**	partridge
†**el pez**	fish (alive)	**la tez**	complexion
el regaliz	licorice		

● A number of feminine words

la armazón	frame, framework; in Am = shelves, bookcase
la bilis	bile
la cárcel	prison
la circular	circular
la crin	horse's mane
la flor	flower
la metrópoli	metropolis
la miel	honey
la sangre	blood
la sien	temple (part of head)
la tos	cough
la tribu	tribe

There are also a number of other words with unpredictable endings, although once the ending is known the gender is obvious.

- ### English *-ive* corresponds to Spanish **-ivo** or **-iva**

la alternativa	alternative
la defensiva	defensive
la iniciativa	initiative
la misiva	missive
la negativa	negative, refusal
la ofensiva	offensive

  BUT

el objetivo	objective

  NOTE ALSO:

los preparativos	preparations

- ### English *-er* corresponds to Spanish **-or** or **-ora**

  There is a good deal of variation in Spanish in the naming of new gadgets:

el aspirador/la aspiradora	vacuum cleaner
el batidor/la batidora	whisk
la freidora	deep–fat fryer
la lavadora	washing machine
el secador	hair dryer
but **la secadora**	tumble–dryer
el tostador/la tostadora	toaster

- ### Others

la característica	characteristic
la década	decade
la herramienta	tool
la paradoja	paradox
la sílaba	syllable

17 Number

17.1 Formation of plurals

(a) Nouns and adjectives ending in an unstressed vowel or stressed **e**, **o** or **u** add **–s**, eg:

libro/**libros**, bueno/**buenos**
carta/**cartas**, inglesa/**inglesas**
estudiante (m/f)/**estudiantes**, triste/**tristes**
pie (m)/**pies**
bici (f)/**bicis**
tribu (f)/**tribus**

(b) Nouns and adjectives ending in a consonant (including **y**) add **–es**, eg:

pared/**paredes**
cortés/**corteses**
árbol (m)/**árboles**
español/**españoles**
rey/**reyes**

(c) Nouns and adjectives ending in a stressed **–á** or **–í** have traditionally added **–es**, eg:

bajá (m)/**bajáes**
rubí (m)/**rubíes**
marroquí/**marroquíes**
esquí (m)/**esquíes**

but nowadays many such words simply add **–s**, eg:

sofá (m)/**sofás**
mamá (f)/**mamás**
papá (m)/**papás**

NOTE: in the formation of plurals the place of the stress and the sound of the final consonant of the singular remain the same, and the spelling must reflect this, eg:

virgen (f)/**vírgenes**
lápiz (m)/**lápices**

Compound nouns

The plurals of compound nouns generally follow the above rules when the noun is a word in its own right, eg:

la bocacalle/**las bocacalles**
el altavoz/**los altavoces**

But in noun + noun groups which consist of two separate words, only the *first* noun pluralizes:

el coche patrulla/**los coches** patrulla
la fecha tope/**las fechas** tope

The gender of nouns is only given where it is not predictable from the principles given in ch. **16**.

R1* vulgar or indecent
R1 informal, colloquial
R2 neutral
R3 formal, written
See also p 3.

† More information about these words or expressions may be found in other sections. Use the Spanish word index to find the page numbers.

Exceptions

(a) Nouns ending in unstressed vowel + **s** have no distinctive plural form, eg:

la crisis/**las crisis**
el lunes/**los lunes**
el virus/**los virus**

(b) Family names optionally add **-s** or **-es** apart from those ending in **-s** or **-z**, which never do, eg:

los Moreno OR los Morenos
los Pérez
los Galmés

(c) Some Anglicisms have the English plural form (though usage is rapidly changing in this area), eg:

gángster/**gángsters**
récord/**récords**
stand/**stands**
BUT
club/**clubs** (R1–2)/**clubes** (R2–3)

(d) One or two learned nouns which derive from Latin formulae have no distinctive plural form, eg:

el déficit/**los déficit**
el ítem/**los ítem**
el superávit/**los superávit**
el ultimátum/**los ultimátum**

(e) One or two nouns have stress on different syllables in singular and plural:

carácter (m)/**caracteres**
régimen (m)/**regímenes**
espécimen (m)/**especímenes**

17.2 Some Spanish plurals which correspond to English singulars

las agujetas	stiffness (of limbs)
por los aires	through the air
las andas (sg in Am)	stretcher, bier, platform for religious tableaux
los aplausos	applause
†**la(s) barba(s)**	beard
las bodas	wedding
los cascotes/los escombros	rubble
los celos	jealousy
los conocimientos (also in sg)	knowledge
(los) Correos	Post Office
las cosquillas	tickling
con creces	with interest (financial), abundantly (gen)
los cubiertos	cutlery/silverware
los datos	information, data

169

los deberes	homework
¡Buenos días!, etc	Good morning!
los efectivos	effective force available (military)
las enaguas	petticoat
a mis expensas, a expensas de	at my expense, at the expense of
las fuerzas	strength
los funerales (also in sg)	funeral
†**los honorarios**	fee
los informes	information
las investigaciones	research
las municiones	ammunition
¡Felices Navidades!	Merry Christmas!
las nieves (R3)	snow
los pertrechos	gear; ammunition
hacer †**progresos**	to make progress
los remordimientos (also in sg)	remorse
las tinieblas	darkness
los transportes (públicos)	(public) transport (ie the transport system)
· **el Ministerio de Transportes**	
BUT	
· **el transporte (de las mercancías)**	transport (= act of transporting) of goods
en vísperas de	on the eve of

17.3 Some Spanish singulars which correspond to English plurals

el alicate (ALSO **los alicates**)	pliers
la braga (ALSO **las bragas**)	panties, knickers
el calzón (ALSO **los calzones**)	shorts (Pen); trousers (US pants) (Am)
el calzoncillo (ALSO **los calzoncillos**)	pants (US underpants, shorts)
la escalera (ALSO **las escaleras**)	stairs
la estadística	set of statistics; statistics as a subject
la gente (ALSO **las gentes** (R3))	people
la malla (ALSO **las mallas** (R1))	tights (ALSO = bathing costume/suit in Am)
el pantalón (ALSO **los pantalones**)	trousers (US pants)
†**el pijama**	pyjamas
la pinza (ALSO **las pinzas**)	pincers (sg ALSO = peg; claw)
la ropa	clothes
la táctica	tactics
la tropa (ALSO **las tropas**)	troops

NOTE ALSO: **la física** (*physics*), **la política** (politics), etc, which appear to be plural (though in fact they are syntactically singular).

17.4   Number concord

Collective nouns

Expressions involving collective nouns are susceptible to some variation in usage:

- *Collective noun + **de** + plural noun*

  Es la primera vez que se reúne (R2)/**reúnen** (R1) **un número de especialistas**
  Un grupo de profesores está (R2)/**están** (R1) **preparando un estudio**
  La mayor parte/La mayoría de las publicaciones está escrita (R2)/**están escritas** (R1) **en castellano**

- *Collective noun + **de** + singular noun*

  La mayoría/El †resto, etc **de la gente dice que…**

  Here a plural verb is not acceptable, even in R3.

Noun – **ser** – noun

ser agrees in number with a following plural noun:
  El problema son los estudiantes
  El ejemplo más frecuente citado son los numerosos y múltiples avances tecnológicos derivados de la II Guerra Mundial
  La revolución eran simplemente unos festivos fuegos artificiales daneses

18 Word order

Spanish is often said to have an extremely flexible word order. It is important to realize, however, that while there is a good deal of freedom which is manipulated for stylistic reasons, differences in word order very often correspond to slight differences in meaning.

18.1 Subject and verb

In Spanish it is very common for the verb to precede the subject. Sometimes its effect is to give the subject a slight emphasis (though the difference is imperceptible to many speakers):

La chica se fue
The girl went (neutral)
Se fue la chica
The girl went

This word order is also preferred in the following circumstances:

(a) Where the subject is much longer than the verb or verb phrase:

Durante estos siglos se fueron formando las lenguas castellana, catalana y galaico-portuguesa
The Castilian, Catalan and Gallaeco-Portuguese languages were formed during these centuries

(b) With verbs such as **faltar**, **sobrar**, **gustar**, **doler**, etc, which do not take a direct object:

Me sobra dinero
I've more than enough money
Nos hace falta dinero
We need money

(c) When a plural subject is used without an article:

Aquí se venden manzanas
Apples are sold here
Vivían leones en el bosque
Lions lived in the wood

(d) With non-finite verbal constructions:

De haberlo sabido antes tu madre
If your mother had known beforehand
Procesado el sargento que mató a un soldado (newspaper headline)
The sergeant who killed a soldier [is] on trial

R1* vulgar or
　　indecent
R1　informal,
　　colloquial
R2　neutral
R3　formal, written
See also p 3.

18.2 Subject, verb and object

The verb may come first according to the principles outlined in the preceding section. Objects may also precede subject and verb, though only one object at a time can be moved in this way, and generally a corresponding pronoun must be used with the verb:

El atentado se lo atribuyó a la banda terrorista
The attack was attributed to the terrorist group
Al hombre le vino la idea de…
The idea of . . . came to the man

Objects involving negative, indefinite and demonstrative pronouns and **tanto** may also precede the verb, especially in R3:

El proyecto que tantos problemas nos ha planteado
The project which has caused us so many problems
Pero quienes se hallaban cerca de la explosión nada oyeron, al principio
But those who were near the explosion heard nothing at first

In R1 there is a very strong tendency to place the 'topics' of a sentence first, the remainder of the sentence then being adapted accordingly:

Ahora, yo esa palabra todavía, su definición exacta, no la sé
Now *I* don't know the exact meaning of *that word*
(Cf R2–3: **Ahora, todavía, no sé la definición exacta de esa palabra**)

Desde un punto de vista…principios digamos…yo es que no estoy plenamente convencida que a la persona que le sacan el corazón, al donante, no creo que esté muerta…
Let's say that from the point of view of principle, *I*'m not fully convinced that *the person whose heart they're taking out, the donor*, I don't think that person's dead . . .
(Cf R2–3: **Digamos que desde el punto de vista de principios, yo no estoy plenamente convencida de que esté muerta la persona a la que sacan el corazón, o sea el donante**)

18.3 Verb, objects and adverb

The adverb usually immediately precedes or immediately follows the verb in Spanish, though it may, as in English, also follow the object:

He leído con interés la noticia/He leído la noticia con interés
I have read the news with interest
Si no me acuerdo mal/Si mal no me acuerdo
If I remember rightly

18.4 Noun and adjective

One adjective

There are some adjectives in Spanish which have slightly different meanings according to whether they precede or follow the noun. The chief of these are:

†**antiguo**	costumbres antiguas *old customs*
	un antiguo presidente *a former president*
†**bárbaro**	los soldados bárbaros *the Barbarian soldiers*
	los bárbaros soldados *the barbaric soldiers*
cierto	indicios ciertos *sure signs*
	cierta falta de confianza *a certain lack of confidence*
	ciertas personas *certain people*
†**diferente**	libros diferentes *different books*
	diferentes libros *several books*
†**distinto**	ideas distintas *distinct ideas*
	distintas ideas *various ideas*
†**grande**	una casa grande *a big house*
	un gran escritor *a great writer*
†**medio**	el hombre medio *the man in the street*
	la clase media *the middle class*
	el dedo medio *the middle finger*
	medio litro *half a litre*
mismo	Roma misma OR la misma Roma (note the article) *Rome herself*
	su mismo pueblo OR su pueblo mismo *his very village*
	el mismo sentido *the same sense*
nuevo	una canción nueva *a new(ly composed) song*
	nos trasladamos a una nueva casa *we moved to another house*
†**pobre**	un barrio pobre *a poor district*
	¡Pobre chico! *Poor (= unfortunate) boy!*
propio	en defensa propia *in self-defence*
	tiene casa propia OR tiene su propia casa *he has his own house*
	sus propias palabras *his very words*
	obra del propio Unamuno *a work of Unamuno himself*
puro	la verdad pura *the unadulterated truth*
	de pura envidia *through sheer envy*

† More information about these words or expressions may be found in other sections. Use the Spanish word index to find the page numbers.

simple	un corazón simple *a simple heart* de simple interés *out of mere interest*
único	Eres una mujer única *You're a unique woman* el único problema *the only problem*
varios	razones muy varias *very varied reasons* varias personas *several people*

More complicated is the situation with other adjectives. Most adjectives in Spanish may be placed before or after the noun, and there is a growing preference among Spanish speakers for the preceding position. Nevertheless, there is usually a slight difference in meaning associated with different adjective positions.

Factors involving a preference for a following position

(a) An adjective following a noun usually has a 'distinctive' overtone, a nuance which is often conveyed in English by contrastive stress, eg:
– ¿Cómo es tu casa?
What's your house like?
– Es una casa pequeña
It's a *small* house
BUT
Vivía en una pequeña casa cerca de la catedral
I lived in a small house near the cathedral (here, nearness to the cathedral is the more 'distinctive' property)

Note the difference between the following sentences:
Las hojas secas se cayeron
The *dry* leaves fell (implies that the others didn't)
Las secas hojas se cayeron
The dry leaves fell (all the leaves were dry, and all fell)

The difference between preceding and following position is not always clear-cut, however, as in the following examples:
Ayer dimos un paseo muy largo
We went for a very long walk yesterday (may imply that we don't usually go for *long* walks)
Ayer dimos un largo paseo por el campo
We went for a long walk in the countryside yesterday (that it was in the countryside is the 'distinctive' information; a walk in the countryside is normally long)

Some adjectives are always essentially 'distinctive' and rarely if ever precede the noun, except for a very special effect. Such adjectives typically denote nationality, membership of a political or religious group, colour, etc, eg:
la ejecutiva socialista
the socialist executive
de nacionalidad libanesa
of Lebanese nationality
vino tinto
red wine

However, for deliberate less 'distinctive' effect even these may sometimes precede the noun, eg:

...apoyado contra la gris pared de una casa (C.-J. Cela)
leaning against the grey wall of a house
En mi propia casa estaban mis octogenarios padres
My 80-year-old parents were in my own house

Conversely, in some contexts an adjective cannot have a 'distinctive' value and must precede the noun, eg:

su admirable buen sentido
her admirable good sense (a person has only 'one' good sense)
tu adorable mujer
your adorable wife (a person has only one wife)
BUT
una mujer adorable
an *adorable* woman (as opposed to others)

(b) When a noun which has a very general meaning and an adjective which has a more specific (and hence more 'distinctive') meaning come together, the adjective tends to follow, eg:

la región craneal
the cranial region
el preso fugado
the escaped convict
dos puntos fundamentales
two fundamental points
un problema geométrico
a geometrical problem

Factors involving a preference for a preceding position

(a) When the adjective is an 'expected' attribute, eg:

un lamentable accidente
a lamentable accident
con enormes dificultades
with enormous difficulty

This usage is frequently employed for stylistic effect, eg:

**El buque ofrece un esmerado servicio del que podemos
disfrutar a lo largo de un maravilloso crucero de ocho
inolvidables días** (advertisement)
The ship offers high–class service which one can enjoy during a
wonderful cruise of eight unforgettable days

(b) When adjective and noun make a familiar or set phrase, eg:

los altos Alpes
the high Alps
un ligero aumento en el coste de la vida
a slight increase in the cost of living
su presunta responsabilidad
his presumed responsibility
el pasado mes de julio
last July
unas recientes declaraciones
recent statements

(c) A preceding position seems to be generally favoured for **difícil**, eg:
> **La extensión real de las propiedades es de difícil precisión**
> It is difficult to be precise about the true extent of the properties

More than one adjective

There are many possibilities available, but the rules for one adjective still basically hold. The most 'distinctive' adjectives will be placed after and furthest away from the noun, eg:
> **la política contemporánea mejicana**
> contemporary *Mexican* politics
> **la política mejicana contemporánea**
> *contemporary* Mexican politics

In cases where one or more of the adjectives may be placed before or after the noun, very subtle differences are possible. The adjective(s) which follow(s) the noun always has/have the more 'distinctive' value. The English translations given convey something of the differences of emphasis.
> **una muñeca manoseada y rota**
> a *worn*, *broken* doll
> **una manoseada y rota muñeca**
> a worn, broken *doll*
> **una manoseada muñeca rota**
> a *broken* worn doll
> **una rota muñeca manoseada**
> a *worn* broken doll

18.5 Numerals and **otro**

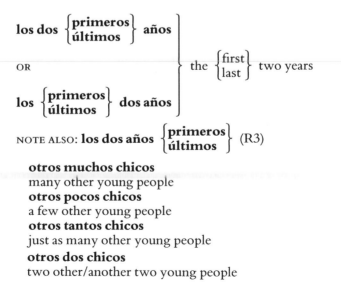

otros muchos chicos
many other young people
otros pocos chicos
a few other young people
otros tantos chicos
just as many other young people
otros dos chicos
two other/another two young people

19 Prepositions

19.1 a

19.1.1 Basic meanings

> *(a) destination, direction; generally corresponds to English to*
>
> **Voy a la costa**
> I'm going to the coast
>
> BUT NOTE:
> **Ayer llegamos a Madrid**
> Yesterday we arrived in (= got to) Madrid
> **Cayó al suelo**
> It fell on (= to) the ground
>
> *(b) point in time (see **19.1.2** below)*

a also introduces the indirect object of the verb and the 'personal' direct object (see **19.1.9** below).

19.1.2 a in time expressions

Spanish **a** corresponds to English *in, at, on* in many time expressions. Note, however, that there are several time expressions which require no preposition; eg: **los sábados** *on Saturdays*, **el día quince** *on the fifteenth*, **el lunes pasado** *last Monday*. See also **en** (**19.8**).

a las dos de la madrugada	at two in the morning
a(l) mediodía	at noon
a (la) medianoche	at midnight
a (las) primeras/altas horas de la noche	in the early hours of the morning
al día siguiente/al otro día	on the following day
a la mañana siguiente	on the following morning
a la noche/mañana/tarde	tonight/tomorrow morning/this afternoon
a principios/comienzos del/de (R1) **año/mes/de la semana**	at the beginning of the year/month/week
a mitad del año	half-way through the year
a mediados de(l) año/mes	in the middle of the year/month
a finales de(l) año/mes	at the end of the year/month
a los diecinueve años	at 19 years of age
a los cinco minutos de llegar/haber llegado	five minutes after arriving
al poco rato	a little later
al mismo tiempo/a la vez	at the same time

> **R1★** vulgar or indecent
> **R1** informal, colloquial
> **R2** neutral
> **R3** formal, written
> *See also p 3.*

a deshora/destiempo	at the wrong time
a tiempo	in time
a primera vista	at first sight

19.1.3 a expressing rate

día a día (see also tras, 19.15)	day by day
uno a uno (ALSO de uno en uno)	one by one
paso a paso	step by step
a docenas/millares	by the dozen/thousand
dos veces a la semana (see also por, 19.13.4)	twice a week
a diario	daily
a razón de cinco por persona	at the rate of five per person
¿A cuánto se vende el coche? (= ¿Cuánto es el coche?)	How much is the car being sold for?
a sesenta pesetas el kilo	at 60 pesetas a kilo
lo vende al litro (R1) (ALSO por litros (R2–3))	she sells it by the litre
vender al por menor/mayor	to sell retail/wholesale
tenemos libros a granel	we've got tons of books (often suggests disorder)
la cosecha ha sido a granel	there's been an abundant crop
a (una velocidad de) cuarenta km/h	at (a speed of) 25 mph
un empate a cero/a un gol	nil–nil/one–all draw

19.1.4 a expressing manner

General

| a la española/a lo español/al estilo español | in the Spanish style |

NOTE: **a lo español** is more abstract than **a la española** and is higher register.

| a mi manera | in my own way |
| a la manera de X | in X's way, after the fashion of X |

BUT: **de una manera/forma/de un modo elegante**

pagar al contado	to pay cash
a mi costa/a toda costa	at my expense/at all costs
a la inversa/al revés	the opposite way, vice versa
a mi juicio/entender/parecer/modo de ver	in my opinion

BUT **en mi opinión**

†a la larga	in the long run
tomar algo a la ligera	to take sth lightly
a la moda (ALSO de moda)	in fashion

† More information about these words or expressions may be found in other sections. Use the Spanish word index to find the page numbers.

19.1.5 Adverbial idioms with **a**

There are many adverbial idioms of manner in Spanish formed on
the patterns **a** + singular noun, **a** + plural noun (without an article)
and **a** + feminine plural adjective or noun. Some of the most
common are:

estar a sus anchas	to be at ease
Le mataron a balazos	They shot him dead
Se lo comió a bocado	She gulped it down by the mouthful
Salió a borbotones	It flooded out
a brazo perdido	fearlessly
a la buena de Dios	randomly, carelessly
a caballo (**de a caballo** in Am R1)	on horseback
Llueve a cántaros	It's pouring with rain
a ciegas	blindly
a ciencia cierta	for sure
a la corta o †**a la larga**	sooner or later
estar al corriente	to be informed
Le metieron a empellones	They pushed him through
Se abrió paso a empujones	He pushed his way through
a escondidas	covertly
a espaldas de uno	behind sb's back
a la fuerza	whether you, we, etc, like it or not
a gatas	on all fours
vivir a lo grande	to live like a king
estar a gusto	to be at ease
Entró a hurtadillas	He crept in
a instancias de (R3)	at the request of
un ataque a mano armada	an armed attack
a medias	partly
a lo mejor	perhaps
llorar a moco tendido (R1)	to cry one's eyes out
a los ojos de uno	in the eyes of sb
a oscuras	in the dark
La echaron a patadas/a puntapiés	They kicked her out
tomar a pecho	to take to heart
a duras penas	with great difficulty
a pie (**de a pie** in Am R1)	on foot
dormir a pierna suelta	to sleep soundly
saber a punto fijo	to know for certain
Le derribó a puñetazos	He hit him until he fell
a quemarropa	point-blank
a rajatabla	completely, strictly
a regañadientes	unwillingly
a sabiendas	knowingly
a solas	alone
Avanzó a tientas	He groped his way forward
Se enfrentaron a tiros	They shot at each other
a todo correr	at full speed

a todo gas (R1)	flat out, at full speed
a todo meter	with great intensity
a tontas y a locas	haphazardly
a trancas y barrancas	with great difficulty
a trechos	occasionally
a troche y moche	anyhow, helter-skelter
a trompicones	in fits and starts
a vista de pájaro	with a bird's-eye view
a voz en cuello/grito	at the top of one's voice

19.1.6 a expressing position

en (**19.8**) is the preposition used for the general expression of position, but **a** appears in many set phrases, eg:

caer al agua	to fall in the water

NOTE: in standard Spanish, **en** is generally used with verbs like **caer** if the 'destination' is uppermost in the speaker's mind; however, **a** is more commonly used in Am R1.

al aire libre	in the open air
al alcance de	within reach of
a bordo de	on board
a medio camino/a mitad de camino	half-way there
al/en contacto con	in contact with
al cuello	around his/her neck
a la derecha	on the right
a escala internacional	on an international scale
Se miró al espejo	He looked at himself in the mirror
al fondo de	at the bottom/end of
BUT **en el fondo**	basically
al hombro	on/over his/her shoulder
a hombros	on his/her back
a la intemperie	in the open air
a la izquierda	on the left
al otro lado	on the other side
a lo lejos	in the distance
a la luz de	in the light of (lit and fig)
a (R2–3)/en (R2) la mesa	at the table
a nivel literario	on the literary level
a orillas (R3) del mar/del río	at the seashore/by the river
NOTE: **en las orillas = R2**.	
tocar una melodía al (ALSO **en el**) **piano**	to play a tune on the piano
al raso	in the open air
a la sombra	in the shade
estar al teléfono	to be on the telephone
BUT **llamar por teléfono**	to telephone, to call (by telephone)

NOTE ALSO the general expression of distance from something:
estar a (dos kilómetros) de (la Universidad)
to be (two kilometres) from (the University)

19.1.7 **a** expressing instrument

hecho a mano/máquina	made by hand/machine
un cuadro al óleo	an oil-painting
un dibujo a pluma/lápiz	a drawing in pen/pencil

19.1.8 Complex prepositional expressions with **a**

a la altura de	on the same latitude as (lit); abreast of (fig)
· **estar a la altura de las circunstancias**	· to rise to the occasion
a/por causa de	because of
a favor de	in favour of
a fuerza de	by dint of, by force of, by means of
· **Le convencí a fuerza de argumentos**	· I convinced him with persuasive arguments
a guisa de (R3)	by way of
al lado de	by the side of
al otro lado de	on the other side of
a lo largo de	along
a nivel de	at the level of
a partir de	starting from (a point in time)
†**a pesar de**	in spite of
a raíz de	immediately after; as a result of, because of
a título de	by way of (eg excuse)
en lo concerniente a/tocante a/(con) respecto a BUT **respecto de**	with regard to
junto (invariable) **a**	close to, next to

19.1.9 'Personal' **a**

The preposition **a** precedes the direct object when the object refers to:

(a) a person, eg:
> **Yo quisiera ver al director**
> I would like to see the director
> **A mí no me interesa**
> It doesn't interest me
> **No vi a nadie**
> I didn't see anyone

(b) a personalized group, eg:
> **Los soldados defienden a la nación**
> The soldiers defend the nation
> **Van a reforzar al gobierno**
> They're going to strengthen the government
> **No haga el error de juzgar a Cuba**
> Don't make the mistake of judging Cuba

(c) an animal which engenders affection, eg:
Llamó al perro
She called the dog

(d) something 'personified', eg:
Llamó en vano a la muerte
He called in vain on death

a is also used to resolve ambiguity. In the following usages it often has a rôle in resolving the potential ambiguities caused by the relative freedom of Spanish word order:
Por fin ha vencido el joven su pasión por el juego
The young man has finally conquered his passion for gambling
Por fin ha vencido al joven su pasión por el juego
The young man's passion for gambling has finally conquered him
Se vio el hombre en el espejo
The man saw himself in the mirror
Se vio al hombre en el espejo
The man was seen in the mirror

But it may be used with objects of other kinds to resolve ambiguity, especially with verbs which express a relation of order of some kind, eg:
El silencio sigue al ruido
Silence follows the noise
El coche alcanzó a la bicicleta
The car overtook the bicycle

The 'personal' **a** is not used:

(a) when a person referred to is treated not as an individual human being, but as a thing or a commodity, eg:
Los romanos arrojaban (a) los cristianos a las fieras
The Romans used to throw the Christians to the wild animals
Prefiero (a) Unamuno
I prefer Unamuno (as an author rather than as an individual)

NOTE: absence of **a** is more prevalent in R1; so strong is the association between a 'personal' object and the use of **a** that the **a** is often used in such cases in R2–3.

(b) when an animal referred to does not engender affection, but is considered from the point of view of usefulness, or food, eg:
He comprado un caballo
I've bought a horse
Cogió un ratón
She caught a mouse

(c) when a person referred to is not known and his or her function rather than 'personality' is being thought of, eg:
Espero un basurero
I'm waiting for a dustman (garbage-collector)
BUT
Espero al basurero
I'm waiting for the dustman (garbage-collector)

Busco un médico que sepa curar a mi hijo
I'm looking for a doctor who can cure my son (any doctor will do)
BUT
Busco a un médico que sabe curar a mi hijo
I'm looking for a doctor (who I already know of) who can cure my son

(d) sometimes when there is also a personal indirect object in the same sentence, since ambiguity might result, eg:
Presentó al director su hija María Amparo
She introduced her daughter María Amparo to the director
BUT NOTE:
Llevo a mis amigos a la estación
I'm taking my friends to the station

With this prepositional phrase there is no possibility of ambiguity.

The following verbs need special care in the use of **a** with their personal objects:

(a) **tener**
Tengo dos hermanos
I've got two brothers (OR a brother and sister)
BUT
Tengo a mi esposa en la cama
I've got my wife (ill) in bed

Tuvo una hija
She had a daughter
BUT
Tuvo a su hija hace seis meses
She gave birth to her daughter six months ago

(b) †**querer**
Quiere un hijo
He wants a son
BUT
Quiere a su hijo
He loves his son

(c) †**perder**
Este niño ha perdido su madre
This child has lost his mother
BUT
Perdió a su hijo
She was the ruin of her son

19.2 ante, delante de, antes de, antes que

	ante	delante de
before (position)	ante	delante de
	face to face with, in the presence of; restricted to R3 in general meaning of before; several fig usages	before, in front of (gen and predominantly lit)
before (time)	antes de	antes que
	gen	when a clause introduced by **antes que** is implied: note that pronouns following remain in the subject form (**yo**, **tú**, etc)

Compareció ante el capitán	He appeared before the captain
ante las circunstancias	in the circumstances
ante la posibilidad de	faced with the possibility of
ante todo	especially
delante de la casa	in front of the house
antes de las cuatro	before four o'clock
Lo hizo antes que yo (lo hiciera)	He did it before me (= before I did)

19.3 bajo, debajo de

Both **bajo** and **debajo de** have the basic meaning of *under*. **Bajo** tends to be restricted to R3 in its literal meaning, but appears in many set phrases in all registers with a figurative meaning.

dos (grados) bajo cero	two (degrees) below zero
bajo la condición de que	on condition that
bajo cuerda	on the side, surreptitiously
bajo la custodia	in custody
bajo la lluvia	in the rain
bajo el mando de	under the command of
bajo sus órdenes	at your command
bajo palabra	on sb's word
bajo pena de muerte	on pain of death
bajo ningún pretexto	on no account
bajo la recomendación de	on the recommendation of
bajo aquel rey	under that king

debajo de is used in all registers with a predominantly literal meaning.

debajo de la mesa	under the table

19.4 con

19.4.1 Basic meanings

(a) association

café con leche
coffee with milk
una cartera con dinero
a wallet containing money

(b) instrument

abrí la lata con un destornillador
I opened the can with a screwdriver

(c) cause

estoy contento con usted
I'm pleased with you

me cansé con tanto escribir
I got tired with writing so much

(d) with adjectives describing behaviour which affects someone else

amable con/para con (R3) **todos**
friendly towards everybody

19.4.2 con in complex prepositional expressions

con arreglo a la ley	in accordance with the law
con miras al futuro	with a view to the future
con motivo/objeto de escaparse	with the intention of escaping
con ocasión de	on the occasion of
con relación a (ALSO **en relación con**)	in relation to
(con) respecto a	with regard to
El barco salió (con) rumbo a Nueva York	The boat left for New York
con vistas a	with a view to

19.4.3 con expressing manner

con cabeza desnuda	bareheaded
con voz ronca	in a hoarse voice

con combines with many abstract nouns to create adverbial expressions, eg:

con claridad	clearly
con desagrado	with displeasure
con locura	madly
con sequedad	drily

NOTE: in Am R1 (especially Central American Spanish), **con** may replace **a**[IO] or **a**, especially with verbs which take a personal direct object, eg:

> **Me presentó con el jefe** [!]
> He introduced me to the boss
> **¡Lléveme con un médico!** [!]
> Take me to a doctor!

19.5 contra, en contra de

These correspond to English *against* (lit and fig). **en contra de** is much more common than **contra** to denote the expression of contrary opinion.

Puso la silla contra la pared	She put the chair against the wall
un remedio contra la tos	a remedy for a cough
la lucha contra el enemigo	the struggle against the enemy
Las posibilidades son una contra diez	It's a ten to one chance
hablar/expresarse/ pronunciarse en contra de una opinión	to speak/to express oneself against an opinion

NOTE: **contra** may have the meaning *near* in Am (especially Argentine Spanish); **¿contra qué?** (= **¿para qué?**) is also an American usage.

19.6 de

19.6.1 Basic meanings

(a) possession; corresponds to English genitive ('s, s') or of

> **Esta casa es de mi padre**
> This house is my father's
> **una calle de Barcelona**
> a Barcelona street

(b) direction from; corresponds to English from

> **de Madrid a Segovia**
> from Madrid to Segovia

NOTE ALSO in time expressions:
> **de mañana en ocho días**
> in a week's time (= eight days from tomorrow)

and **de...en**, corresponding to English *from . . . to*:
> **de año en año**
> from year to year
> **de vez en cuando**
> from time to time

[IO] **a**[IO] introduces the indirect object

[PERS] **a**[PERS] denotes the Spanish personal **a**

[!] These forms are in regular use but might be considered 'incorrect' in an examination.

$\ggg\rightarrow$

(c) origin *(fig associated with (b))*

Es de Caracas
He's from Caracas

(d) material from which something is made *(again, fig associated with (b))*

la estatua de mármol
the marble statue

(e) introducing an agent *(see also **por**, **19.13.5**)*

estaba cubierta de una lona
it was covered in/by a tarpaulin
manchado de sangre
bloodstained
es amado de todos
he's loved by everyone
un cuento de García Márquez
a short story by García Márquez

This usage is found especially with past participles which would be accompanied by **estar** (see **27.5**), but extends to others which primarily express a mental state (the use of **por** indicating a more active involvement by the agent).

(f) cause *(esp with abstract nouns)*

Murió de tristeza
He died of grief
Lloró de alegría
She cried out of/for happiness

(g) concern; corresponds to English about

No sé nada de eso
I don't know anything about that

(h) introducing a descriptive or specifying phrase

el chico del pelo largo	the long-haired boy
la casa de al lado	the house next door
sordo del oído izquierdo	deaf in his left ear
español de nacimiento	Spanish by birth
peluquero de profesión	a hairdresser by trade

The phrase may indicate type, purpose or content:

un buque de (also **a** R1 Pen and R1–2 Am) **vapor**	a steamship
una máquina de escribir	a typewriter
una taza de té	a cup of tea

(i) linking nouns in apposition

la ciudad de Buenos Aires	the city of Buenos Aires
el bribón de mi hermano	my rogue of a brother

19.6.2 **de** in adverbial expressions of time

de antemano	beforehand
de día	by day
de inmediato	immediately
de joven	as a youngster
(muy) de mañana	(very early) in the morning
de momento	for the moment
de niño	as a child
de noche	by night

19.6.3 **de** in adverbial expressions of position

estar de pie	to be standing
estar de rodillas/hinojos (R3)	to be kneeling

19.6.4 **de** in expressions of price and measurement

un sello (Pen)/una estampilla (Am) de (a) treinta pesetas/pesos	a 30–peseta/peso stamp
El precio del coche es de ocho mil dólares	The price of the car is $8,000
El aumento es del diez por ciento	The increase is 10%
La distancia es de cien km	The distance is 100 km
El peso es de cinco kilos	The weight is 5 kilos
más de diez (see **30.1**)	more than ten

19.6.5 **de** with professions

Hace de camarero	He works as a waiter

See also **estar**, **meterse** (**20.9**)

19.6.6 **de** in adverbial expressions of manner

General

de todas formas/maneras/de todos modos (BUT en todo caso)	in any case
de cierto modo/de cierta manera	in a certain way
NOTE: en cierto modo	in some way or other (see **19.8.5**)
vestido de luto/paisano/ militar/marinero	dressed in mourning, in civilian clothes, in military, naval uniform
la conozco de vista/nombre	I know her by sight, name
tirarse de cabeza/de pie (al agua)	to dive, to jump (into the water)

19.6.7 Common idioms and expressions involving de

Me lo dio de balde	He gave it to me free
See also **en balde** (**19.8.5**)	
caer de bruces	to fall on one's face
de buenas a primeras	suddenly
de costumbre	usually
de buena fe	in good faith
de buena/mala gana	willingly/unwillingly
de golpe	suddenly
de buen grado (R2–3)	willingly
mirar de hito en hito	to stare at
de improviso	unexpectedly
de un lado, …, de otro, …	on the one hand, …, on the other …
Es de lejos el mejor	It's the best by a long way
de memoria	by heart, from memory
estar de moda	to be in fashion
de nuevo	again
de oídas	by hearsay
de oído	by ear
de ordinario	usually
estar abierto de par en par	to be wide open
venir de perillas	to come at an opportune moment
de pronto	suddenly
Me lo dieron de regalo	They gave it to me as a present
de repente	suddenly
Tengo tiempo de sobra	I've more than enough time
de un tirón	all in one movement
Lo bebió de un trago	He gulped it down in one mouthful
de trecho en trecho	occasionally
de veras/verdad	truly
estar de viaje	to be travelling
estar de visita	to be visiting

19.6.8 de expressing direction to or from

el camino de la ciudad	the way to the town
el tren de Valencia	the Valencia train (ie to Valencia)
el autocar procedente de Córdoba	the bus from Córdoba
de acá para allá (R1)	here and there
más acá de Salamanca	this side of Salamanca
más allá de Zamora	the other side of Zamora

19.6.9 'Grammatical' uses of **de**

(a) Before **que** with some verbs, adjectives and nouns (see **20.4** and **26.10**):

Me extraño de que no lo sepa
I'm surprised he doesn't know

Estoy seguro de que vendrá
I'm sure she will come

Pronto me di cuenta de que habían salido
I soon realized that they'd gone

NOTE: in R1, **de** is often omitted. In journalistic R3, on the other hand, **de** is sometimes erroneously used between a verb and a following **que...** (eg **se dice de que** ⌷); this is known as **dequeísmo**.

(b) In constructions involving adjectives meaning *easy* and *difficult*:
Este libro es muy difícil de leer (= **Es muy difícil leer este libro**)
This book is very difficult to read

(c) In superlative constructions:
el edificio más alto del mundo
the highest building in the world

19.6.10 Complex prepositions with **de**

acerca de	concerning
alrededor de	around
†**cerca de** (**cerca a** Am R1)	near

ALSO **el embajador cerca de la corte inglesa**   the ambassador to the English court

BUT NOTE: **junto a** (p 182) and the adjectives †**cercano a**, **contiguo a** and **inmediato a**. The adjective †**vecino** is found with **a**, though **de** is preferred.

enfrente de	opposite
de parte de	on behalf of
· **de mi parte**	· on my behalf

19.7 **desde**

desde has the basic meaning of *from* (a particular point) and hence overlaps with basic meaning (b) of **de** (**19.6.1**). It is used in expressions of position and time, and may also be used figuratively:

Desde la habitación se ve la costa
From the room you can see the coast
Está descontento desde ayer
He's been unhappy since yesterday
No lo hago desde hace tres meses
I haven't done it for three months
desde el más rico hasta el más pobre (R2–3)
from richest to poorest
NOTE: **de...a** is preferred to **desde...hasta** in R1.

⟫⟫→

desde mi punto de vista
from my point of view
desde muy antiguo
from olden times

In Am R1 **desde** is sometimes used to mark a point in past time:
Desde el lunes llegó [!]
He arrived on Monday

19.8 **en**

19.8.1 Basic meanings

(a) position above; corresponds to English on *(see also **encima de** (**19.9** and **19.14**) and **sobre** (**19.14**))*	
en el tejado	on the roof

(b) position within; corresponds to English in	*reference to a point within a period of time; corresponds to English* in *or* at
en/dentro de la caja — in the box	**en la actualidad** — at present
NOTE: **entre** is sometimes used in R1 in this sense.	**en la antigüedad** — in antiquity
en primera división — in the first division	**en aquel entonces/en aquellas fechas** — at that time
means of transport	**en breve** (R2–3) — soon
en tren/coche/bici(cleta)/moto(cicleta)/ barco/avión/autobús	**en (el** (R2–3)) **invierno** — in (the) winter
BUT **en el avión del presidente**	**en junio** — in June
	en Semana Santa/ Navidad(es) — in Holy Week/at Christmas
	en tiempo de guerra — in time of war
	en tiempos del rey — in the king's time
	No he dormido en toda la noche — I haven't slept all night
	No he hecho tal cosa en toda mi vida — I haven't done such a thing in my life

metaphorical position; corresponds to English in (a state)	
en estado de crisis	in a state of crisis
el gobierno en el poder	the government in power

(c) location; corresponds to English at *and* in	*reference to a point in time (see also **a**, **19.1.2**); often corresponds to English* on
en la cárcel/en prisión — in prison	**en el día trece** — on the 13th
en casa — at home	**el día en que** (**el día que** (R1)) — the day when/on which
en la estación — at the station	**de hoy en cuatro días** — in four days' time
en Málaga — in Málaga	
en todas partes — everywhere	

(d) movement within; corresponds to English into	
El tren entró en el túnel	The train went into the tunnel
poner en órbita	to put into orbit

19.8.2 **en** in expressions of measurement

aumentar, disminuir, etc, **en un diez por ciento**	to increase, decrease, etc, by 10%
firme en mal estado en diez km	bad road surface for 10 km

19.8.3 **en** indicating material   (see also **de, 19.6.1**)

La estatua es en mármol
The statue is made from marble

en focuses attention on the material, while **de** is more a simple description: **una estatua en mármol** = *a statue made out of marble*, **una estatua de mármol** = *a marble statue*.

19.8.4 **en**, corresponding to English *from*, with nouns indicating receptacles

fumar en pipa	to smoke a pipe (as a habit)
beber café en una taza	to drink coffee from a cup
comer en un plato	to eat from a plate

19.8.5 Common idioms and expressions involving **en**

en antena	on the air
en ausencia de	in the absence of
en balde	in vain
(SOMETIMES **de balde** in R1)	
en beneficio de	for the benefit of
en busca de	in search of
BUT **a la búsqueda de**	
en calidad de colega	as a colleague
en cambio	on the other hand
en carnes (vivas)	(stark) naked
en carretera	on the (main) road
en todo caso	in any case
en concreto	in fact, specifically
†**estar en condiciones de**	to be in a position to
en consecuencia	consequently
BUT **por consiguiente**	
en contestación/respuesta a	in reply to
en correo aparte	under separate cover
en cuanto a (algo/hacer algo)	as for (sth/doing sth)
en cuclillas	squatting
en cueros (vivos)	(stark) naked
en derredor de	around
emisión en diferido	recorded broadcast
emisión en directo	live broadcast
en especial	especially
en esto	thereupon
licenciado en filosofía y letras	bachelor of arts
en función de	in terms of

en honor de	in honour of
en lugar/vez de	instead of
en cierto modo	in some way or other
en nombre de	on behalf of
en mi opinión	in my opinion
BUT **a mi juicio, a mi entender**	
en parte	in part
en pie de guerra	on a war footing
salieron en plan de reyes	they went out like royalty
en presencia de	in the presence of
fue el primero/segundo, etc/último en hacerlo	he was the first/second, etc/last to do it
arguyó en pro de la reforma	he argued for (the) reform
en la †**radio**	on the radio
en razón de	by reason of, because of
en relación con	in relation to
(ALSO **con relación a**)	
†**en resumen**	in short
frenar en seco	to brake sharply
en seguida	immediately
en serio	seriously
en (la) televisión	on (the) television
(ALSO **por la televisión**)	
en torno a	with regard to, concerning
en trance de	in the process of
en tropel	in a mass
en lo que va de año	as far as this year is concerned
en vano	in vain
en virtud de	by virtue of
en vivo	live (eg television broadcast)
en voz alta/baja	aloud/in a low voice

19.9 encima de

encima de has the basic literal meaning of *on, above, on top of,* and is preferred to **en** (**19.8**) and **sobre** (**19.14**), where a high position is involved. **arriba de** is often used for **encima de** in this sense in Am.

encima de mi cabeza	above my head
Saltó encima de la cama	She jumped on (to) the bed

It also has the figurative meaning corresponding to **además de**:
   Encima de ser tonto, es desobediente
   As well as (on top of) being stupid, he's disobedient

19.10 enfrente de, frente a

In the basic meaning of *opposite*, **frente a** is slightly higher register than **enfrente de**, eg:

enfrente de/frente a (R2–3) **la casa**
opposite the house

NOTE ALSO the following special meaning of **frente a** (all registers):
Hubo un accidente frente a Bilbao
There was an accident off (the coast of) Bilbao

19.11 hacia

	literal		*figurative*	
direction	**hacia Cáceres**	towards Cáceres	**sus sentimientos hacia los animales/su padre**	his feelings towards animals/his father
	miró hacia atrás/ arriba	she looked back/up		
in time expressions	**hacia octubre**	towards (= about) October		

19.12 hasta

	literal		*figurative*	
direction	**hasta allí/ aquí**	there (= to there)/here (= to here)	**Estaba cansado hasta tal punto que...**	I was so tired that . . .
	desde Lisboa hasta Madrid (see **19.7**) (R2–3)	from Lisbon to Madrid		
time	**¡Hasta luego!** **hasta entonces** **No lo habrá terminado hasta mañana**		So long! up till then He won't have finished until tomorrow	

NOTE: the use of **no** in this construction, and consequently its meaning, vary considerably with register and regional variety, eg:

Hasta las tres no iré (standard)
I'll not go until three o'clock
Hasta las tres iré (R1–2, esp Central America, Colombia)
I'll not go until three o'clock

No saldré hasta que llegue (standard)
I'll not leave until he comes
No saldré hasta que no llegue (R1 Pen and Am)
I'll not leave until he comes

19.13 **para** and **por**

Since **para** and **por** are both the equivalents of English *for* in some of their meanings, English speakers do not always know which one to use. For this reason, it is helpful to present them contrastively, although they are quite different in their basic meanings.

19.13.1 Basic meanings

para	*por*
(a) purpose **¿Para qué sirve?** What is it for? **He venido a la biblioteca para estudiar** I've come to the library to study	*(a) cause* **¿Por qué lo hiciste?** Why did you do it? **La castiga por no estudiar** He punishes her for not working **Le han despedido por perezoso** They've dismissed him for being lazy **Por tu culpa he perdido el tren** It's your fault I've missed the train
(b) destination **Lo compré para ti** I bought it for you **un garaje para dos coches** a garage for two cars	*(b) on behalf of, for the sake of, in substitution for* **Lo hice por ti** I did it for you (= for your sake) **una misa por su alma** a mass for (the sake of) his soul **Hazlo por caridad** Do it for (the sake of) charity **Firma por su esposa** He signs for (= on behalf of) his wife **Lo cambiaron por un coche nuevo** They exchanged it for a new car **Le envié por (a por (R1)) vino** I sent him for wine **Pasa por lista** She is considered intelligent NOTE the following constructions with **razón**: **la razón de/para su salida** the reason for his leaving **la razón por (la) que/por la cual salió** the reason why he left

(c) in expressions of place, **para** again indicates destination	*(c)* through, along, around
Sale para Madrid He's leaving for Madrid **Voy para casa** I'm going home **Caminé para el árbol** I walked towards the tree	**Fui a Madrid por Valladolid** I went to Madrid via Valladolid **Mire por la ventana** Look out of the window **Se paseaba por la calle** She was walking along the street **¿Hay un banco por aquí?** Is there a bank (around) here? **Está por Pamplona** It's near Pamplona

19.13.2 **para** and **por** in time expressions

para	*por*
Se va para una semana He's going away for a week (= he intends to be away for a week) **Vendré para el veinticinco de mayo** I'll come (in time) for 25 May	**Viene por tres días** He's coming for three days (= for a period of three days' duration) **Vamos a aplazarlo por un mes** Let's put it off for a month **Vendré por el veinticinco de mayo** I'll come about 25 May **por la noche** at night **por el momento** (ALSO **de momento**) for the moment **por primera vez/por vez primera** (R3) for the first time **Es todo por ahora** That's all for the time being
Va para dos años que murió (R1) It's been nearly two years since he died **Nos veremos para el año que viene** (R1) We'll see each other some time next year	

19.13.3 Other uses of **para**

para is the equivalent of English *to* and *for* in expressions of excess (*too . . . to/for*) and sufficiency (*enough . . . to/for*), eg:

Eso es demasiado para mí
That's too much for me
No tengo dinero suficiente (como) para comprártelo
I don't have enough money to buy it for you

Es para volverse loco
It's enough to drive you mad
No es para creerlo
You really can't believe it

19.13.4 **por** expressing rate   (see also **a**, **19.1.3**)

por docenas	by the dozen
día por día	day by day
ocho por ciento	8%
a cien km por hora	at 100 km an hour

19.13.5 **por** expressing agent   (see also **de**, **19.6.1**)

La carta fue escrita por un holandés
The letter was written by a Dutchman

19.13.6 **por** in expressions of manner and means

por adopción	by adoption
por aire/carretera/	by air/road/rail/sea/land
ferrocarril/mar/tierra	
por carta	by letter
por correo	by mail
por (la) radio/(la) televisión	on (the) radio/(the) television
(ALSO **en (la) televisión**)	
Lo conocí por el sombrero	I knew him by his hat
llamar por teléfono	to telephone
BUT **estar al teléfono**	to be on the telephone
(19.1.6)	(momentarily)

19.13.7 **por** in adverbial idioms of manner

por cierto	certainly; of course
por consiguiente	consequently
BUT **en consecuencia**	
(19.8.5)	
por el (ALSO **al**) **contrario**	on the contrary
por desgracia	unfortunately
por escrito	in writing
por fortuna	luckily
por lo general/por regla	in general
general	
por un lado/una parte	on the one hand
por otro lado/otra parte	on the other hand
por separado	separately
por supuesto	of course
por lo tanto	therefore
por último	at last
por lo visto	apparently

19.13.8   **por** with other prepositions

por used before a preposition indicating location adds the idea of movement:

Corrieron por entre los coches
They ran among the cars
Pasó por detrás de la silla
He passed behind the chair
El avión voló por debajo del puente
The plane flew under the bridge
Saltó por encima de la mesa
He jumped over the table

19.13.9   Complex prepositions with **por**

mi abuelo por parte de mi padre
my grandfather on my father's side
Me lo pidió por mediación de su amigo
He asked me for it through his friend

19.14   **sobre**

sobre has the basic meaning of *on top of*, and is an alternative to **en** in basic meaning (a) (**19.8.1**) and to (**por**) **encima de** (**19.9** and **19.13.8**), eg:

Hay un libro sobre/en la mesa	There's a book on the table
Puso un ladrillo sobre/encima de otro	He put one brick on top of another
mil metros sobre el nivel del mar	1,000 metres above sea level
un grado sobre cero	one degree above zero
sobre (R3)/**en el cielo español**	in the Spanish sky
El reactor voló sobre/por encima de la ciudad	The jet flew over the town

In addition, **sobre** has a range of figurative usages, many, but not all, of which correspond to English *on*:

un libro sobre Cervantes	a book on Cervantes
sobre las cinco de la tarde (ALSO **a eso de las cinco**)	at about five o'clock
ocho sobre diez	eight out of ten
Dice tontería sobre tontería	He says one stupid thing after another

Adverbial phrases with **sobre**

sobre ascuas	on tenterhooks
sobre aviso	on one's guard
sobre manera	exceedingly
sobre todo	especially

19.15 tras (tras de in Am R1), detrás de (atrás de in Am R1), después de, después que

after (position)	detrás de
	behind (gen and
	    predominantly lit)
		tras
		gen R3, but R1–3 in some set
		    expressions (see below)

Caminaron uno tras otro
    (R1–3)   *They walked one behind the other*

tras (R3)/**detrás de la puerta**   *behind the door*

Iba tras (R3) **el/detrás del**
    caballo   *She followed on after the horse*

after (time)	después de gen	tras gen R3, but R1–3 in some set expressions (see below)
	después que when a clause introduced by después que is implied	

NOTE: pronouns following **después que** remain in subject form (**yo**, **tú**, etc).

día tras día (R1–3)   *day after day*
    (ALSO **a**, **19.1.3**)

Leía libro tras libro (R1–3)   *He read book after book*

tras (R3)/**después de las seis**   *after six o'clock*

tras (R3)/**después de dos**   *after two months' absence*
    meses de ausencia

Lo hice tras (R3)/**después que**   *I did it after him*
    él

19.16 a través de

a través de corresponds to English *through* in most senses:
    a través de una celosía
    through a blind

Lo supe a través de la radio
    I found out through the radio

Se puede hacer a través del banco
    You can do it through the bank

Lo puedes encargar a través de mi profesor
    You can order it through my teacher

It is also equivalent to English *across* when this implies a vague distance from one side of something to the other, eg:
    Corrió a través de los campos/del bosque
    She ran across the fields/the wood

Compare:
una carrera campo a través
a cross–country race

NOTE: where a precise distance is implied, the notion of *across* requires a different construction (see ch. **21**), eg:
Cruzó la calle corriendo
She ran across the road
Atravesó el río nadando/a nado
She swam across the river

NOTE: *across* in the sense of *on the other side* is usually rendered by Spanish **al otro lado de**, eg:
El transatlántico estaba anclado al otro lado de la bahía
The liner was anchored across (= on the other side of) the bay

19.17 Accumulation of prepositions

Prepositional phrases may sometimes be used rather like nouns, and be preceded themselves by other prepositions. Such usage is most common in R1, eg:
No es de por aquí (R1)
He's not from around here
Estará la casa arreglada para dentro de dos meses (R1)
The house will be sorted out within two months
Fue a por vino (R1)
He went to get wine
de a ratos (Am R1)
from time to time
No se meta usted de por medio
Don't poke your nose in here
la casa de al lado
the house next door

20 Prepositional constructions with verbs, nouns and adjectives

This is one of the most complex areas of Spanish grammar. The following sections outline some general principles and draw attention to the many differences between Spanish and English. All verbs, nouns and adjectives listed in this section are included in the Spanish word index at the end of the book.

NOTE: the raised equals sign by a verb ($^=$) indicates that in order for the verb to take an infinitive or gerund complement the subject of the verb and the implied subject of its dependent infinitive or gerund must be identical. For example, in **aprendí (yo) a hacerlo (yo)**, **yo** is the subject of both **aprendí** and **hacer** (cf English *I learned how I should do it*).

20.1 Verbs with no preposition before an infinitive

20.1.1 Infinitive as subject of the verb

If the infinitive is the subject of the verb, no intervening preposition is used. †**aburrir (a uno)** (*to be boring (to sb)*) is such a verb: in the sentence **Me aburre hacer eso**, **hacer eso** is the subject of **me aburre**. Notice that the most usual English equivalent of such sentences is often not parallel in structure: **Me aburre hacer eso** might be translated as *I'm bored doing that* in preference to the more literal *Doing that bores me*.

agradar a^{io} uno	to please sb
†**alegrar a^{io} uno**	to gladden sb
†**antojarse a^{io} uno**	
· **Se me antoja hacerlo**	· I feel like doing it
apasionar a^{io} uno	to arouse passion/enthusiasm in sb
apetecer a^{io} uno	to appeal to sb
atraer a^{io} uno	to attract sb
†**bastar a^{io} uno**	to be enough for sb
†**caber**	to fit, to be appropriate
· **Cabe destacar que...**	· It should be pointed out that . . .
†**convenir a^{io} uno**	to be fitting for sb
†**corresponder a^{io} uno**	to be up to sb
· **Me correspondió contestar**	· It was up to me to reply
costar a^{io} uno	to cost sb effort
· **Cuesta manejar tantas cifras**	· It's difficult to cope with so many figures
†**cumplir a^{io} uno hacer algo**	to behove sb to do sth
†**encantar a^{io} uno**	to be pleasing/delightful to sb
†**entusiasmar a^{io} uno**	to arouse enthusiasm in sb
†**extrañar a^{io} uno**	to surprise sb

$^=$ The subject of the main verb must be the same as that of its dependent infinitive.

^{io} **a^{io}** introduces the indirect object
PERS **a^{PERS}** denotes the Spanish personal **a**

† More information about these words or expressions may be found in other sections. Use the Spanish word index to find the page numbers.

†**hacer falta a**[io] **uno**	to be lacking to sb (lit)
· **Hace falta matricularse**	· You have to register
fascinar a[io] **uno**	to fascinate sb
†**fastidiar a**[io] **uno**	to annoy sb
†**gustar a**[io] **uno**	to be pleasing to sb (lit)
· **Me gustaría saberlo**	· I would like to know

NOTE: **gustar de hacer algo/algo**, *to like doing sth/sth*, is restricted to R3; **gustar hacer algo/algo**, with the same meaning, is common, however, in Am R1.

†**importar a**[io] **uno**	to be important/to matter to sb (lit)
· **¿Te importa cerrar la ventana?**	· Would you mind closing the window?
incumbir a[io] **uno** (R3)	to be incumbent upon sb
interesar a[io] **uno**	to interest sb
merecer/valer la pena	to be worthwhile
†**molestar a**[io] **uno**	to be a nuisance to sb
†**ocurrirse a**[io] **uno**	to occur to sb (lit)
· **Se me ocurrió ir**	· I made up my mind to go
†**quedar a**[io] **uno**	to remain for sb
†**sobrar a**[io] **uno**	to be superfluous
†**tocar a**[io] **uno**	to fall to sb (fig)
· **Te toca pagar**	· It's your turn to pay

20.1.2   Infinitive as direct object

When the following infinitive has essentially the same function as a direct object noun, there is no intervening preposition:

†**Fingió**[=] **tener miedo**
He pretended to be afraid

Compare:
Fingió sorpresa
He feigned surprise

Other verbs of this class are:

†**aceptar**[=]	to undertake to do sth/sth
†**acordar**[=]	to agree to do sth/on sth
anhelar[=]	to long to do sth/for sth
BUT **el anhelo por/en**	
ansiar[=]	to long to do sth/for sth
BUT **el ansia** (f) **de/para**	
†**aparentar**[=]	to make as if to do sth/to feign sth
†**conseguir**[=]	to manage to do sth/to succeed in doing sth/to obtain sth
†**desear**[=]	to want to do sth/sth
BUT **el** †**deseo de; deseoso de**	
†**escoger**[=]	to choose to do sth/sth
†**evitar**[=]	to avoid doing sth/sth
†**intentar**[=]	to try to do sth/to attempt sth
BUT **el intento de/para**	
jurar[=]	to swear to do sth/sth

lamentar$^=$	to regret to do sth/sth
†**lograr**$^=$	to succeed in doing sth/to get sth
†**necesitar**$^=$	to need to do sth/sth
BUT la †**necesidad de**	
†**parecer**$^=$	to seem to do sth/sth
†**pedir**$^=$	to ask to do sth/for sth
planear$^=$	to plan to do sth/sth
†**preferir**$^=$	to prefer to do sth/doing sth/sth
†**pretender**$^=$ (R2–3)	to want to do sth/to try to do sth/to claim to do sth/to seek sth
prever$^=$/**tener**$^=$ **previsto**	to foresee doing sth
†**probar**$^=$ (R3 with inf)	to try to do sth/sth
†**procurar**$^=$ (R2–3)	to try to do sth/sth
prometer$^=$	to promise to do sth/sth
†**proponerse**$^=$	to propose to do sth/doing sth/sth
†**proyectar**$^=$ (R2–3)	to plan to do sth/sth
BUT **el proyecto de hacer algo**	
†**querer**$^=$	to want to do sth/sth
†**resolver**$^=$	to resolve to do sth
BUT **resolverse**$^=$ **a/para hacer algo, estar resuelto a hacer algo**	
†**saber**$^=$	to know how to do sth/sth
†**sentir**$^=$	to regret doing sth/to do sth/sth
†**solicitar**$^=$ (R3)	to ask to do sth/for sth
†**temer**$^=$	to fear doing sth/to do sth/sth

20.1.3 Verbs of ordering

A number of verbs of ordering take an infinitive without a preposition as an alternative to the **que** + subjunctive construction (see **26.2.2**), eg:

†**aconsejar a**^{io} **uno**	to advise sb to do sth
†**consentir a**^{io} **uno**	to allow sb to do sth
†**dejar a**^{io} **uno**	to let sb do sth
†**hacer a**^{io} **uno**	to make sb do sth
†**impedir a**^{io} **uno**	to prevent sb from doing sth
†**mandar a**^{io} **uno**	to order sb to do sth

BUT **mandar a uno a hacer algo** = *to send sb to do sth*. In Am R1 the distinction is sometimes obscured, **a** being used in both constructions.

†**ordenar a**^{io} **uno**	to order sb to do sth
†**permitir a**^{io} **uno**	to allow sb to do sth
†**prohibir a**^{io} **uno**	to forbid sb to do sth
†**sugerir a**^{io} **uno**	to suggest doing sth to sb

IO   **a**^{io} introduces the indirect object
PERS **a**^{PERS} denotes the Spanish personal **a**

$^=$ The subject of the main verb must be the same as that of its dependent infinitive.

20.1.4   Verbs of perception (eg **oír** and [†]**ver**)

Examples:

> **Oí cantar a María**
> I heard Mary sing(ing)
> **Oí cantar una canción**
> I heard a song (being) sung
> **Oí cantar una canción a María**
> I heard Mary sing(ing) a song

20.1.5   Verbs of saying

Several verbs of saying may take an infinitive in R2–3 with no intervening preposition as an alternative to the **que** + clause construction, eg:

> **Confirmó que lo había hecho/Confirmó haberlo hecho**
>   (R2–3)
> He confirmed having done it/that he had done it

Other verbs of this class:

afirmar[=]	to affirm that . . .
confesar[=]	to confess doing sth/that . . .
[†]**creer**[=]	to think that . . .
[†]**decir**[=]	to say that . . .
[†]**declarar**[=]	to declare that . . .
[†]**dudar**[=]	to doubt if/whether/that . . .
[†]**manifestar**[=]	to state that . . .
[†]**pensar**[=]	to think that . . .
[†]**reconocer**[=]	to recognize that . . .

20.1.6   Other verbs

[†]**dignarse**[=]	to deign to do sth
osar[=] (R2–3)	to dare to do sth
rehuir[=] (R2–3)	to avoid doing sth
rehusar[=] (R3)	to refuse to do sth

20.2   **a** before an infinitive

As with the use of **a** in isolation (see **19.1.1**), there is often the notion of metaphorical movement towards a goal. **a** tends to be used with verbs which carry a 'positive' meaning.

20.2.1   Attainment and figurative motion

acertar[=] **a**	to manage to do sth/to succeed in doing sth

> NOTE: **acertar a hacer algo** = *to happen to do sth*: **Un cartero acertó a pasar**   *A postman happened to pass.*

[†]**alcanzar**[=] **a**	to manage to do sth/to succeed in doing sth
aprender[=] **a**	to learn (how) to do sth

[†]**apresurarse**⁼ **a** (ALSO **por, con**) to hasten to do sth
  ALSO **apresuramiento a** (ALSO **en**) **hacer algo**
[†]**arriesgarse**⁼ **a** to risk doing sth
 aspirar⁼ **a** to aspire to do sth
[†]**atinar**⁼ **a** to manage to do sth/to succeed
    in doing sth
[†]**atreverse**⁼ **a** to dare to do sth
[†]**decidirse**⁼ **a** to decide to do sth
  ALSO **estar**⁼ **decidido a** = *to be decided on doing sth*
  BUT **decidir**⁼ **hacer algo** with same meaning, and **la** [†]**decisión**
    de hacer algo
[†]**llegar**⁼ **a** to succeed in doing sth/to end
    up doing sth
[†]**matarse**⁼ **a** to kill oneself doing sth
[†]**precipitarse**⁼ **a** (ALSO **en**) to hasten to do sth
 rebajarse⁼ **a** to stoop to doing sth
 tender⁼ **a** to tend to do sth

20.2.2 Verbs of beginning

[†]**comenzar**⁼ **a**
[†]**echarse**⁼ **a**
[†]**empezar**⁼ **a**
[†]**meterse**⁼ **a**
[†]**ponerse**⁼ **a**
[†]**principiar**⁼ **a** (R3)

See also *to begin* in ch. **2.**

ALSO:

[†]**lanzarse**⁼ **a** to rush into doing sth
[†]**pasar**⁼ **a** to go on to do sth
 · **Pasó a pedir más dinero** · He went on to ask for more
    money
[†]**romper**⁼ **a** to burst out doing sth

20.2.3 Agreement

[†]**acceder**⁼ **a** to agree to do sth/to doing sth
[†]**avenirse**⁼ **a** to agree to do sth (of two or
See also *to agree* in ch. **2.** more people)

20.2.4 Encouragement, help or other influence

[†]**acostumbrar a**^{PERS} to accustom sb/oneself to doing
  uno/acostumbrarse⁼ **a** sth
[†]**animar a**^{PERS} **uno a** to encourage sb to do sth
 autorizar a^{PERS} **uno a** (ALSO to authorize sb to do sth
  para)
[†]**ayudar a**^{PERS} **uno a** to help sb to do sth
 brindarse⁼ **a** (ALSO **para**) to offer to do sth
 comprometerse⁼ **a** (ALSO to undertake to do sth
  para)

> ⁼ The subject of the main verb must be the same as that of its dependent infinitive.

condenar a[PERS] **uno a**	to condemn sb to do sth/to doing sth
consagrarse= **a**	to devote oneself to doing sth
contribuir= **a**	to contribute towards doing sth
†**convidar a**[PERS] **uno a** (ALSO with no PREP in Am R1)	to invite sb to do sth
dedicarse= **a**	to dedicate oneself to doing sth
†**determinar a**[PERS] **uno a**	to determine sb to do sth
disponerse= **a** (ALSO **para**)	to prepare to do sth
empujar a[PERS] **uno a**	to push sb into doing sth
†**enseñar a**[PERS] **uno a**	to teach sb to do sth
entregarse= **a**	to devote oneself to doing sth
exhortar a[PERS] **uno a** (R3)	to exhort sb to do sth
†**forzar a**[PERS] **uno a**	to force sb to do sth
habituar a[PERS] **uno a**/ **habituarse**= **a**	to accustom sb/oneself to doing sth
impulsar a[PERS] **uno a**	to impel sb to do sth
incitar a[PERS] **uno a**	to incite sb to do sth
inclinarse= **a**	to be inclined to do sth
ALSO **inclinación a** (ALSO **por**)	
inducir a[PERS] **uno a**	to lead sb to do sth
instar a[PERS] **uno a** (R3)	to urge sb to do sth
†**invitar a**[PERS] **uno a** (ALSO **para**; ALSO with no PREP in Am R1)	to invite sb to do sth
ALSO **invitación a** (ALSO **para**)	
estar= †**listo a** (ALSO **para**)	to be ready to do sth
†**llevar a**[PERS] **uno a**	to lead sb to do sth
†**mentalizarse**= **a** (ALSO **para**)	to make up one's mind/to decide to do sth
†**mover a**[PERS] **uno a**	to move sb to do sth
obligar a[PERS] **uno a**	to oblige sb to do sth
BUT **la obligación de hacer algo**	
†**ofrecerse**= **a** (ALSO **para**)	to offer to do sth
†**persuadir a**[PERS] **uno a** (ALSO **para**)	to persuade sb to do sth
†**prepararse**= **a** (ALSO **para**)	to prepare to do sth
ALSO **estar**= †**preparado a** (ALSO **para**) = *to be prepared to do sth*	
prestarse= **a**	to lend oneself to doing sth
proceder= **a**	to proceed to doing sth
†**tentar a**[PERS] **uno a**	to tempt sb to do sth

20.2.5 With verbs of motion

†**Fui a verla**
I went to see her
†**Salió a recibirme**
He came out to welcome me
†**Se sentó a pensar**
She sat down to think
†**Vengo a decirte que...**
I've come to tell you that . . .

20.2.6 **a** for **para** and **por**

In R1, and increasingly in R2–3, **a** may be used for **para** and **por** (see
20.5.4) in the following types of construction:
una cuestión a $\boxed{!}$ (R1)/**para** (R2–3) **resolver**
una †**cuenta a** $\boxed{!}$ (R1)/**por** (R2–3) **pagar**

20.2.7 **a** + infinitive as imperative

a + infinitive has the force of an imperative in R1:

¡ A comer!
Let's eat!
¡A dormir!
Let's sleep!
¡A ver!
Let's see!
¡A pasarlo bien!
Have a good time!

20.3 **a** before a noun

20.3.1 Indirect object **a** rendered by a preposition other than *to* in English

With verbs which have the general meaning of 'to take away',
Spanish **a**^{IO} corresponds to English *from*, eg:
Lo compré a^{IO} **un gitano**
I bought it from a gipsy

Other verbs of this class are:

arrebatar	to snatch away
confiscar	to confiscate
disimular	to hide
escamotear	to whisk away
esconder	to hide
†**exigir**	to demand
†**ganar** (R3)	to win
†**hurtar**	to steal
ocultar	to hide
ocupar	to seize
†**pedir**	to ask for
†**pedir prestado**	to borrow
†**quitar**	to take away
†**reclamar** (R3)	to claim
†**restar**	to take away
†**robar**	to steal
†**sacar** (R1)	to get out of
†**solicitar** (R2–3)	to ask for
sonsacar	to extract (eg information)
†**sustraer**	to take away

a[io] may also be rendered by other prepositions in English, eg:

imponer	⎫	to impose sth on sb
inculcar	⎬ **algo a**[io] **uno**	to inculcate sth in sb
infundir (R2–3)	⎭	to instil sth in sb
producir una impresión a[io] **uno**		to make an impression on sb
[†]**regatear**	⎫ **algo a**[io] **uno**	to keep sb short of sth
reprochar	⎭	to reproach sb for sth

20.3.2   Noun + **a** + noun

Several nouns which represent actions or attitudes require **a** before a noun which functions as the direct object of the corresponding verb, eg:

la operación a Reagan
the operation on Reagan

Compare:

Operaron a Reagan
They operated on Reagan

Other examples:

su [†]**afición al dinero** (ALSO **por**)	his love of money
ALSO **estar aficionado a algo**	
la agresión a Nicaragua (ALSO **contra**)	aggression against Nicaragua
el amor a un hijo (ALSO **por**)	love for a child
su apoyo al Primer Ministro	his support for the Prime Minister
el asalto a Cádiz	the attack on Cadiz
un ataque al gobierno	an attack on the government
un atraco a un banco	a bank raid
el boicot a África del Sur	the boycott of South Africa
un [†]**comentario al** *Quijote* (ALSO **del**)	a commentary on the *Quixote*
Hizo muchas críticas a los medios informativos	He made many criticisms of the media
el culto al ejercicio físico	the cult of physical exercise
su [†]**denuncia a los responsables**	his denouncing of those responsible
la entrevista al Primer Ministro (ALSO **con**)	the interview with the Prime Minister
un [†]**interrogatorio al sospechoso**	an interrogation of the suspect
mi odio a los dictadores	my hatred for dictators
la opresión a los judíos (ALSO **sobre**)	the oppression of the Jews
el reconocimiento a Shakespeare (ALSO **por, de**)	recognition of Shakespeare
el rechazo a los liberales (ALSO **de**)	the rejection of the liberals

209

su †renuncia a la sucesión (ALSO de)	his renunciation of the succession
un repaso a la lección (ALSO de)	review of the lesson
el robo a una bolsa	the theft of a handbag
mi †temor a la muerte (ALSO de)	my fear of death
See **20.9**.	

NOTE: with such nouns, **de** marks the subject of the corresponding verb; contrast the following examples with those given above:

el amor de un hijo	a son's love
el odio de clases	class hatred (ie hatred of one class by another)

20.3.3 With verbs of smell and taste

oler a algo	to smell of sth
†saber a algo	
tener †gusto a algo	to taste of sth

20.4 **de** before an infinitive or noun

de may be thought of as the 'opposite' of **a**. It tends to be associated with metaphorical movement away from something.

20.4.1 Cessation

†abstenerse= de	to abstain from doing sth/sth
†acabar= de	to have just + PP/to finish doing sth

NOTE: †**acabar de** has the meaning of *to have just* when used in the Present and Imperfect; in other tenses it has the meaning of *to finish*:

Acabo de llegar
I've just arrived
Acababa de llegar
I'd just arrived
Cuando acabó de vestirse...
When he had finished dressing . . .

NOTE ALSO: **no acabar de** = *to fail to* (see **22.1**):
Estudio mucho pero no acabo de entenderlo
I study a lot but I fail to understand it

cesar= de	to stop doing sth
†dejar= de	to stop doing sth
desistir= de	to desist from doing sth/sth
†despedirse de	to take one's leave of sb/sth
†parar= de	to stop doing sth
†terminar= de	to stop doing sth

> = The subject of the main verb must be the same as that of its dependent infinitive.

20.4.2 'Negative' idea

A number of verbs have unfavourable or 'negative' meanings.

†**acusar a**ᴾᴱᴿˢ **uno de**	to accuse sb of doing sth
†**burlarse de**	to make fun of sb/sth
ALSO **burlar a**ᴾᴱᴿˢ **uno** (R3) = *to deceive sb*	
†**cuidarse bien de**	to take good care not to do sth
culpar aᴾᴱᴿˢ **uno de**	to blame sb for doing sth/sth
desconfiar de	to distrust sb/sth
BUT **desconfianza en algo/uno**	
†**desesperarse**⁼ **de**	to despair of doing sth/sb/sth
desinteresarse⁼ **de** (ALSO **por**)	to lose interest in doing sth/sth
BUT **desinterés por algo**	
†**disuadir a**ᴾᴱᴿˢ **uno de**	to dissuade sb from doing sth/sth
excusarse⁼ **de hacer algo/algo** (ALSO **por algo**)	to apologize for doing sth/sth
†**guardarse**⁼ **de**	to be careful not to do sth
librarse de	to escape from sb/sth
mofarse de (R2–3)	to make fun of sb/sth, to scoff at sb/sth
privar(se) de	to deprive (oneself) of sth
privar aᴾᴱᴿˢ **uno de**	to forbid sb to do sth/to deprive sb of sth
†**quejarse de**	to complain about sth
recelar de (R2–3)	to be suspicious of sb
†**renegar de**	to forsake sb/sth (esp faith)
resarcirse de	to make up for sth
vengarse de	to take revenge on sb/for sth
zafarse de	to dodge sth

BUT NOTE:

†**negarse**⁼ **a**	to refuse to do sth
†**negativa a**	refusal to do sth
†**renunciar a**	to renounce sth
†**renuncia a**	renunciation of sth
†**resistirse**⁼ **a**	to resist doing sth/sth

20.4.3 Causation

†**aburrirse de** (ALSO **por, con**)	to be bored by sth
admirarse de	to wonder at sth
†**alegrarse de** (ALSO **por, con**)	to be gladdened by sth
†**arrepentirse**⁼ **de**	to repent of doing sth/sth
asombrarse de	to be amazed at sth
asustarse de (ALSO **por, con**)	to be frightened by sth
†**avergonzarse**⁼ **de**	to be ashamed of doing sth/sth/sb
†**cansarse**⁼ **de**	to tire of doing sth/sth/sb
ALSO **cansarse con uno**	
estar †**contento de** (ALSO **con**)	to be happy with sth/sb
estar †**descontento de** (ALSO **con**)	to be unhappy with sth/sb
enamorarse de	to fall in love with sb

escandalizarse de	to be scandalized by sth
espantarse de	to be scared of sth
†extrañarse de	to be surprised at sth
†fatigarse= de	to get tired of doing sth/sth
†gloriarse de	to be proud of sth
hartarse= de	to be fed up with doing sth/sth
ALSO estar= †harto de	
†jactarse= de	to boast of doing sth/sth
maravillarse de	to marvel at sth
pagarse de	to be pleased with sth
preciarse= de	to pride oneself on sth/to boast of doing sth
†preocuparse de (ALSO con, por)	to worry about sth/to give special attention to sth (Am)
†reírse de	to laugh at sth
†sonreírse de	to smile at sth
sorprenderse de	to be surprised at sth
ufanarse= de (R3) (ALSO con)	to be proud of doing sth/sth

20.4.4 'Advantage'

†aprovecharse de	to take advantage of sth
beneficiarse de	to benefit from sth
†disfrutar de ⎫ (ALSO with	
†gozar de ⎭ no PREP)	to enjoy sth

20.4.5 'Instrument' (**de** is often the equivalent of English *with*)

†acomodarse de ⎫	
apercibirse de ⎭	to provide oneself with sth
†cargar aᴾᴱᴿˢ uno de (ALSO with con fig)	to weigh sb down with sth
colmar aᴾᴱᴿˢ uno de	to fill sb up, to overwhelm sb with sth
encargar aᴾᴱᴿˢ uno de	to entrust sb with sth/sth to sb
ALSO **encargar algo a uno** with the same meaning; and	
encargarse de = *to take charge of sth*	
henchirse de	to swell (intr) with sth
pertrecharse de	to equip oneself with sth
saciarse de	to be satisfied with sth, to have one's fill of sth
vestir aᴾᴱᴿˢ uno de (ALSO refl)	to dress sb in sth
vivir de	to live on sth

20.4.6 With verbs of change

†cambiar	to change
· **Quieren cambiar de casa**	· They want to change house(s)
mudar	to change
variar	to vary in sth
· **Las dos paredes varían de color**	· The two walls vary in colour

> = The subject of the main verb must be the same as that of its dependent infinitive.

20.4.7 Other uses of **de**

†**el deber de hacer algo**	the duty to do sth
tener ganas de hacer algo	to want to do sth
†**Ya es hora de hacer algo**	It's time to do sth
la voluntad de hacer algo	the will to do sth
digno de algo/hacer algo	worthy of sth/doing sth
seguro de algo/hacer algo	sure of sth/of doing sth
†**susceptible de hacer algo**	capable of doing sth

20.5 **por** before an infinitive or noun

Although many of the uses of **por** can be related to the basic meanings of the preposition (**19.13.1**), it is sometimes difficult for English speakers to perceive the connection.

20.5.1 **por** = *on account of*

†**aburrirse por**	to be bored by sth
†**apurarse⁼ por**	to worry about sth/doing sth
felicitar aᴾᴱᴿˢ **uno por**	to congratulate sb on doing sth/sth
(dar las) gracias por	(to give) thanks for doing sth/sth
†**indignarse por** ⎫	
†**irritarse por** (ALSO **con, contra**) ⎬	to get angry about sth
obsesión por (ALSO **para**)	obsession for doing sth/sth
BUT **tener la obsesión de** = *to be obsessed by sth/doing sth*	
pasión por	passion for doing sth/sth
†**preocuparse⁼ por** (ALSO **de, con**)	to worry about doing sth/sth
†**protestar por**	to protest about sth

20.5.2 **por** = *by*

With verbs of beginning and ending, **por** + inf or ger alone may be used, eg:

Acabé por leerlo or **acabé leyéndolo**
I ended up by reading it

†**acabar⁼ por** (ALSO + ger)	to end up doing sth
†**comenzar⁼ por** (ALSO + ger) ⎫	
†**empezar⁼ por** (ALSO **con**, + ger) ⎬	to begin by doing sth
†**terminar⁼ por** (ALSO + ger)	to end up doing sth

20.5.3 **por** = *in favour of*

abogar por	to plead for sb
†**brindar por** (ALSO **a**)	to drink to sb
†**decidirse**⁼ **por**	to decide in support of/on doing sth/sth

    BUT **la** †**decisión de** = *the decision to do sth*

optar⁼ **por**	to opt for doing sth/sth
†**votar**⁼ **por**	to vote in support of/for doing sth/sth

20.5.4 With verbs and nouns of 'effort'

afanarse⁼ **por** (ALSO **en**)	to strive to do sth
ALSO **afán** (m) **por** (ALSO **de**)	
†**apurarse**⁼ **por** (ALSO **en**)	to hasten to do sth
un comezón (m) **por**	an itch to do sth
†**entusiasmarse**⁼ **por** (ALSO **con**)	to get enthusiastic about doing sth/sth
ALSO **entusiasmo por** (ALSO **para**)	
†**esforzarse**⁼ **por** (ALSO **en**)	to strive to do sth
ALSO **esfuerzo por** (ALSO **en, para**)	
†**esmerarse**⁼ **por** (ALSO **en**)	to take pains to do sth
ALSO **esmero en**	
†**hacer**⁼ **por**	to try to do sth
tener⁼ **ilusión por** (ALSO **para**)	to look forward to doing sth
luchar⁼ **por** (ALSO **para**)	to fight to do sth
ALSO **lucha por**	
†**matarse**⁼ **por**	to kill oneself doing sth/for sth
†**morirse**⁼ **por**	to be dying to do sth, to be crazy about sth/sb
hacer⁼ **lo posible por** (ALSO **para**)	to do one's utmost to do sth
†**darse**⁼/†**tener**⁼ **prisa por** (ALSO **en** (**20.7**) and **a**)	to hasten to do sth
pugnar⁼ **por**	to fight to do sth/for sth
rabiar⁼ **por**	to be dying to do sth/for sth
reventar⁼ **por**	to be bursting to do sth/for sth
suspirar⁼ **por**	to long to do sth/for sth

Note also

mil cosas por hacer	a thousand things to be done

Compare: **estar por** (**20.9**, **27.9**) and **quedar por** (**20.9**).
See also: **a** (**20.2.6**).

> ⁼ The subject of the main verb must be the same as that of its dependent infinitive.

20.6   **para** before an infinitive or noun

20.6.1   Ability and inability

aptitud para	aptitude for doing sth/sth
autorizar aᴾᴱᴿˢ **uno para** (ALSO **a**)	to authorize sb to do sth
ALSO **autorización para**	
tener⁼ **capacidad para**	to have talent for doing sth/sth
ALSO **la (in)capacidad para** (ALSO **de**), †**capaz para** (ALSO **de**)	
estar⁼ **capacitado para** (ALSO **a**)	to be qualified to do sth
tener⁼ **dificultad para**	to have difficulty in doing sth
†**hábil para**	competent to do sth/at sth, qualified to do sth

ALSO **tener**⁼ **la habilidad para** = *to have the capacity to do sth/for
sth*, **habilitar a**ᴾᴱᴿˢ **uno para** = *to qualify sb to do sth/for sth*

estar⁼ **impedido para**	to be prevented from doing sth
imposibilitar aᴾᴱᴿˢ **uno para**	to make it impossible for sb to do sth
impotencia para	inability to do sth
tener⁼ **libertad para** (ALSO **de**)	to be free to do sth
permiso para	permission to do sth
prepararse⁼ **para**	to prepare oneself to do sth/for sth
ALSO **preparado para** (ALSO **a**)	
presto para (ALSO **a**) ⎫	ready, quick to do sth
pronto para (ALSO **a**) ⎭	

20.6.2   Sufficiency (see also **19.13.3**)

†**bastar para**	to be enough to do sth
· **Me bastan cien pesos para hacerlo**	· A hundred pesos are enough for me to do it
†**faltar para**	to be necessary to do sth/for sth
· **Me falta una para las cien**	· I need another one to make a hundred
· **Me faltan dos días para terminarlo**	· I need two days to finish it

20.7   **en** before an infinitive or noun

20.7.1   **en** corresponding to English *in, into, on*

†**apoyarse en**	to lean on sth (lit and fig)
hacer⁼ **bien en**	to do well in doing sth/to do sth
†**coincidir**⁼ **en**	lit to coincide in doing sth
· **Coincidimos en no decir nada**	· We both said nothing
complacerse⁼ **en**	to take pleasure in doing sth
concentrarse⁼ **en**	to concentrate on doing sth/sth

†**creer en** — to believe in sb/sth
  NOTE: **creer a**[PERS] **uno** = *to believe sb (ie to believe what sb says)*
†**deleitarse**= **en** (R3) (ALSO **con**, +ger) — to delight in doing sth/sth
ejercitarse en — to practise sth, to train in sth
†**embarcarse en** — to get involved in sth/to get on sth (eg a bus) (Am)
empeñarse= **en** — to insist on doing sth/sth, to persist in doing sth/sth
  ALSO **empeño en**
entrar en (ALSO **a** (R1, esp Am), but see **20.9**) — to enter sth
†**entretenerse**= **en** — to pass the time (in) doing sth
†**esperar en** — to hope, to believe in sb/sth
†**incidir en** — lit to fall on sth (eg light on water); fig to have an effect on sb/sth
incurrir en — to incur sth/ to commit sth (fig)
  · Incurrimos en el error — · We committed an error
influir en (ALSO **sobre**) — to influence sb/sth
  BUT **influir con uno para que haga algo** = *to influence sb to do sth*
ingresar en (ALSO **a** (R1 Am)) — to go into sth, to be admitted to sth (eg hospital), to enlist in sth (eg army)
insistir= **en** (ALSO **para**) — to insist on doing sth/sth
  ALSO **insistencia en**
tener= **interés en** (ALSO **por**)
interesarse= **en** (ALSO **por**)
estar= **interesado en** (ALSO **por**) — to be interested in doing sth/sth
ser= **lento en** — to be slow in doing sth/sth
†**participar en** — to participate in sth
penetrar en (ALSO **a** (R1, esp Am)) — to penetrate sth (lit)
  BUT **penetrar a** = *to penetrate sth (fig), eg* **penetrar al misterio**
perseverar= **en** (R3) — to persevere in doing sth/sth
persistir= **en** (R3) — to persist in doing sth/sth
ser= **el primero, último en** — to be the first, last in doing sth
†**darse**=/†**tener prisa en** (ALSO **por**) — to hurry in doing sth
†**recrearse**= **en** (ALSO +ger) (R3) — to amuse oneself (in) doing sth
ser= **unánime en** (R3) — to be unanimous in doing sth

> = The subject of the main verb must be the same as that of its dependent infinitive.

20.7.2 With verbs of 'persistence'

obstinarse= **en** — to persist in doing sth
  ALSO **obstinación en**
perseverar= **en** (R3) — to persevere in doing sth
persistir= **en** (R3) — to persist in doing sth
  ALSO **persistencia en**

20.7.3 With verbs of 'hesitation'

†**dudar**= **en**
vacilar= **en** (ALSO **para**) — to hesitate in doing sth/to do sth
  ALSO **vacilación en** (ALSO **para**)

20.7.4 With verbs of 'noticing'

fijarse en ⎫
†**reparar en** ⎰   to notice sth

Note also

†**consentir**= **en**   to consent to doing sth/sth

20.8 Verbs followed by the gerund

†**continuar**= ⎫
†**seguir**=   ⎰   to continue doing sth
†**llevar**= (**tiempo**) (see also **24.6**)
  · **Llevo dos horas escribiendo**   · I've been writing for two hours

20.9 Varying prepositions

Several Spanish verbs, nouns and adjectives have a range of prepositional structures with following infinitives and nouns. Change of preposition usually involves a change of meaning.

†**acabar**	**acabar de** (p 210), **por/+** ger (p 213) AND **Acabó con palabras de agradecimiento** He ended with words of thanks **Las palabras que acaban con/por a** The words which end in a **Acabó con las malas costumbres** He put an end to the evil customs **La fiesta acabó en desastre** The party ended in disaster
acomodarse	**acomodarse de** (p 212) AND **Se acomodó**= **a leer** He settled down to read
acostumbrar	**acostumbrar a**PERS **uno a** (p 206) AND **Acostumbro**= (R3) **acostarme tarde** I usually go to bed late
aferrarse	**¿Por qué te afierras a esta hipótesis?** Why do you stick to this theory? **Se aferró en su error** He persisted in his error
†**amenazar**	**Amenaza**= **con llover** It's threatening to rain **Me amenazó de** (ALSO **con**) **un machete** He threatened me with a machete

†**apoyar**	cf †**apoyarse** and †**apoyo** **Apoyo esta opinión** I support this view **La columna apoya sobre el pedestal** The column is supported on the pedestal
†**armarse**	**Se armó con un fusil** (lit) He armed himself with a rifle **Se armó de valor** (fig) He armed himself with courage
arriesgarse	**arriesgarse a** (p 206) AND **Se arriesgó en una misión desesperada** He ventured upon a desperate mission
†**asirse**	**Se asió a la cuerda** (R2–3) He seized the rope NOTE: **Asió la cuerda** is more common in R1–2. **Se asió con el intruso** He grappled with the intruder **Se asió de provisiones** She got hold of provisions
atinar	**atinar a** (p 206) AND **Has atinado= en decir eso** You were right to say that **Atinó con la solución** She hit on the answer
†**atreverse**	**atreverse a** (p 206) AND **Se atrevió con el director** He was rude to the principal
†**avenirse**	**avenirse a** (p 206) AND **Tenemos que avenirnos en una solución** We must agree on a solution **No se aviene con mi amigo** He doesn't get along with my friend
†**bastar**	**bastar hacer algo** (p 202), **para** (p 215) AND **Basta con telefonearle** (R1–2) You need only telephone him **Basta con tu presencia** (R1–2) Your presence is enough
†**hacer caso**	**¡Haz caso a las señales de tráfico!** Pay attention to the road signs! **Hace caso del niño** He looks after the child

coincidir	**coincidir en** (p 215) AND **Coincido con usted** I agree with you
comenzar	**comenzar a** (p 206), **por**/+ ger (p 213)
compensar	**compensar algo/una cosa con otra** (p 225) AND **Le compensaron de sus esfuerzos** They compensated him for his efforts **Le compensaron con 6.000 pesetas por el reloj perdido** They gave him 6,000 pesetas compensation for the lost watch
†**concordar**	**El verbo concuerda con el sujeto** The verb agrees with the subject **Todos concordamos en que no será aconsejable** We all agree that it would not be advisable
†**confiar**	**Confió la carta a su hija** He entrusted the letter to his daughter **Confío en mi amigo** I trust my friend ALSO **Su †(des)confianza en su amigo** BUT **Me confié a mi amigo** = *I confided in my friend*
consentir	**consentir a**¹⁰ **uno/hacer algo** (p 204), **consentir**= **en** (p 217)
†**convenir**	**convenir** (p 202) AND **Convine**= **con él en ir** I agreed with him to go **Convinieron en un precio** They agreed on a price
tener cuidado	**¡Ten**= **cuidado de escribir de forma legible!** Take care to write legibly! **Hay que tener cuidado con el perro** You must be careful of the dog ALSO **el †cuidado en** (ALSO **con**) **hacer algo** = *care in doing sth*
cuidar	**Mi hermana cuida a**ᴾᴱᴿˢ **los niños** My sister looks after the children **Cuida de nuestra casa cuando estamos ausentes** She looks after our house while we're away ALSO †**cuidarse de algo** = *to take care of sth*
chocar	**chocar con, contra** (p 228) AND **chocar con uno** to fall out with sb **chocar a**ᴾᴱᴿˢ **uno** to shock sb

dar	**Le dio por regresar temprano** He took it into his head to come back early **Lo dio por terminado** He considered it finished **Di con él en la calle** I bumped into him in the street **Mi habitación †da al mar** My room looks on to the sea **El coche dio contra un árbol** The car struck a tree **Has †dado con/en la solución** You've found the answer

> = The subject of the main verb must be the same as that of its dependent infinitive.

†decidir	**Decidí= ir** I decided to go BUT **la †decisión de ir** = *the decision to go* **decidir de/sobre algo** to decide (about) sth (Cf **decidirse a** (p 206), **por** (p 214))
dejar	**dejar** (p 204), **dejar= de** (p 210)
desesperarse	**desesperarse= de** (p 211) AND **desesperarse por algo** to despair at sth
determinar	**determinar a** (p 207) AND **Determiné= hacerlo en seguida** I decided to do it immediately
†dudar	**dudar= en** (p 216) AND **Dudo de su buena voluntad** I doubt his good will **Duda= entre aceptar y rechazar** He's hesitating between accepting and refusing
†echar	**Echó= a correr** He began to run **Se echó= a llorar** She began to cry **Echaron por el camino de...** They took the direction of... NOTE the idiom **echarse de ver** = *to be obvious.*
†empezar	**empezar= a** (p 206), **por/ + ger** (p 213)
entender	**No entiendo de matemáticas** I don't understand mathematics **Se entiende en inglés** He can make himself understood in English **Me entiendo a la perfección con ella** I get along perfectly well with her

entrar	**entrar en (a)** (p 216) AND **Entró al colegio el año pasado** She started school last year
†**esperar**	**esperar** (p 225), **en** (p 216), **a** (p 225)
†**estar**	**Estoy**= **por salir ahora** I'm inclined to go out now **Lo demás está por escribir** The rest remains to be written **Estaba**= **para morirse** He was on the point of death **No estoy para chistes** I'm not in the mood for jokes **Las manzanas están a cien pesetas** The apples are a hundred pesetas **Está con fiebre muy alta** She's got a high fever **Una gran parte de la población estaba con los gobernantes** Much of the population was on the side of the governors **estar de camarero** to have a job as a waiter
†**faltar**	**faltar para** (p 215) AND **Faltaron a la cita** They didn't turn up for the date **Falta a su palabra** He breaks his promise **Faltan dos cucharas** There are two spoons missing ALSO **estar falto de** (R3) = *to be lacking in*
†**fatigarse**	**fatigarse**= **de** (p 212) AND **fatigarse**= + ger/**en** + inf to get tired (in) doing sth
gusto	**gusto a** (p 210) AND **¡Mucho gusto en conocerle!** Pleased to meet you! **el gusto por/de la música** the taste for music
†**hacer**	**hacer** (p 204), **por** (p 214) AND with nouns: **Hace de camarero** He works as a waiter **No me hago al calor** I can't get used to the heat **Los militantes se hicieron con el poder** The militants took power
†**indignarse**	**indignarse por** (p 213) AND **Se indignó conmigo** He became indignant with me

inspirar	**inspirar algo a[10] uno** to inspire sth in sb **inspirarse en/de algo** to be inspired by sth
†ir	**Tu corbata no va bien con el color del traje** Your tie doesn't go with the colour of your suit **Va para primer ministro** He hopes to be Prime Minister **En lo que va de año...** As far as this year goes . . .
libre	**El hombre no es libre de matar** Man is not free to kill (axiomatic) **Está libre para marcharse** He is free to go (permission)
†echar mano	**echar mano a algo** to get hold of sth **echar una mano a uno** (R1) to give sb a hand **echar mano de algo** to have recourse to sth
†meterse	**meterse= a** (p 206) AND **¡No te metas conmigo!** Don't provoke me! **Se metió de secretaria** She took a job as a secretary
†tener miedo	**Tengo miedo al/del profesor** I'm afraid of the teacher **Tengo miedo de que no lo haga** I'm afraid he won't do it **Tengo= miedo de hacerlo** (ALSO, though less commonly, **a**) I'm afraid of doing it
†mirar	**mirar** (p 225) AND **mirar a algo** to contemplate, to think about sth **mirar por uno/algo** to look after sb/to be concerned about sth
motivo	**el motivo de su rechazo** the reason for its rejection **No tienes motivo para quejarte** You've no reason to complain
ocuparse	**La madre se ocupó de la cena** Mother dealt with dinner **Me ocupaba en/de enviar cartas a todos mis amigos** I spent my time sending letters to all my friends

†**participar**	**participar en** (p 216) AND **Participan de la misma opinión** They share the same opinion
†**pasarse**	**Se pasó de lista** She was just a bit too clever **Me paso sin pan** I do without bread
†**pensar**	**Pienso**= **hacerlo esta tarde** I intend to do it this afternoon **Estoy pensando en mis estudios** I'm thinking of my studies **¿Qué piensas de la película?** What do you think of the film? **Hay que pensarlo bien** A lot of thought must be given to it
†**persuadir**	**persuadir** (p 207) AND **persuadir a**PERS **uno de algo/de que…** to persuade sb of sth/that . . .
†**poner**	**La pusieron a estudiar en el instituto** They sent her to study at the institute **Lo han puesto a 200 pesetas** They have priced it at 200 pesetas **Le pusieron de dependiente** They found him a job as a shop assistant
†**protestar**	**protestar por** (p 213) AND **Protesta de su inocencia** He protests his innocence **Vamos a protestar contra la reforma** Let's protest against the reform
quedar = The subject of the main verb must be the same as that of its dependent infinitive.	**Le quedaron veinte duros al**IO **chico** The boy had 20 duros left **Hemos quedado**= **en (de (R1 Am)) aplazarlo hasta mañana** We've agreed to put it off until tomorrow **Quedamos en el día trece** We agreed on the thirteenth **Quedamos para mañana** We arranged to meet tomorrow **Quedan diez páginas por leer** There are ten pages left to read **Quedan seis semanas para Navidad** It's six weeks to Christmas
†**quedarse**	**Se quedó con el coche** He kept the car **La fiesta se quedó**= **en beber** The party was reduced to drinking

tener razón	**Tuvo= razón para hacerlo** She had reason to do it **Tuvo= razón en hacerlo** She was right to do it
rebajarse	**rebajarse= a** (p 206) AND **El alumno se rebajó de la clase de latín** The pupil was excused from the Latin class
†**reclamar**	**reclamar a**[io] (p 208) AND **reclamar contra algo** to protest against sth
†**reparar**	**reparar en** (p 217) AND **reparar algo** to repair sth
responder	**Voy a responder a la pregunta** I'll answer the question **Éste responde a la descripción** This man answers the description **No respondo de mi hermano** I'm not responsible for my brother **Respondo por él** I can vouch for him
servir	**Esta herramienta no sirve para nada** This tool is good for nothing **Puede servir de plato** It can serve as a plate
†**temor**	**su temor a la oscuridad** his fear of the dark **mi temor de que lleguen a saberlo** my fear that they will get to know
†**tentar**	**tentar a**[PERS] **uno a** (p 207) AND **tentar= (a) hacer algo** (R2–3) to try to do sth BUT **la tentativa de hacer algo**
†**terminar**	**terminar= de** (p 210), **por/+** ger (p 213); ALSO with **con** as **acabar**
†**tratar**	**tratar= de hacer algo** to try to do sth **Me trató de mal educado** He called me ill-bred **El conferenciante trató de/sobre un tema apasionante** The lecturer dealt with a fascinating subject **tratar con uno** to have dealings with sb **tratar en algo** to deal in sth

> = The subject of the main verb must be the same as that of its dependent infinitive.

†**ver**	**ver** (p 205) AND **Veré⁼ de terminarlo** I'll try and get it finished

20.9.1 No preposition in Spanish: preposition in English

Spanish verbs not listed above which take no preposition before a following infinitive or noun but correspond to English verbs which do:

†**acordar algo**	to agree on sth
†**agradecer algo a**ᴵᴼ **uno**	to thank sb for sth
BUT NOTE: **estar agradecido a**ᴵᴼ **uno por algo** = *to be grateful to sb for sth*	
†**aguardar algo/a**ᴾᴱᴿˢ **uno**	to wait for sb/sth
BUT **aguardar a que** + subj	
ambicionar hacer algo/algo	to have the ambition of doing sth/to strive after doing sth/sth
†**aprobar algo**	to approve of sth
†**aprovechar algo**	to take advantage of sth
BUT **aprovecharse de algo** with the same meaning	
buscar algo/aᴾᴱᴿˢ **uno**	to look for sth/sb
†**callar algo**	to keep quiet about sth
comentar algo	to comment on sth
BUT **un comentario a algo** (p 209)	
compadecer aᴾᴱᴿˢ **uno**	to sympathize with sb
BUT **compadecerse de uno** with the same meaning	
†**compensar algo/una cosa con otra**	to compensate for sth/for sth with sth else
See also **20.9**	
contratar algo/aᴾᴱᴿˢ **uno**	to sign a contract for sth/to take sb on
costear algo	to pay for sth
†**desaprobar algo**	to disapprove of sth
equivocar algo	to make a mistake about sth
BUT **equivocarse de algo** with the same meaning	
· **Equivocamos la fecha/Nos equivocamos de fecha**	· We got the date wrong
escuchar algo	to listen to sth
†**esperar algo/a**ᴾᴱᴿˢ **uno**	to wait for sth/sb
BUT **esperar a que** + subj	
NOTE: **esperar que** + indic/subj (**26.3**, **26.8**) = *to hope that*	
incendiar algo	to set fire to sth
†**intervenir a**ᴾᴱᴿˢ **uno**	to operate on sb
llorar algo	to weep over sth
†**mirar algo/a**ᴾᴱᴿˢ **uno**	to look at sth/sb
BUT **mirar a algo** = *to gaze at sth*	
operar aᴾᴱᴿˢ **uno**	to operate on sb
padecer algo	to suffer from sth
pagar algo	to pay for sth
BUT **Pagué cien pesetas por el periódico** = *I paid a hundred pesetas for the newspaper*	

ᴵᴼ **a**ᴵᴼ introduces the indirect object
ᴾᴱᴿˢ **a**ᴾᴱᴿˢ denotes the Spanish personal **a**

† More information about these words or expressions may be found in other sections. Use the Spanish word index to find the page numbers.

pedir algo a[IO] **uno**	to ask sb for sth
[†]**pisar algo**	to tread on sth
[†]**pisotear algo**	to trample on sth
presidir algo	to preside over sth
[†]**profundizar (en) algo**	to go deeply into sth
[†]**recorrer una ciudad**	to go round (= visit) a town
suscribir algo	to subscribe to sth

BUT **suscribirse a algo** with the same meaning

velar a[PERS] **uno** (ALSO **por**)	to watch over sb
votar algo	to vote for sth

BUT **votar por uno** = *to vote for sb* (**20.5**)

20.9.2   Preposition in Spanish: no preposition in English

Spanish verbs taking a preposition before a following infinitive or noun corresponding to English verbs which take no preposition:

[†]**abusar de algo**	to abuse sth
[†]**acordarse de algo** (**de** often omitted ⚠ in R1)	to remember sth

NOTE **recordar algo** with same meaning, and see **recordar** below. In Am R1 **recordarse de** and **recordar de** are often used.

[†]**amenazar**[=] **con hacer algo** (see p 217)	to threaten to do sth
anteponerse a algo	to precede sth
anticiparse a algo ALSO **anticipar algo**	to anticipate, to get there before sth
[†]**apoderarse de algo**	to take hold of sth
[†]**apropiarse de algo**	to appropriate sth
asemejarse a uno	to resemble sb
[†]**asirse a algo**	to seize sth
[†]**asistir a algo**	to attend sth
carecer de algo	to lack sth
[†]**cargar con algo**	to take sth
· **Debo cargar con la responsabilidad**	· I must take the responsibility
casarse (see **29.3**) **con uno**	to marry sb
condescender[=] **en hacer algo** (R3)	to condescend to do sth
contactar con algo/uno	to contact sth/sb
[†]**contestar (a) una carta**	to answer a letter

NOTE: **contestar algo** has the additional meaning of *to contest sth.*

contravenir a algo	to contravene sth
[†]**cumplir con algo**	to fulfil sth

BUT **su cumplimiento de la orden** = *his execution of the order*

[†]**disponer de algo**	to have sth at one's disposal
[†]**dudar de algo** (see **20.9**)	to doubt sth
[†]**encaramarse a/en algo**	to climb sth
ensayarse[=] **a/para hacer algo**	to practise doing sth
enterarse de algo	to find sth out

> [=] The subject of the main verb must be the same as that of its dependent infinitive.

†**entrevistarse con uno**	to interview sb
BUT **una †entrevista a/con uno**	
excederse en algo	to overdo, to exceed sth
fiarse de algo/uno	to trust sth/sb
incorporar algo a algo	to incorporate sth into sth
†**jugar a(l tenis**, etc)	to play (tennis, etc)
motejar aPERS **uno de algo**	to label sb sth
†**necesitar de algo/uno**	to need sth/sb
ALSO **necesitar algo/a**PERS **uno** with same meaning	
BUT **la †necesidad de algo/uno** = *the need for sth/sb*	
†**negarse**= **a hacer algo**	to refuse to do sth
ALSO **la †negativa a hacer algo**	
obsequiar aPERS **uno con algo**	to give sb sth as a present
(**con** often omitted in Am)	
olvidarse de hacer algo/algo	to forget to do sth/sth
NOTE the following constructions with **olvidar** and **olvidarse**:	
Olvidé las llaves ⎫ **Se me olvidaron las llaves** ⎬	I forgot my keys
Me olvidé de hacerlo ⎫ **Se me olvidó hacerlo** ⎬	I forgot to do it
parecerse a uno	to resemble sb
percatarse de algo	to notice sth
†**posesionarse de algo**	to take possession of sth, to seize sth
†**precisar de algo** (R3)	to need sth
presumir de algo/ADJ	to think oneself sth/ADJ
· **Presume de artista/listo**	· He thinks himself an artist/clever
†**protestar de algo**	to protest sth
· **Protesta de su inocencia**	· He protests his innocence
†**recordar algo a uno**	to remind sb of sth
†**renunciar**= **a hacer algo/algo**	to renounce doing sth/sth
ALSO **la †renuncia a hacer algo/algo**	
†**resistirse**= **a hacer algo/algo**	to resist doing sth/sth
rivalizar con uno/algo	to rival sb/sth
servirse de algo	to use sth
sobrevivir a uno/algo	to survive sb/sth
†**sustituir a algo/uno**	to substitute for sth/sb
unirse a algo	to associate oneself with sth

20.9.3 Some prepositions which do not correspond in Spanish and English

†**agarrarse a algo** (ALSO **de** (R1))	to cling on to sth
apiadarse de uno	to take pity on sb
atenerse a algo/uno	to abide by sth/to rely on sb
atentar contra algo/uno	to make an attempt on sth/sb
· **Atentó contra la vida del rey**	· He made an attempt on the king's life
ALSO **un atentado contra algo/uno**	
calificar algo/aPERS **uno de** (ALSO **como**) ADJ	to describe sth/sb as ADJ
†**compadecerse de uno**	to sympathize with sb

hacer compañía a uno	to keep sb company
confinar con algo (R3)	to border on sth
†**consentir en hacer algo/algo**	to consent to doing sth/sth
ALSO **el consentimiento en algo** (ALSO **para, de**) = *consent to sth*	
consistir en hacer algo/algo	to consist of doing sth/sth
BUT **constar de hacer algo/algo** with similar meaning	
contar con uno/algo	to count on sb/sth
†**chocar con/contra algo/uno**	to bump into sth/sb
depender de uno/algo	to depend on sb/sth
†**diferente a** (⊡ , but common)/**de algo**	different from sth
dimitir de (**presidente**)	to resign as (president)
ALSO **dimitir** (**la presidencia**) = to resign (from) (the presidency)	
disparar a/contra uno	to fire at/on sb
NOTE: **disparar un tiro/un fusil** = *to fire a shot/a rifle.*	
†**distinto a/de algo**	different from sth
†**encararse con/a algo/uno**	to face up to sth/sb
†**encontrarse con algo/uno**	to meet sth/sb
†**enfrentarse con/a** ⊡ **algo/uno**	to face up to sth/sb
examinarse de (**en** R1 Am) **algo**	to take an exam in sth
†**informar de/sobre algo**	to report on sth
informarse sobre algo	to enquire into sth
†**inquirir** (**sobre**) **algo**	to enquire into sth
†**lindar con algo**	to border on sth
†**pasar de** (**diez**)	to be more than, to exceed (ten)
†**preguntar por uno**	to ask for/after sb
prescindir⁼ **de hacer algo/uno/algo** (R3)	to do without doing sth/sb/sth
rebasar de (**diez**)	to be more than, to exceed (ten)
responsabilizarse de algo	to make oneself responsible for sth
ALSO †**responsable de algo**	
soñar con uno/algo (often with no preposition in Central American R1)	to dream of sb/sth
NOTE: **soñar en hacer algo/algo** = *to daydream about* + ger/*sth.*	
†**sustituir X por Y**	to substitute Y for X (lit to substitute X with Y)
†**tardar**⁼ **en hacer algo**	to take time to do sth/in doing sth
ALSO **tardanza en hacer algo**	
tirar de algo†	to pull on sth
NOTE: **tirar algo** = *to throw sth.*	
toparse con algo (R2–3)	to run up against sth
traducir a (**un idioma**)	to translate into (a language)
†**tropezar con uno/algo**	to bump into sb/sth
†**vecino de algo**	next door to sth
ALSO **vecino a** (p 191)	

⁼ The subject of the main verb must be the same as that of its dependent infinitive.

21 Constructions with verbs of movement

English and Spanish differ greatly in the ways they express *manner* and *direction* of movement. English tends to use a verb to express *manner* and a preposition to express *direction*; in Spanish, the verb normally expresses *direction* while a gerund or other adverbial phrase expresses *manner*. For example:

She ran / across the road
manner   direction
Atravesó la calle / corriendo
direction   manner

Other examples:

He crawled towards the wall
Avanzó a gatas hacia la pared
She hobbled back to the kitchen
Volvió cojeando a la cocina
He burst in
Entró volando
She swam across the river
Cruzó el río nadando/a nado
I crept downstairs
Bajé de puntillas la escalera
He cycled back
Volvió en bicicleta
They climbed over the wall
Pasaron por encima del muro

The chief *direction* verbs of Spanish are:

atravesar	(to go) across
avanzar hacia algo	(to go) towards sth
†**bajar**	(to go) down
†**continuar**	(to go) on
cruzar	(to go) across
†**dar la vuelta a algo**	(to go) around sth
†**entrar en algo**	(to go) in(to) sth
†**pasar**	(to go) past
pasar por debajo de algo	(to go) under sth
pasar por encima de algo	(to go) over sth
†**salir de algo**	(to go) out of sth
†**seguir**	(to go) on
†**subir**	(to go) up
†**volver**	(to go) back

Spanish does, however, have some *direction* adverbs, eg:

Anduvieron calle abajo
They walked down the street
Corrieron escaleras arriba
They ran up the stairs
Anduvieron campo a través
They went across the fields

and many *manner* verbs, eg:

Gateó hacia la valla
She crawled towards the fence
Irrumpió en la casa
He burst into the house
Pasearon a lo largo del río
They walked along the river

22 Negation

22.1 General

A Spanish sentence is negated by placing **no** before the verb or auxiliary (and associated pronouns, if any), eg:

Juan no lo hizo
John didn't do it
No quiero volver a verte
I don't want to see you again

'Scope' of negation can be limited by placing **no** in front of individual elements, eg:

No todos acudieron
Not everyone came
Estoy dispuesto a no hacerlo
I'm ready not to do it
Te lo digo no porque tu madre esté enfadada sino porque quiero saber la verdad
I'm telling you not because your mother is angry but because I want to know the truth

NOTE, however, that in one or two verbal expressions **no** does not give an exactly opposite meaning, eg:

†**Acabo de entender por qué lo hizo**
I've just realized why he did it
BUT
No acabo de entender por qué lo hizo
I fail to understand why he did it
†**Dejé de fumar**
I gave up smoking
BUT
No dejé de rezar las oraciones (R3)
I didn't neglect to say my prayers

22.2 Negation of adjectives

Often an adjective can be negated by using a negative prefix **in-** or **des-**, eg: **cómodo/incómodo**, **conocido/desconocido**. If such a ready-made word does not exist (always check in a dictionary if you are uncertain), a variety of negatives, **no**, **nada** and **poco**, can be used.

no is used for straightforward negation:

un corazón no corrompido
an uncorrupted heart
objetivos no logrados
unattained objectives

poco is used where there is a sense of gradation, and means roughly *not very*, eg:

> **una idea poco original**
> an unoriginal idea
> **un paisaje poco típico**
> an atypical countryside

nada is stronger than **poco** and means roughly *not at all*, eg:

> **una costumbre nada frecuente**
> a not at all frequent custom
> **un empleo nada lucrativo**
> a not at all well-paid job

NOTE ALSO the use of **sin** + inf in an adjectival sense, meaning *not yet*, eg:

> **una cuestión sin resolver**
> an unresolved question
> **una calle sin pavimentar**
> an unpaved street

22.3 Negative pronouns, adjectives and adverbs

These expressions (**nada, nadie, jamás, nunca, tampoco, ni, ni siquiera, ni...ni..., ninguno** (**alguno** R3 following the noun)) are inherently negative. If used after a verb, the verb has to be preceded by **no** or another negative pronoun or adjective, eg:

> **No encontró nada** BUT **Nada encontró** (R3)
> He found nothing
> **No lo supo nadie** BUT **Nadie lo supo**
> No one knew
> **No había leído ningún libro/libro alguno** (R3)
> He had not read any books
> **No tengo ni bolígrafo ni lápiz**
> I haven't got either a ballpoint pen or a pencil

BUT

> **Ni tú ni yo sabemos hacerlo**
> Neither you nor I know how to do it

NOTE: **ni...ni...** may be used with verbs:

> **Ni fumo ni bebo**
> I neither smoke nor drink

22.4   Expressions which require **no** before the verb

Spanish has a number of other expressions which have the value of a negative and require **no** before the verb:

No dijo palabra
He didn't say a word (anything)
No he dormido en toda la noche
I haven't slept all night
En mi vida no vi tal cosa
I've never seen such a thing
No me gustó en absoluto
I didn't like it at all

22.5   Other negative contexts

The negative and inherently negative expressions referred to in the preceding sections are also required in the following contexts: **sin, antes de, más...que, ser imposible**:

sin decir nada a nadie
without saying anything to anyone
antes de hacer ningún gesto
before making any expression
más alto que nunca
taller than ever
Es imposible contestar nada
It's impossible to answer anything

23 Use of tenses

Tenses in Spanish have three kinds of function: (a) temporal
(referring to times: past, present, future, etc), (b) modal
(representing attitudes: commands, politeness, supposition, etc) and
(c) aspectual (the way in which an action or state is viewed:
continuous, repeated, within 'fixed' limits, etc). The following table
gives a summary of the main functions of the Spanish tenses within
these categories.

23.1 Present tense (**hago**, etc)

Temporal functions

Any kind of PRESENT, including reference to a general state of
affairs which includes the PRESENT, eg:
  Ahora terminan su trabajo
  They're finishing their work now
  Ahora sé qué hacer
  Now I know what to do
  Leo el periódico
  I'm reading the newspaper
  Hoy hace mucho frío
  It's very cold today
  Siempre llego a las cinco
  I always arrive at five
  Los Andes son muy altos
  The Andes are very high

FUTURE (especially R1; see also modal functions), eg:
  El tren sale a las seis
  The train leaves at six

IMMEDIATE PAST (especially R1), eg:
  ¿Qué me cuentas?
  What have you just told me?
  Te traigo un regalo
  I've brought you a present

PAST continuing to PRESENT, eg:
  Vivo aquí desde hace dos meses
  I've been living here for two months

PAST (as R1 equivalent for Preterite and Imperfect), eg:
  Luego salgo del bar y estoy en la calle
  Then I left the bar and was in the street

Also regularly with **por poco (no)**, eg:
  Por poco le mato
  I nearly killed him

Modal functions

IMPERATIVE (see also **23.2** and
26.2)
  **¿Me hace el favor de
    repetirlo?**
  Would you please repeat it?

'DUENESS' in FUTURE, eg:
  Mañana vamos a la playa
  Tomorrow we are going (=
    we have arranged to go) to
    the beach

INTENTION in FUTURE, eg:
  ¿Qué escribo?
  What shall I write?

ABILITY in general PRESENT, eg:
  Habla tres idiomas
  She speaks three languages
  **Desde esta ventana se ven las
    montañas**
  From this window you can see
    the mountains

23.1.1   Present and Perfect

With adverbs marking a period of time back from the PRESENT (English *for*, Spanish **desde**, **desde hace**, etc) standard Spanish uses the Present when the action or state is continuous, eg:

Te espero aquí desde hace una hora	
Hace una hora que te espero aquí	I've been waiting here
Llevo esperándote aquí una hora	for you for an hour
Tengo una hora esperándote aquí	
(Am, esp R1)	

But where the period of time is that of something which has *not* happened, either Present or Perfect can be used, and in R1 the Imperfect may be used, eg:

Hace dos meses que no te veo/he visto	It's two months since I
Hace dos meses que no te veía (R1)	saw you
Hace(n) dos meses a que no te veía (R1 (Am))	

23.2   Future tense (**haré**, etc)

Temporal function	*Modal functions*
FUTURE (but increasingly rare in R1), eg: **Mañana lo sabremos** Tomorrow we'll know	INTENTION, eg: **De eso no te diré más** I won't say any more to you about it IMPERATIVE (see also **23.1** and **26.2**), eg: **¡Sí que lo harás!** Oh yes you *will* do it! SUPPOSITION in PRESENT, eg: **Ahora estará aquí** He must be here now

23.3   Future Perfect tense (**habré hecho**, etc)

Temporal function	*Modal function*
Anteriority in FUTURE, eg: **Lo habré terminado cuando le veamos** I will have finished it when we see him	SUPPOSITION (anterior to PRESENT), eg: **Habrá llegado ahora** He must have arrived now

23.4 Conditional tense (**haría**, etc)

Temporal function	*Modal functions*
FUTURE in PAST, eg: **Dijo que pronto lo sabríamos** He said that we would soon know	POLITENESS, eg: **¿Tendría usted la bondad de contestarme?** Would you be kind enough to answer me? SUPPOSITION (in PAST), eg: **Serían las ocho cuando salimos** It must have been eight o'clock when we left HYPOTHESIS in PRESENT or FUTURE (see **26.7**), eg: **Se lo diría de buena gana si lo supiera, pero...** I would willingly tell you if I knew, but . . .

23.5 Conditional Perfect tense (**habría hecho**, etc)

Temporal function	*Modal functions*
Anteriority to FUTURE in PAST, eg: **Dijo que lo habría terminado antes de que llegara** She said she would have finished before he arrived	SUPPOSITION (anterior to PAST), eg: **Ya habría llegado cuando salimos** She must have arrived when we left HYPOTHESIS in PAST (see **26.7**), eg: **Se lo habría dicho, pero tú me lo impediste** I would have said so, but you stopped me

23.6 Imperfect and Preterite (**hacía**, etc; **hice**, etc)

The basis of the contrast between Imperfect and Preterite is aspectual. Both tenses can represent a single action or state or the repetition of an action or state.

The Preterite is basically the aspect of sequential action ('what happened next'); it implies that the action, state, or repeated action or state is thought of:

(a) as taking place within a single 'closed' period of time, eg:
Estuve dos meses en Madrid
I spent two months in Madrid
Aquella semana fui cada día a la universidad
That week I went to the university every day

(b) as beginning at a particular moment, eg:
> **Luego supimos la verdad**
> Then we got to know the truth

(c) as being part of a sequence of events, eg:
> **Felipe V fue el primero de los Borbones (otros le sucedieron)**
> Philip V was the first of the Bourbons (others succeeded him)
> **Entonces hubo un estrépito grande (seguido de un silencio)**
> Then there was a loud noise (followed by silence)

The Imperfect is basically the aspect of an ongoing action or state ('description in the past'). It represents actions, states, or repetitions of actions or states as being in progress and hence situated in an 'open' period of time, eg:
> **Estaba en Madrid (ya había estado allí unos meses) cuando oí las noticias**
> I was in Madrid (I had been there some months) when I heard the news
> **Ya lo sabíamos (antes que nos lo dijeras)**
> We already knew (before you told us)
> **Felipe V era típicamente Borbón**
> Philip V was a typical Bourbon
> **Iba muchas veces al río porque me gustaba nadar**
> I went to the river a lot because I liked swimming
> **Había un estrépito grande (ya había empezado) cuando entré en la sala**
> There was a loud noise going on (it had already started) when I went into the room

NOTE: the Imperfect is often used in journalistic R3 in place of the Preterite, eg:
> **El trece de febrero de 1939 atravesaba la frontera francesa**
> He crossed the French border on 13 February 1939

23.6.1 Imperfect tense (**hacía**, etc): other uses

Modal function

POLITENESS, eg:
> **Quería saber si…**
> I wanted to know if . . .

23.6.2 Preterite tense (**hice**, etc): other uses

Aspectual function

SUDDENNESS (idiomatic, with **acabarse**) (R1), eg:
> **Otros dos, y se acabó**
> Two more, and that's it

23.7 Perfect tense (**he hecho**, etc)

Temporal function

PAST where relevance to the PRESENT is implied, typically with adverbs such as **hoy**, **este año**, **ahora mismo**, which include reference to the PRESENT (understood), eg:
¿Todavía no has terminado?
Haven't you finished yet?
No le he visto esta semana
I haven't seen him this week

23.7.1 Perfect and Preterite

In general, the distinction between Perfect and Preterite in Spanish corresponds to that made in English between the Perfect and Simple Past (*have done/did*). But there are slight differences in register and regional variety in both languages. British English *I've already done it* corresponds to American English *I already did it*; American Spanish prefers **¿qué pasó?** to Peninsular **¿qué ha pasado?** Standard Peninsular and American usage prefer the Preterite for PAST events which are not related to the PRESENT, ie where adverbs such as **ayer**, **el año pasado**, **hace…**, etc can be understood, although amongst Madrid speakers there is currently a preference for **lo he hecho ayer** over **lo hice ayer**.

23.8 Pluperfect tense (**había hecho**, etc)

Temporal functions	*Modal function*
Anteriority to PAST, eg: **Lo había terminado cuando llegó** I had finished when she arrived PAST in the PAST, eg: **Dijo que ya lo había hecho** He said he had already done it	SURPRISE (R1 Arg), eg: **¡Había sido usted!** So it's you!

23.9 Past Anterior tense (**hube hecho**, etc)

Temporal function	*Aspectual function*
In a temporal clause, anteriority to PAST expressed by the Preterite, eg: **Cuando lo hubo terminado, salió** (R3 only; in R1–2 the Preterite or an alternative construction tends to be used) When he had finished, he left	SUDDENNESS in PAST, eg: **En un instante lo hubo terminado** (R2–3 only) He had finished it in an instant

23.10 -ra tense (**hiciera**, etc)

Temporal functions	*Modal functions*
PAST (R3 Am), eg: **La noticia que este diario diera** (= **dio, ha dado**) **tiene confirmación** The news this paper gave has been confirmed Anteriority in PAST (R3, esp Am), eg: **Le entregó la carta que escribiera** (= **había escrito**) She gave him the letter she had written	POLITENESS (restricted to **querer** in Pen), eg: **Quisiera saber si...** I would like to know if... **¿Adónde fuéramos esta noche?** (Am) Where should we go tonight? HYPOTHESIS (see **23.5**), eg: **Hubiera jurado que era él** I could have sworn it was him

24 Periphrastic verb-forms

The following periphrastic verb-forms are used to a certain extent in all registers, but are especially common in R1, often replacing the verb-forms in **23.1–10** above. They tend to be fairly specific in temporal, modal or aspectual value, and there are often restrictions on the tenses in which they can be used.

The English translations offered in this section are necessarily approximate, and do not always bring out the full value of the Spanish.

24.1 **ir a** + infinitive

Only used in Present and Imperfect.

Temporal functions	*Modal function*
FUTURE and FUTURE in PAST, eg: **Voy a salir** I'm going to leave **Iba a salir** I was going to leave	OBLIGATION, eg: **¡Cómo lo voy a saber!** How should I know!

24.2 **acabar de** + infinitive

Only used in Present and Imperfect: otherwise it has the meaning of *to finish* + ger.

Temporal functions	*Modal function*
RECENT PAST and RECENT PAST in PAST, eg: **Acabo de salir** I've just left **Acababa de salir** I'd just left	POLITENESS (in negative), eg: **No acabamos de entender por qué...** We can't understand why . . .

24.3 **estar** + gerund

Aspectual value

> CONTINUOUS action, eg:
> **Estoy leyendo**
> I'm reading
>
> NOTE: **estar** + gerund exists in all tenses, even in the Preterite, eg: **Toda aquella mañana estuvimos haciendo visitas** = *We were visiting all that morning*. Note, however, that the Spanish Present Continuous *cannot* refer to the future, as can English, eg: **Lo estoy haciendo** = *I'm doing it (now)*; but *I'm doing it tomorrow* = **Lo voy a hacer mañana**.
>
> NOTE: many purists condemn **estar siendo**, although it is in common usage, especially in R1, eg: **Esta lectura está siendo** (R1)/**resultando** (R2) **muy difícil** = *This reading is proving very difficult*.

24.4 **ir** + gerund

Aspectual values

> GRADUAL action (implying adverbs such as **cada vez más/menos, poco a poco**, etc), eg:
> **El tiempo va mejorando**
> It's clearing up
>
> GRADUAL BEGINNING of an action, eg:
> **Ya voy viendo**
> I'm beginning to see

24.5 **venir** + gerund

Only used in Present and Imperfect.

Temporal values	*Aspectual value*
PAST continuing to PRESENT (Present), FAR PAST continuing to PAST (Imperfect), eg: **Vengo diciéndolo desde hace mucho tiempo** I've kept saying so for some time	REPETITION

24.6 **llevar** + gerund

Aspectual function

> The STAGE reached by a CONTINUOUS action or state, eg:
> **Lleva estudiando en Madrid dos meses**
> She's been studying for two months in Madrid

24.7 **tener** + past participle

Aspectual functions   *Modal value*

COMPLETION (only with transitive verbs; the PP agrees with the object), eg: **Lo tengo bien pensado** I've got it thought out **Tengo escritas dos cartas** I've got two letters written REPETITION (with transitives and intransitives), eg: **Ya te tengo dicho que no hagas eso** I've told you repeatedly not to do that	MORAL 'HOLD', eg: **Te tengo prohibido que digas cosas así** I've forbidden you to say things like that

24.8 **llevar** + past participle

Aspectual function

The STAGE reached in a REPEATED action or state, eg:
Llevamos publicados tres libros de la serie
We've got three books in the series published

24.9 **ir** + past participle

Aspectual functions

The STAGE reached in a REPEATED action or state (a kind of passive equivalent of **llevar** + PP), eg:
Van publicados tres libros de la serie
Three books in the series have been published

A RESULTANT STATE (comparable with **estar** + PP – see **27.5**), eg:
Van preparados para un desastre
They're prepared for a disaster

25 Modal auxiliaries

English has a relatively large number of auxiliary verbs (eg *will*, *would*, *may*, *might*, *shall*, *should*, *must*, *ought*) and verbal expressions (*to be to*: 'we were to arrive at nine'; *to have to*: 'we had to go'). Their main function is to express intentions or opinions (commands, possibility, etc). There is no straightforward match between these and their Spanish equivalents: Spanish has a rather smaller number of auxiliary verbs (eg **deber**, **poder**, **querer**) and verbal expressions (**tener que hacer algo**, **haber de hacer algo**). The major differences between Spanish and English are:

1 Spanish auxiliaries may usually be used in all tenses (eg **puede**, **podía**, **podría**, **ha podido**, **pudo**, etc) while English auxiliaries have a maximum of two (which may in any case have independent modal values, eg *may*, *might*) and sometimes only one (eg *must*).

2 In English the Perfect auxiliary *have* can accompany only the infinitive, whereas in Spanish it can accompany either the auxiliary or the infinitive, eg:

He may have done it $\begin{cases} \textbf{Podría haberlo hecho} \\ \textbf{Habría podido hacerlo} \end{cases}$

There is a good deal of overlap in the values of modal auxiliaries in both Spanish and English: English *It will be six o'clock* or *It must be six o'clock*; Spanish **Debes hacerlo** or **Tienes que hacerlo**. Also, an auxiliary may have several modal functions: English *can* is associated with ABILITY and POSSIBILITY; Spanish **deber** with OBLIGATION and INFERENCE.

The following tables are presented according to categories of meaning rather than taking each modal auxiliary separately, and the equivalences given are necessarily rather vague. They are not exhaustive but cover the most problematic areas of usage. Judgments about 'strength' and 'weakness' of meaning derive from native speakers, but it is unlikely that all speakers would agree about these.

⟫→

25.1 Obligation

	weakest
You might (at least) tell him!	**(Por lo menos) podrías/podías decírselo**
You ought to tell him	
You should tell him	**Has de** (R3 and regional)/**Deberías/Debieras** (R3) **decírselo**
You are to tell him	**Debías decírselo**
You have to tell him	**Tienes que decírselo**
You must tell him	**Debes decírselo**
	strongest

	weakest
You might (at least) have told him	**(Por lo menos) podrías/podías/pudieras** (R3)/**has podido/pudiste habérselo dicho**
You should have told him	**(Por lo menos) podías/podrías/pudiste/habrías podido/hubieras podido** (R3)/**habías podido/has podido decírselo**
You were to tell him	**Habrías debido** (R3 preferred)/**Hubieras debido** (R3)/**Habías debido** (R3 preferred)/**Has debido** (R3 preferred) **decírselo**
You had to tell him	
	Debiste/Debías decírselo
	Debiste habérselo dicho
You ought to have told him	**Tenías que decírselo/Tenías que habérselo dicho** (R2)
You *should* have told him	**Deberías/Debías/Debieras** (R3) **habérselo dicho**
	strongest

Notes

1 The choice of tense for the auxiliary in Spanish (eg **has debido**, **debías**, **debiste**, etc) corresponds to the tense that would be appropriate for a simple verb, eg:

Se lo dije ayer
I told him yesterday
Se lo debí haber dicho ayer
I should have told him yesterday
> NOTE: **Se lo debía haber dicho ayer** is also possible when thought of as an 'ongoing state' (see **23.6**).

Pudiste decírselo ayer
You might have told him yesterday!

Estaban en Nueva York
They were in New York
Debían estar en Nueva York
They had to be in New York

Ha ayudado a mucha gente
He's helped lots of people
Ha debido ayudar a mucha gente
He's had to help lots of people

2   **debía** and **podía** may additionally function as alternatives to **debería** and **podría** in modal auxiliary expressions.

3   Tenses other than those given in the above examples may be used if the context demands them; for example, a future tense may be used for the modal auxiliary when reference is to the future:
Deberás hacerlo la semana que viene
You'll have to do it next week

25.2 Ability

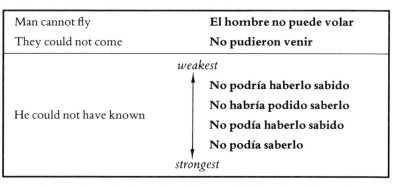

| Man cannot fly | **El hombre no puede volar** |
| They could not come | **No pudieron venir** |

weakest

He could not have known
No podría haberlo sabido
No habría podido saberlo
No podía haberlo sabido
No podía saberlo

strongest

NOTE: a learned ability is rendered in Spanish by **saber hacer algo**, eg:
I can swim
Sé nadar

poder hacer algo is used only for a physical ability, eg:
I can swim a kilometre
Puedo nadar un kilómetro

A general property is rendered in Spanish by a simple verb, eg:
From here you can see the sea
Desde aquí se ve el mar

25.3 Inference

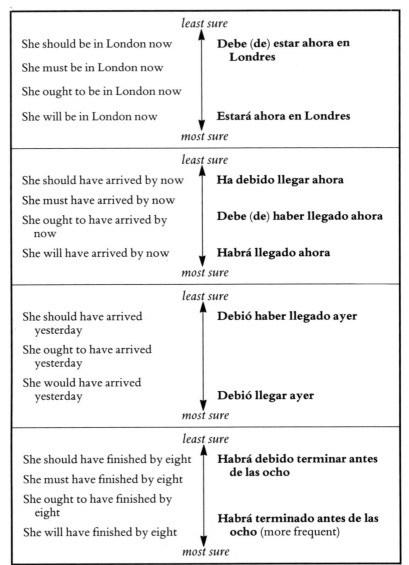

NOTE: purists draw a distinction between **deber hacer algo** and **deber de hacer algo** on the basis that **deber de hacer algo** indicates inference and **deber hacer algo** obligation. While **de** is admitted by speakers in certain cases, as above, it appears always to be optional and is sometimes considered clumsy and pedantic, especially with compound tenses of **deber**.

25.4 Possibility

They may come	**Pueden venir**
They might come They could come	**Podrían venir**
They may have come	**Pueden haber venido**
They might have come They could have come	**Podrán haber venido** **Pudieron haber venido**

26 The Subjunctive

It should be stressed that in the Spanish of all registers and regions all the tenses of the Subjunctive are actively used today. In the Imperfect and Pluperfect Subjunctive, the **-ra** form is commoner than the **-se** form, especially in R1, and particularly in R1 Am. However, there *are* alternatives to many Subjunctive constructions which tend to be preferred in R1–2.

There are various uses of the Subjunctive, and it is essential *not* to think of the Subjunctive itself as having one characteristic 'meaning'. It is helpful to realize at the outset that in Spanish there are both contexts in which the Subjunctive is obligatory (in the same way that a plural adjective is obligatory with a plural noun) and contexts in which there is a choice between Subjunctive and Indicative. In the former case, the Subjunctive itself is automatically required and so has no distinctive meaning; in the latter case, there is usually a difference in meaning between Subjunctive and Indicative, and English speakers sometimes find this difficult to grasp.

In the following sections, the uses of the Subjunctive are grouped according to the meaning or syntax of the contexts in which they are found. The possibility of choice between Subjunctive and Indicative is indicated by an asterisk (*), and explained more fully in notes. Alternatives to the Subjunctive constructions are also given, and are of two kinds: (a) optional alternatives which are on the whole more commonly used in R1–2, though unless otherwise indicated both constructions are actively used in all registers, and (b) obligatory alternatives which are demanded by certain conditions. The chief kind of obligatory alternative is the use of an infinitive when the subject of the main verb and the subject of the complement verb are identical, for example with **querer**. **Quiero que lo haga** could never be used to mean *I want to do it* (where **yo** is the subject of **quiero** and also of **haga**): this notion must be rendered by **Quiero hacerlo** or **Lo quiero hacer**.

NOTE: only a brief account of usage with infinitive complements is included in this section; see ch. **20** for further information.

R1*	vulgar or indecent
R1	informal, colloquial
R2	neutral
R3	formal, written
See also p 3.	

26.1 Sequence of tenses in Subjunctive constructions

The basic sequence-of-tense patterns are given in the following table:

Am	Spanish-speaking Latin America
Arg	Argentina
Mex	Mexico
Pen	Peninsular Spain
See also p 1.	

main clause	*subordinate clause*
Present/Perfect Future/Future Perfect	Present/Perfect Subjunctive
Imperfect/Pluperfect Preterite Conditional/Conditional Perfect	Imperfect/Pluperfect Subjunctive

Examples:
Pide que se lo digamos
She asks us to tell her
Me gustaría que lo hicieses
I'd like you to do it
Me alegro de que hayas llegado temprano
I'm glad you've arrived early
No había pensado que fuera tan difícil
I hadn't thought it was so difficult
Negó que lo hubieran hecho
He denied that they had done it

However, this sequence of tense may sometimes be broken if there is a shift in point of view in the course of the sentence (the same thing may happen in English in parallel structures), eg:

Negó (in the past) **que existiera/exista** (universal principle) **una relación directa entre la gravedad y el magnetismo**
He denied that there was/is a direct relationship between gravity and magnetism
Se pidió (in the past) **a Reagan que buscara/busque** (he hasn't done it yet) **una solución**
Reagan was asked to find a solution

See also the note on sequence of tense on pp 266–7.

26.2 Commands and related structures

26.2.1 Direct commands

The Subjunctive is used for all direct commands except the **tú** and **vosotros** (Pen) positive imperatives (**haz**, **haced**).

Subjunctive expression	*Alternative/Remarks*
¡Hága(n)lo!	**¡a hacerlo!** (R1–2), **¡lo harás!** (R1–3), **¡haciéndolo!** (R1), etc
¡No lo hagas! **¡No lo hagáis!** (Pen) **¡No lo haga(n)!**	**¡No lo harás!**, etc (R1–3), **¡Ni hacerlo!** (R1), **¡Nada de hacerlo!** (R1), **¡Sin hacerlo!** (R1)
¡Que venga(n)! **¡Empecemos ahora!** (R2–3) but with **ir(se)**: **¡Vámonos!**	**¡Vamos a empezar ahora!** (R1–2)

Notes

1 The Subjunctive may be used as an alternative to the **tú** and **vosotros** (Pen) imperatives to express a wish: **¡Que te diviertas mucho!** or **¡Diviértete mucho!**

2 The infinitive is increasingly used in place of the rather odd–sounding Peninsular **vosotros** imperative, thus **¡Sentaros!** for **¡Sentaos!** It is also commonly used to soften the tone of the imperative: **¡Escribirme!, ¡Telefonearme mañana!**

3 There are a number of other expressions involving imperatives which may conveniently be mentioned here, eg:

> **hágalo o no lo haga**
> whether she does it or not
> **dijera lo que dijera**
> whatever she might have said
> **viniera de donde viniera**
> wherever he came from
> **sea como sea/fuere**
> be that as it may
> > NOTE: **fuere** is the old Future Subjunctive, still occasionally preserved in this expression.
> **venga cuando venga**
> come when he may/whenever he comes
> **Te vistas como te vistas**
> Dress as you like

The use of the Subjunctive after **como** and **cuando** in the last three examples is related to the use with -*ever* expressions (see **26.9**).

26.2.2 Indirect command, request, necessity

The Subjunctive is used in the complements of verb and verbal expressions which express influence.

Subjunctive-requiring expression	Alternative/Remarks
†**aconsejar que** *to advise* · **le aconsejé que lo hiciese**	**aconsejar a uno** + inf · **le aconsejé hacerlo**
†**agradecer que** *to thank, to be grateful* · **Le agradezco (que) me escriba** I would be grateful if you would write to me	BUT NOTE the infinitive construction when the complement refers to the past: · **Le agradezco el haberme escrito** I am grateful to you for writing
†**animar a uno a que** *to encourage*	**animar a uno a** + inf
†**conseguir que** *to manage, to get*	BUT **conseguir hacer algo** obligatory when subjects of main verb and complement verb are identical

★ These expressions also take the Indicative. *See notes on p 248.*

Subjunctive-requiring expression	Alternative/Remarks
†★**decidir que** *to decide*	BUT **decidir** + inf obligatory when subjects of main verb and complement verb are identical
· **Decidí que lo hiciese** I decided that he should do it	· **Decidí hacerlo** I decided to do it
†★**decir que** *to tell*	See p 205 for **decir** + inf
†★**declarar que** (R3) *to state*	See p 205 for **declarar** + inf
decretar que (R3) *to decree*	
†**desear que** *to want, to wish, to desire*	BUT **desear** + inf obligatory when subjects of main verb and complement verb are identical
†**disponer que** (R2–3) *to stipulate*	
es esencial que (impersonal) *it is essential*	**es esencial** + inf
★**establecer que** *to establish*	
†**evitar que** *to avoid*	BUT **evitar** + inf obligatory when subjects of main verb and complement verb are identical
†**exigir que** *to demand, to require*	NOTE ALSO: **exigir a uno** + inf, eg: · **Exigí al chico volver en seguida**
†**hace falta que** (impersonal) *it is necessary* · **Hace falta que llegue a tiempo** I need to arrive in time	**hace falta** + inf, eg: · **Hace falta llegar a tiempo** It's necessary to arrive in time NOTE that the infinitive construction avoids specification of a subject.
es imperativo que (impersonal) *it is imperative*	**es imperativo** + inf
es importante que (impersonal) *it is important*	**es importante** + inf

Subjunctive-requiring expression	*Alternative/Remarks*
†**lograr que** *to manage, to get*	BUT **lograr** + inf obligatory when subjects of main verb and complement verb are identical
†**mandar que** *to order*	**mandar** + inf NOTE these constructions: · **Le mandé hacerlo/Se lo mandé hacer** I ordered him to do it · **Lo mandé hacer/Mandé hacerlo** I ordered it to be done
†**es mejor que** (impersonal) *it is better*	**es mejor** + inf
es necesario que (impersonal) *it is necessary*	**es necesario** + inf
†**necesitar que** *to need*	BUT **necesitar** + inf obligatory when subjects of main verb and complement verb are identical
†**ordenar que** *to order*	**ordenar a uno** + inf
†**pedir que** *to ask*	BUT **pedir** + inf obligatory when subjects of main verb and complement verb are identical
†**precisa que** (impersonal) (R3) *it is necessary*	**precisa** + inf
precisar que (R3) *to need*	BUT **precisar** + inf obligatory when subjects of main verb and complement verb are identical
es preciso que (impersonal) *it is necessary*	**es preciso** + inf
presionar para que *to press*	
†*****pretender que** *to expect, to suggest*	See p 204 for **pretender** + inf
†**querer que** *to want*	BUT **querer** + inf obligatory when subjects of main verb and complement verb are identical
†**reclamar que** *to demand, to require*	

***** These expressions also take the Indicative. *See notes on p 248.*

Subjunctive-requiring expression	Alternative/Remarks
recomendar que *to recommend*	
[†]**resolver que** (R2–3) *to resolve*	BUT **resolver** + inf obligatory when subjects of main verb and complement verb are identical
[†]**rogar que** *to ask*	**rogar a uno** + inf
[†]**suplicar que** *to ask, to implore*	**suplicar a uno** + inf
[†]**urge que** (impersonal) (R3) *it is urgent*	**urge** + inf
es urgente que (impersonal) *it is urgent*	**es urgente** + inf
más vale que (impersonal) *it is better, it is preferable*	**más vale** + inf

Notes

1 When the asterisked verbs listed above do not express a command, the Indicative is used. Contrast the following pairs of examples:

Decidí que dimitiera
I decided he should resign
Decidí que eso era mejor
I decided that was better

Juan me dijo que saliera
John told me to leave
Juan me dijo que saliste
John told me that you left

Ha declarado que los impuestos sean abolidos
He has declared that taxes should be abolished
Ha declarado que el Gobierno no sirve para nada
He has declared that the government is no good

Hemos establecido que todos los ciudadanos tengan derecho a su opinión
We have established that all citizens shall have a right to their opinion
Hemos establecido que el hidrógeno es combustible
We have established that hydrogen burns

Pretende que todos estén de acuerdo
He expects everyone to agree
Pretende que todos estaban de acuerdo
He claims that everyone was in agreement

2 **que** is often omitted after **agradecer**, **pedir**, **rogar** and **suplicar** in R3, eg:

Rogamos se sirva contestar cuanto antes
Please reply as soon as possible

26.2.3 Suggestion

This may be viewed as a kind of weak or polite command.

Subjunctive-requiring expression	Alternative/Remarks
†**basta que** (impersonal) *it is enough*	**basta** + inf (as for **hace falta** + inf, p 251)
★**convencer a uno para que** *to persuade*	**convencer a uno para** + inf
†**conviene que** (impersonal) *it is fitting, it is advisable*	**conviene** + inf (as for **hace falta** + inf, p 251)
†**convidar a uno a que** (R2–3) *to invite*	**convidar a uno a** + inf (R1–3)
†**disuadir a uno de que** *to dissuade*	**disuadir a uno de** + inf
†**importa que** (impersonal) *it matters*	**importa** + inf (as for **hace falta** + inf, p 251)
†★**indicar que** (R2–3) *to indicate*	
★**insinuar que** (R2–3) *to insinuate, to hint*	
†**invitar a uno a que** (R2–3) *to invite*	**invitar a uno a** + inf (R1–3)
†**persuadir a uno que** *to persuade*	**persuadir a uno a/para** + inf
†**proponer a uno que** *to propose*	**proponer a uno** + inf
proponerse que *to propose*, (in Perfect) *to be determined*	BUT **proponerse** + inf obligatory when subjects of main verb and complement verb are identical
· **Te has propuesto que no lo sepa** You're determined she won't know	· **Me propongo salir** I propose to go out
es suficiente que (impersonal) *it is sufficient*	**es suficiente** + inf (as for **hace falta** + inf, p 251)

★ These expressions also take the Indicative. *See notes on p 248.*

Subjunctive-requiring expression	Alternative/Remarks
†★**sugerir que** *to suggest*	**sugerir a uno** + inf

Note

When the asterisked verbs listed above do not have the force of a weak command, the Indicative is used. Contrast the following pairs of examples:

Le convencí para que fuese
I persuaded him he should go
Le convencí de que tenía razón
I convinced him that he was right

Me indicó/insinuó/sugirió que me sentara
He indicated/hinted/suggested that I should sit down
Me indicó/insinuó/sugirió que quería hacerse profesor
He indicated/hinted/suggested that he wanted to become a teacher

26.2.4 Permission and prohibition

Subjunctive-requiring expression	Alternative/Remarks
†**aprobar que** (R2–3) *to approve*	
†**consentir que** *to allow, to tolerate*	**consentir a uno** + inf BUT **consentir en** + inf obligatory when subjects of main verb and complement verb are identical
· **No consiento que hable** I won't allow him to speak	· **No le consiento salir** I won't allow him out · **Consiento en ir** I agree to go
†**dejar que** *to allow, to let*	**dejar a uno** + inf
†**desaprobar que** (R3) *to disapprove* **Desaprueba que lo haga yo** She disapproves of my doing it	
†**impedir que** *to prevent*	**impedir a uno** + inf
oponerse a que (R2–3) *to oppose*	BUT **oponerse a** + inf obligatory when subjects of main verb and complement verb are identical

Subjunctive-requiring expression	*Alternative/Remarks*
†**permitir que** *to permit, to allow*	**permitir a uno** + inf
†**prohibir que** *to forbid, to prohibit*	**prohibir a uno** + inf

26.2.5 Conjunctions expressing purpose or intention

Subjunctive-requiring expression	*Alternative/Remarks*
a fin de que (R2–3) *in order that*	
★**de forma/manera/modo que** *so that*	
para que *in order that*	**para** + inf (R1) · **Lo hizo para saberlo yo** He did it so that I would know BUT **para** + inf obligatory when subjects of main verb and complement verb are identical

Notes

1 **de forma/manera/modo que** take the Indicative when they express consequence. Contrast the following:

   Lo recité muy despacio, de forma/manera/modo que lo aprendieran
   I recited it very slowly in order that they might learn it
   Lo recité muy despacio, de forma/manera/modo que lo aprendieron
   I recited it very slowly, so (consequently) they learned it

2 **para que** introducing a complement of sufficiency (see **19.13.3**) also takes the Subjunctive, eg:

   Faltan/Quedan dos horas para que lleguen
   It'll be two hours before they arrive

★ These expressions also take the Indicative. *See notes on p 248.*

26.2.6 Other expressions of influence

Subjunctive-requiring expression	Alternative/Remarks
†**forzar a uno a que** *to force*	**forzar a uno a** + inf
†**hacer a uno que** *to make*	**hacer** + inf NOTE these constructions: · **Le hice leerlo/Se lo hice leer** I made him read it · **Lo hice leer/Hice leerlo** I had it read
obligar a uno a/para que *to oblige, to compel*	**obligar a uno a** + inf
†**preferir que** *to prefer*	BUT **preferir** + inf obligatory when subjects of main verb and complement verb are identical

26.3 Expressions of emotion

Spanish uses a Subjunctive in the complement of the following verbs and verbal expressions whatever the truth or otherwise of the complement. Expressions of emotion should be carefully distinguished from expressions of opinion, which are dealt with in **26.5** below.

Subjunctive-requiring expression	Alternative/Remarks
†**alegra a uno que** (impersonal) *it makes sb happy*	**alegra a uno** + inf
†**alegrarse de que** *to be happy, to be glad*	BUT **alegrarse de** + inf obligatory when subjects of main verb and complement verb are identical
es bueno que (impersonal) *it is nice, it is good*	**es bueno** + inf
†**celebrar que** (R3) *to be glad*	BUT **celebrar** + inf obligatory when subjects of main verb and complement verb are identical
†★**confiar en que** (R2–3) *to trust*	

Subjunctive-requiring expression	Alternative/Remarks
†**encanta a uno que** (impersonal) *it delights*	**encanta a uno** + inf
†★**esperar que** *to hope*	BUT **esperar** + inf obligatory when subjects of main verb and complement verb are identical
es de esperar que (impersonal) *it is to be hoped*	
extraña a uno que (impersonal) *it surprises*	**extraña a uno** + inf
es de †extrañar que (impersonal) *it is surprising*	
extrañarse de que *to be surprised*	
es †extraño que (impersonal) *it is surprising*	**es extraño** + inf
es inevitable que (impersonal) *it is inevitable*	**es inevitable** + inf
es inútil que (impersonal) *it is useless*	**es inútil** + inf
es justo que (impersonal) *it is right*	**es justo** + inf
es (una (R1)) lástima que (impersonal) *it is a pity*	**es lástima** + inf
es lógico que (impersonal) *it is natural*	**es lógico** + inf
†**es mejor que** (impersonal) *it is better*	**es mejor** + inf
†**tener miedo que** *to be afraid*	BUT **tener miedo de** + inf obligatory when subjects of main verb and complement verb are identical

Subjunctive-requiring expression	Alternative/Remarks
†**molesta a uno que** (impersonal) *it annoys*	**molesta a uno** + inf
es natural que (impersonal) *it is natural*	**es natural** + inf
es una pena que *it is a shame*	**es una pena** + inf
es raro que (impersonal) *it is odd*	**es raro** + inf
†**sentir que** *to regret*	BUT **sentir** + inf obligatory when subjects of main verb and complement verb are identical
†*★**temer que** *to fear*	BUT **temer** + inf obligatory when subjects of main verb and complement verb are identical
es de temer que (impersonal) *it is to be feared*	
es triste que (impersonal) *it is sad*	**es triste** + inf

NOTE, however, **lo triste es que** + Indicative:
> **Es triste que no lo sepa**
> It's sad she doesn't know
> **Lo triste es que no lo sabe**
> The sad thing is that she doesn't know

Note

confiar en and **esperar** frequently, but by no means always, take the Indicative when the complement is in the future; in such circumstances there is a choice between Indicative and Subjunctive which is often difficult to appreciate from an English point of view:
> **Espero/Confío en que haya tenido/tenga éxito**
> I hope/trust he has been/will be successful
> **Espero/Confío en que tendrá éxito**
> I hope/trust he'll be successful (I'm sure he will)

†**temer(se)** takes the Indicative when the 'fear' is only conventional or polite and not a genuine emotion:
> **Temo que vaya a caer**
> I'm afraid (genuinely) that he'll fall
> (**Me**) **temo que usted no tiene razón**
> I'm afraid (polite) that you're wrong

26.4 Expressions involving a negative idea

26.4.1 Verbs and verbal expressions of denial and doubt

Subjunctive-requiring expression	Alternative/Remarks
no es †cierto que (impersonal) *it is not certain*	NOTE: **no es cierto** (impersonal) **si** + Indicative.
descartar que (R2–3) *to rule out*	
desmentir (R3) **que** *to deny*	BUT **desmentir** + inf obligatory when subjects of main verb and complement verb are identical
†dudar que *to doubt* · **Dudo que tenga mucho dinero** I doubt he has much money	NOTE: **dudar si** + Indicative (R1–2). · **Dudo si llegará a tiempo** I doubt if he will arrive in time
NOTE: perhaps because of the mixing of these constructions, **dudar que** sometimes takes the Indicative in R1 ⌐!⌐.	
es dudoso que (impersonal) *it is doubtful*	NOTE: **es dudoso** (impersonal) **si** + Indicative.
†ignorar que *to be unaware*	NOTE: **ignorar si** + Indicative.
NOTE: as for **dudar**.	
es †increíble que (impersonal) *it is incredible*	
†negar que *to deny*	BUT **negar** + inf obligatory when subjects of main verb and complement verb are identical
NOTE: **negar que** sometimes takes the Indicative in R1 ⌐!⌐.	
no querer decir que *not to mean*	
no es seguro que (impersonal) *it is not certain* · **No es seguro que vaya** It's not certain that she will go	NOTE: **no es seguro** (impersonal) **si** + Indicative.
See **27.6** for **ser/estar seguro** with a personal subject.	
no es verdad (impersonal) *it is not true*	

★ These expressions also take the Indicative. *See notes on p 248.*

26.4.2 'Negative' conjunctions

Subjunctive-requiring expression	Alternative/Remarks
sin que *without*	**sin** + inf
· **Lo hizo sin que yo lo supiera**	· **Lo hizo sin saberlo yo** He did it without my knowing
He did it without my knowing	BUT **sin** + inf obligatory when subjects of main verb and complement verb are identical
	· **Lo dije sin darme cuenta** I said it without realizing

26.5 Expressions of opinion and thought

The complements of verbs of thinking such as **admitir**, **comprender**, **concebir**, †**creer**, †**figurarse**, †**imaginarse**, †**parecer** (impersonal), †**pensar** and †**suponer** normally have Indicative verbs in their complements (but see **26.7** below). There are circumstances, however, in which the Subjunctive is used.

26.5.1 Apparent negation

When the verb is apparently negated, eg **No creo que sea verdad**. In fact, this is simply the equivalent of the construction **Creo que no es verdad**, and it is not **creer** itself that is being negated. This 'transferring' of the negative element from the complement verb to the main verb necessitates in Spanish the complement verb going into the Subjunctive, eg:

Me †parece que este problema no tiene solución
No me parece que este problema tenga solución
} I don't think this problem has a solution

Me †imagino que no ha salido todavía
No me imagino que haya salido todavía
} I don't suppose he's left yet

26.5.2 Doubt or hesitation

The Subjunctive is used where there is a strong element of doubt or hesitation concerning the complement, eg:
Creo que sea verdad (especially R1)
I think it may be true
Admito que no tenga razón
I admit he may not be right

Conversely, the 'negative-transferred' constructions discussed in the previous section may have the Indicative if the truth of the complement is being strongly asserted, eg:

Pedro no cree que la Tierra es redonda
Pedro doesn't think the Earth is round (but it is)

Extreme care should be taken in using constructions such as these.

26.5.3 Emotional overtone

The Subjunctive is used where the verb has an emotional overtone, eg:

Comprendo que no lo hayas querido hacer
I can understand that you shouldn't have wanted to do it

Extreme care should be taken in using constructions such as these.

26.6 Expressions of possibility and probability

Subjunctive-requiring expression	Alternative/Remarks
acaso (R2–3) *perhaps*	
es posible que (impersonal) *it is possible*	**es posible** + inf
posiblemente *possibly*	
es probable que (impersonal) *it is probable*	
puede (ser) que (impersonal) *maybe, perhaps*	BUT **poder** + inf obligatory when subjects of main verb and complement verb are identical
NOTE: **pueda (ser) que** + Subjunctive is also encountered in R1 (Pen) and R1–2 (Am).	
*quizá(s) *perhaps*	
*tal vez *perhaps*	

Note

Both Subjunctive and Indicative are used with **quizá(s)** and **tal vez**, the choice depending on the 'remoteness' of the possibility; this distinction is difficult to gloss in English:

Quizás/Tal vez viene
Perhaps he's coming

> * These expressions also take the Indicative. *See notes on p 248.*

Quizás/Tal vez venga
Perhaps he may come

Quizás/Tal vez ha venido
Perhaps he has come (I'm not sure)
Quizás/Tal vez haya venido
He may have come (but I rather doubt it)

The Indicative is used when **quizás/tal vez** follows the verb parenthetically, eg:
Iré, tal vez/quizás
I'll go, perhaps

Note that the other common expression with the meaning of *perhaps*, **a lo mejor**, takes the Indicative, and is the commonest in R1.

26.7 Hypothetical expressions

26.7.1 Verbs and expressions of imagining and wishing

Subjunctive-requiring expression	*Alternative/Remarks*
†*★**figurarse que** *to imagine*	
†*★**imaginarse que** *to imagine*	
¡ojalá (que)! (in R1 **que** is usually omitted) *if only* · **¡Ojalá tuviéramos tiempo!** If only/I wish we had time!	
se presume que (impersonal) *it is presumed*	
es de presumir que (impersonal) *it is to be presumed*	
★suponer que *to suppose*	NOTE ALSO that the Future and Conditional tenses can express the idea of supposition (see **23.2** and **23.4**).

Notes

1   The verbs marked with an asterisk also function as verbs of thinking (see **26.5**), in which function they normally take the Indicative.

2 Notice the sequence of tense with the following expressions:

¡ **Figúrate que venga mañana!**
Imagine he's coming tomorrow!
¡ **Suponga que estuviera aquí!**
Suppose he were here!
¡ **Ojalá hubiera podido venir!**
I wish he could have come!

26.7.2 Conjunctions of supposition, provision and concession

Subjunctive-requiring expression	*Alternative/Remarks*
a (la) condición (de) que *on condition that*	**si** (p 266) will often have the same value
a no ser que *unless*	
★**a pesar de que** *in spite of*	BUT **a pesar de** + inf is more usual when subjects of main verb and subordinate verb are identical, eg: · **A pesar de ser rico, no quería darme nada** In spite of being rich, he wouldn't give me anything
★**aun cuando** *even if, even though*	**si bien** + Indicative (= *while, although*) is closely related in meaning
★**aunque** *although*	Compare **si bien** (as above)
bien que *although*	Compare **si bien** (as above)
★**como** *if* · **Como lo vuelvas a hacer, te castigaré** If you do it again I will punish you	**si** (p 266) will often have the same value
como si *as if*	Always with the Imperfect or Pluperfect Subjunctive **como si lo supiera todo** as if she knew everything
con tal (de) que *provided that*	**si** (p 266) will often have the same value

★ These expressions also take the Indicative. See notes on p 248.

Subjunctive-requiring expression	Alternative/Remarks
*con que *provided that* · **Con que se haga con antelación, no hay problema** Provided you do it in advance, there's no problem	**si** (p 266) will often have the same value BUT **con** + inf is more usual when subjects of main verb and subordinate verb are identical, eg: · **Con levantarse temprano puede verlo** If you get up early you may see him
*dado que *given that*	
en caso de que *in case*	BUT **(en) caso de** + inf is more usual when subjects of main verb and subordinate verb are identical
excepto que *unless*	
más que (R1 Am) *although*	
ni aunque (R1–2) *even though*	
ni que (R1) · **Ni que fuera tuyo** Anyone would think it was yours	
salvo que *unless*	
siempre que *provided that*	
*supuesto que *supposing that*	**si** (p 266) will often have the same value
en el supuesto de que *supposing that*	

Notes

1 **a pesar de que**, **aun cuando**, **aunque** and **dado que** take the Indicative when they introduce an established fact rather than a hypothesis, eg:

A pesar de que me lo dijo ayer, no me acuerdo de su nombre
Despite the fact she told me yesterday, I can't remember her name

Aun cuando no tenía el menor interés en el tema, criticó a todos
Even though he hadn't the slightest interest in the matter, he criticized everyone
Aunque está aquí, no lo quiero ver
Even though he's here, I don't want to see him
Dado que es tan inteligente, ¿por qué no sabe contestar?
Given that he's so bright, why doesn't he know the answer?

2   **como, conque** (note the spelling) and **supuesto que** take the Indicative when expressing cause, eg:
Como no tengo dinero, no puedo ir
Since I've no money, I can't go
¿Conque quieres escapar?
So you want to escape?
Supuesto que no quiere venir, vamos a salir sin él
Since he doesn't want to come, we'll go without him

26.7.3   Conditional sentences

The Imperfect or Pluperfect Subjunctive (but never the Present Subjunctive) is used after **si** when the condition is unlikely or impossible. The commonest patterns are:

FUTURE: **Si viniera mañana, se lo diríamos**
If he came tomorrow, we would tell him
PRESENT: **Si estuviera aquí, se lo diríamos**
If he were here, we would tell him
PAST: **Si hubiera estado allí, se lo habríamos dicho**
If he had been there, we would have told him

In the **si** clause, the **-ra** form may be replaced by the **-se** form in R2–3, and in the main clause, the Conditional is sometimes replaced by the **-ra** form. The several other combinations of tenses in conditional sentences which were to be found in Spanish literature until quite recently should nowadays be avoided.

There are, however, several equivalents in R1 which involve other tenses:
Si viniera mañana, se lo decíamos ⚠️ (FUTURE)
If he came tomorrow, we would tell him
Si vendría ⚠️ **mañana, se lo diríamos** (R1 Arg) (FUTURE)
If he came tomorrow, we would tell him
Que estuviera aquí ahora, se lo decíamos ⚠️ (PRESENT)
If he were here now, we would tell him

NOTE ALSO the many more specific conditional conjunctions on pp 264–5 above, and the common **de** + inf construction:
De haberlo sabido, se lo habríamos dicho (PAST)
If we had known, we would have told him

NOTE: the Subjunctive is not used when the condition is open, eg:
Si viene, se lo diremos
If he comes, we shall tell him
Si sabe la respuesta, nos la dirá
If he knows the answer, he will tell us

⚠️ These forms are in regular use but might be considered 'incorrect' in an examination.

Si viene aquí, lo vemos
Whenever he comes here, we see him
Si iba allí, lo veíamos
Whenever he went there, we saw him
Dije que si venía, se lo diríamos (reporting '**si viene, se lo diremos**')
I said that if he came, we would tell him
Dije que si sabía la respuesta, nos la diría (reporting '**si sabe la respuesta, nos la dirá**')
I said that if he knew the answer, he would tell us

26.8   Temporal clauses

The Subjunctive is used in all temporal clauses which refer to the FUTURE, eg:

En cuanto/Una vez que/Cuando, etc, **venga Juan, vamos a avisarle de lo ocurrido**
As soon as/Once/When, etc, John comes, let's tell him what happened

NOTE: the 'future' idea may be in reported speech or envisaged from a 'past' point of view, eg:

Dije que en cuanto llegáramos a casa, íbamos a telefonear a nuestros amigos
I said that as soon as we arrived home, we would telephone our friends
Iba a esperar en la estación hasta que viniera el autobús
She was going to wait at the station until the bus came

Compare the use of the Indicative when the temporal clause refers to the PAST or to a repeated action:

En cuanto vino Juan le avisamos de lo ocurrido
As soon as John came we told him what had happened
Siempre espero aquí hasta que viene el autobús
I always wait here until the bus comes
Siempre esperaba allí hasta que venía el autobús
She always waited there until the bus came

antes (de) que is the only temporal conjunction which is *always* followed by the Subjunctive, eg:

Voy a salir antes de que llegue
I'm going before she arrives
Oí las noticias antes de que llegara
I heard the news before he got here
Siempre oigo las noticias antes de que llegue
I always hear the news before he gets here

Notes

1   **antes de**, **después de**, **hasta** and **luego de** are preferably followed by an infinitive when the subjects of the main verb and temporal clause verb are identical, eg:

Lo supimos después de llegar
We found out after arriving

and, increasingly, may be followed by an infinitive and subject pronoun even when the subjects are not identical, eg:

Lo supimos después de llegar él
We found out after he had arrived

2 **desde que** and **luego que** are increasingly used with the **-ra** form, and occasionally with the **-se** form, of the Subjunctive, in journalistic and literary R3, eg:

Es ésta la segunda crisis de Gobierno desde que Kurt Waldheim fuera elegido en junio pasado
This is the second government crisis since Kurt Waldheim was elected last June

3 **después de que** is increasingly followed by the Subjunctive in all registers, eg:

La reunión comenzó después de que acabara el Consejo de Ministros
The meeting began after the Council of Ministers ended

4 A 'pleonastic' (logically superfluous) **no** is sometimes used with **hasta que** and **mientras**, eg:

Me quedaré aquí mientras no lo haga $\boxed{!}$
I'll stay here while she does it

5 Notice also the complements of **aguardar** and **esperar** (see also p 225), which are similar to FUTURE temporal clauses:

Estoy aguardando/esperando (a) que venga el autobús
I'm waiting until the bus comes

26.9 Relative clauses

The Subjunctive is used in a relative clause which refers to a non-existent, indefinite or hypothetical antecedent. It is also used in R3, although more and more rarely, in a relative clause which refers to a superlative antecedent.

Non-existent antecedent

No hay nadie que sepa la respuesta
There's no one who knows the answer

Indefinite or hypothetical antecedent

Busco un (= cualquier) médico que me sepa curar
I'm looking for a doctor (= any doctor) who can cure me

Notes

1 The personal **a** is often omitted in this construction, since the object is not thought of as an individual (**19.1.9**). Contrast the above example with the following:

Conozco a un médico que me sabe curar
I know a doctor who can cure me

2   The Subjunctive construction is used in Spanish more often than
     might appear necessary to English speakers. It frequently has a more
     polite overtone than the Indicative, and avoids the presentation of
     the relative clause as a fact, eg:

Los que no hayan entendido pueden preguntar otra vez
Those who haven't understood (if there are any) can ask again
Nada de lo que diga me ofende
Nothing of what she may say (if anything) offends me
el incierto límite futuro que el destino nos tenga asignado
the uncertain future limit which destiny may have assigned us

Superlative antecedent

el mejor libro que hayamos leído (R3)
the best book we have ever read

The Subjunctive used in the equivalent of English -*ever* expressions

quienquiera que sea/fuese	whoever it may be/might have been
dondequiera que ande/anduviera	wherever he goes/went
cuando quiera	when(ever) you wish
por estúpidos que sean/fuesen	however stupid they are/were
por más dinero que gane/ganara	however much money he earns/earned
por muchos que tenga/tuviera	however many she has/had
lo que me paguen	whatever they pay me
donde vayas	wherever you go

NOTE ALSO the following idioms:

que yo sepa	as far as I know
que yo recuerde	as far as I remember

See also **26.2**.

26.10   Noun clauses

The Subjunctive is used in noun clauses which correspond to the uses
described in **26.2–7** above.

el deseo de que lo haga	the *wish* that she does it
la necesidad de que nos demos cuenta de lo ocurrido	the *necessity* of our realizing what has happened
la esperanza de que lo lea	the *hope* that he may read it
la duda de que lo sepa	the *doubt* whether she knows
la posibilidad de que se escape	the *possibility* he may escape
había el peligro de que cayese	there was the *danger* of his falling

The Subjunctive is also regularly found after **el hecho de que**, even when the clause refers to an established fact about which no 'emotion' or 'opinion' is being expressed, eg:

> **El hecho de que los cristianos fueran mayoría era en gran parte sociológico**
> The fact that the Christians were a majority was largely sociological

Notice also:

> †**Ya era hora de que hicieran lo que les diera la gana**
> It was time they did what they liked

27 **ser** and **estar**

The idea that the contrast between **ser** and **estar** is based on considerations of 'permanence' and 'temporariness' seems to be entrenched in the minds of many English-speaking students. Although it has a limited usefulness where the adjectival complements of the two verbs are concerned, it is a very inadequate general principle. In fact, no single rule of thumb will satisfactorily describe the difference between **ser** and **estar** in English terms. The approach taken here is to examine the several contexts in which they appear and to look at the basis of the contrast, where there is one, within each of these.

27.1 With nouns, pronouns, infinitives and clauses

ser	estar
• Always used: **Soy médico** I am a doctor **¿Quién es el director?** Who is the head? **No es nada** It's nothing **Ver es creer** Seeing is believing **Eso es lo que quería saber** That's what I wanted to know NOTE: **Durante la guerra mi padre fue coronel de artillería** During the war my father was a colonel in the artillery (though a 'temporary' state of affairs)	• One or two idiomatic usages which derive from the use of **estar** with ADJECTIVES or PAST PARTICIPLES (see **27.5–6**), eg: **Estás (hecho) un hombre** (of a child) You've turned into a man **estar pez** (R1) to be an ignoramus

27.2 With adverbs of place

ser	estar
• Used with subjects which represent an event, eg: **La clase es en la otra sala** The class is (taking place) in the other room	• Normally used, eg: **El Museo del Prado está en Madrid** The Prado Museum is in Madrid **¿Dónde estamos ahora?** Where are we now? **La misma idea está en la otra novela** The same idea is in the other novel
• Reorganization of a sentence for the purposes of stress, using **ser**, may also result in its apparently being used with an adverb or adverbial phrase of place, eg: **Donde te vi fue en la Calle Mayor** It was in the Calle Mayor that I saw you **Fue en Londres donde nos conocimos** It was in London that we met	NOTE: **La enciclopedia está siempre en el mismo estante** The encyclopaedia is always on the same shelf

NOTE: adjectives indicating position, since they represent inherent characteristics (see **27.6** below), take **ser**:
Mi país es lejano BUT **Mi país está lejos**
Mi piso es cercano al Ayuntamiento BUT **Mi piso está cerca del Ayuntamiento**

27.3 With other adverbs

ser	estar
	• Always with **bien** and **mal**, eg: **No está mal** It's not bad

27.4 With a gerund

ser	estar
NOTE: **fui llegando**, etc, are forms of **ir llegando** (see **24.4**).	● Always used in the formation of the progressive tenses, eg: **Estaba leyendo el periódico cuando entró** I was reading the paper when she came in **Estaba llora que llora (R1)/llora que llora (R1)** I was crying my eyes out

27.5 With a past participle

ser	estar
● Used to form the straightforward passive: **El árbol fue cortado por el leñador** (= **El leñador cortó el árbol**) The tree was cut down by the woodcutter ● Many past participles can be used as adjectives, and **ser** is accordingly used where it would be the appropriate choice with an ADJECTIVE (see **27.6**), eg: **La ropa era muy usada** They were very worn clothes (**La ropa estaba muy usada** = The clothes had been worn a lot) **Este estudiante es muy instruido** This is a very well-informed student (**Este estudiante está muy instruido** = This student has been very well-educated)	● With **estar**, the past participle indicates a state, never an action. The state **(a)** results from the action of a transitive verb, eg: **Este pan está vendido** This bread is sold (= has been sold and is awaiting collection) **El vaso está roto** The glass is broken (= has previously been broken) **La ventana estaba abierta** The window was open (= it had been opened) **(b)** is associated with a reflexive or intransitive verb, eg: **Está levantado** He is up (= **se ha levantado**) **Estamos aburridos** We're bored (= **Nos aburrimos**) **Está muerto** He's dead (= (**Se**) **Ha muerto**)

ser	estar
• Some adjectival past participles used with **ser** have an 'active' meaning, eg: **La película era aburrida** The film was boring **El joven es muy atrevido** The young man is very daring (BUT **atrevido** also has an 'active' meaning with **estar**: **El joven está muy atrevido** = *The young man is behaving very daringly.*) NOTE ALSO in this category: **callado** *quiet* **cansado** *tiring, tiresome* **confiado** *trusting* **descreído** *disbelieving* **disimulado** *cunning* †**divertido**, **entretenido** *entertaining* †**osado** *daring* **pesado** *dull, boring* **sufrido** *long-suffering*	**Está callado** He's quiet (= (**Se**) **Ha callado**) BUT NOTE: **Es callado** = *He's a quiet (sort of) person.* NOTE: many past participles in this category are translated by English present participles (the Spanish present participle is *never* used adjectivally): **acostado** *lying down* **acurrucado** *huddling, nestling* **agachado** *bending over* **agachapado** *crouching* **agarrado (a algo)** *grasping (sth)* **arrimado (a algo)** *leaning (on sth)* **arrodillado** *kneeling* **colgado** *hanging* **dormido** *sleeping* **echado** *lying down* **inclinado** *leaning* **repantigado** *lolling* **sentado** *sitting* **suspendido** *hanging* **tendido** *lying down* **tumbado** *lying down*
• Contrast the following: **Esta novela fue escrita por Galdós** This novel was written by Galdós (straightforward passive)	**Aquí está escrito que...** It says here that . . . (= it has been written)
El grupo fue dividido en cuatro secciones The group was divided into four sections (straightforward passive)	**El capítulo está dividido en tres partes** The chapter is divided into three parts (description; it has been divided . . .)
Esa niña es muy distraída That girl is very absent-minded (adjective)	**Aunque intenté concentrarme, estaba muy distraído** Although I tried to concentrate, I was very absorbed in other things (my mind was wandering at that time)

NOTE: many examples of contrast between **ser** and **estar** are extremely difficult to appreciate, and hence to render, in English, eg:

No es permitido decir cosas así	**No está permitido salir**
One isn't allowed to say things like that (it's not generally permissible)	You can't go out (it's been forbidden)
¿Es usted casado o soltero?	**No estoy casado todavía**
Are you married or single? (Into which category do you fall?)	I'm not married yet (**todavía** implies a change of state is possible)

27.6 With an adjective

ser	estar
(a) With adjectives which classify the subject into a category (typically nationality, religion, etc), eg: **Mi mujer es francesa** My wife is French **Mi profesor de inglés es estructuralista** My English teacher is a structuralist **El tigre es carnívoro** The tiger is a carnivore	**(a)** With adjectives which, like the past participles in **27.5**, represent a 'resultant' state, eg: **Este pastel está muy dulce** This cake is very sweet (it tastes sweet) (**Este pastel es dulce** = This is a sweet kind of cake)
(b) Where the adjective is an inherent property of the subject, eg: **La nieve es blanca** (All) snow is white, *not* The snow is white **El hielo es frío** (All) ice is cold, *not* The ice is cold	NOTE: **Estoy siempre tan nervioso** I'm always so nervous (though apparently 'permanent'; things are always making me nervous)
(c) Where the adjective is a possible physical or moral property of the subject, even though this may not be 'inherent' or 'permanent', eg: **Juanito es muy alto** Johnny is tall (**Juanito está muy alto** = Johnny looks tall) **Nuestros vecinos son ricos** Our neighbours are rich	**(b)** With adjectives which do not represent a normally 'inherent' property of the subject, eg: **La sala está vacía** The room is empty (rooms are not necessarily empty) **Mi padre está ocupado** My father is busy (people are not necessarily busy) **El agua está fría** The water is/feels cold (water can be hot as well) **Las uvas están verdes** The grapes are/taste unripe (grapes are not necessarily unripe)

ser	estar
Soy viejo I'm old **El libro es triste** The book is sad (its contents are sad)	NOTE: **Está enfermo desde niño** He's been ill since he was a child (even though this is 'permanent', illness is not an inherent quality of people)
(d) Where the adjective expresses a measurement, quantity or comparison, eg: **Los tomates son muy caros** Tomatoes are very expensive (BUT **Los tomates están muy caros** = Tomatoes are very expensive at the moment) **La calle es estrecha** The street is narrow **Juana es muy distinta de su hermana menor** Juana is very different from her younger sister	**(c)** Where there is some qualification or comparison of an otherwise 'inherent' notion, eg: **Este niño está muy alto para su edad** This child is tall for his age **Estos zapatos me están pequeños** These shoes feel tight
(e) Where the subject is a proposition or its equivalent, eg: **Este problema es dificilísimo** This problem is very difficult **Comunicarle eso sería delicado** Telling him that would be difficult	**(d)** Where it is desired to give an impression of suddenness or irony: **¡Qué alto estás!** How tall you look! **Hoy la nieve está blanquísima** The snow looks really white today **Está muy viejo ahora** He's looking very old now

NOTE: again, there are examples of contrast between **ser** and **estar** which are difficult to appreciate.

En este país todos somos libres We are all free in this country	**Este taxi ¿está libre?** Is this taxi free?
Este estudiante es muy listo This student is very clever	**¿Estamos listos?** Are we ready?
Es claro que no sabe It's clear he doesn't know	**¿Está claro?** Is that clear? (**estar claro** is generally more emphatic than **es claro**, and so more typical of R1–2)
La casa es nueva The house is newly built (**La casa está nueva** = The house still looks new)	**Este sombrero está todavía nuevo** This hat is still new (= unworn)

ser	estar
Esta muchacha es viva This girl is lively	**Todos estamos vivos** We're all alive (compare **estar muerto, 27.5**)
No es seguro de sí mismo He's unsure of himself (a characteristic)	**No está seguro de poder ir** He's not sure he can go (an attitude) **Estoy muy contento aquí** I'm very happy here (**contento** is never normally used with **ser**)

27.7 With a prepositional phrase

ser	estar
● As with ADJECTIVES, eg: **Ese libro es para mí** That book is for me **Soy de Málaga** I'm from Málaga **Eso es por el bien de todos** That is for everyone's good	● As with ADJECTIVES, eg: **Está con la gripe** He's got flu **Estoy sin dinero** I'm without money **Estamos en armonía** We're in harmony **El cuarto está a oscuras** The room is in darkness **Hoy está de mal humor** She's in a bad mood today **Mi abuela estaba de luto** My grandmother was in mourning

27.8 In isolation

ser	estar
● Implies existence or identity, eg: **Todo lo que es** Everything that is (= exists) **¿Quién es?** Who is it?	● Implies location or state (of health), eg: **¿Está D. Jaime?** Is D. Jaime there? **¿Cómo estás?** How are you?

⟫→

	estar
	• It also appears in set phrases: **¿Estamos?** Are we agreed? **Ya está** That's it, it's finished **Déjale estar** Leave him alone

27.9 Idioms with prepositions, etc

ser	estar
• **ser de**: *to come from, to be made of, to belong to*, eg: **La familia es de Madrid** The family is from Madrid **La mesa es de madera** The table is made of wood **Los fantasmas no son de este mundo** Ghosts are not of this world	• **estar a** + date, price or other measurement, eg: **Estamos a quince de mayo** It's 15 May **Las manzanas están a veinte pesos el kilo** Apples are 20 pesos a kilo **El termómetro está a cuarenta grados** The thermometer reads 40 degrees
• †**ser de** (impersonal): *to become of*, eg: **¿Qué será de mí?** What will become of me?	• **estar de** + profession, eg: **Estaba de profesor en una escuela de idiomas** He was doing the job of a teacher in a language school
• **ser para** (impersonal) (R1): *to be enough to*, eg: **Es para morirse ya de risa** It's enough to make you die of laughter	• **estar en**: *to consist of, to intend to*, eg: **El secreto está en no contestar** The secret lies in not answering **Estoy en decirle la verdad** I intend to tell you the truth
• **ser que** (impersonal): emphasis or question device, eg: **Es que no sé** I don't really know **¿Es que el tren va a salir?** Is the train going to leave?	• **estar a uno en** + quantity (R1): *to cost sb sth*: **Este traje me está en mil duros** This suit cost me a thousand duros

estar

- **estar con**: *to agree with*, eg:
En esta opinión estoy con usted
In this view I'm in agreement with you

- **estar para**, **estar a punto de**, **estar al** (R1) + inf: *to be about to*, eg:
El tren está para/a punto de/al salir
The train is about to leave

- **estar (como) para** (R1): *to be in the mood for*, eg:
No estoy para debates
I'm not in the mood for arguments

- **estar por** + inf: *to be inclined to*, eg:
Estamos por comenzar ahora
We're inclined to start now

- **estar por** (impersonal) + inf: *to remain to*, eg:
La novela perfecta está por escribir
The perfect novel remains to be written

- **estar por** + noun: *to be in favour of, to be keen on* (R1), eg:
Yo estoy por la playa
I'm all for the beach
Juan está por María
Juan really likes María

- **estar que** (R1): intensifying device, eg:
Estoy que me caigo
I'm falling good and proper

28 Pronouns

In the following sections, pronouns are divided into two categories:

(a) UNSTRESSED: **me, te, se, le, lo, la, nos, os, les, los, las**. These pronouns never receive stress; they are always dependent upon a verb.

(b) DISJUNCTIVE: **yo, mí, tú, ti, usted, él, ella, ello, sí, nosotros/as, vosotros/as, ustedes, ellos, ellas**. These pronouns may be stressed, and they function as subjects of verbs or objects of prepositions.

NOTE: after a preposition, choice between **yo** (subject)/ **mí** (object), **tú** (subject)/ **ti** (object) varies. The object form is used in the majority of cases (**para mí, detrás de ti**), but the subject form is used after **como, salvo, excepto** and **según** (**según yo, como tú**, etc), and effectively after **entre** (**entre tú y yo**). In conjunction with another noun or pronoun, the subject form tends to be used, although it is preferable to repeat the preposition.

> **para mí** AND **para él y para mí** (preferred) BUT **para él y yo**
> **delante de mí** (ALSO **delante mío** (R1)) AND **delante de él y**
> **delante de mí** BUT **delante de él y yo**

28.1 Order

The order of unstressed pronouns relative to each other is governed by two principles:

Order by form

se	te os	me nos	**le** } become **se** if occurring with **les** } another pronoun of this group **lo** **la** **los** **las**

Te lo dije ayer
I told you yesterday
Se la envié
I sent it to him
Se me escapa la fecha
The date escapes me
¡Cómetemelo!
Eat it up for me!

Notes

1 **se** sometimes follows **te/os, me/nos** in R1 [!] (see p 5).

2   **se** (from **les**) **lo/la** sometimes becomes **se los/las** in R1 Am and even
R2 Am, eg:
    Eso pasó como se los ⎡!⎤ digo a ustedes
    It happened as I told you

Order by function

indirect object	direct object

If there is a conflict between the principles of order by form and
order by function, then a preposition and disjunctive pronoun
construction must in theory be used:
    Te me recomendó
    He recommended me to you
BUT
    Te recomendó a mí
    He recommended you to me

However, such cases are rare: a disjunctive pronoun construction is
generally preferred for all sequences involving first- and second-
person pronouns.

28.2 Pronouns and verb

The unstressed pronouns *precede* all finite verbs except the positive
imperative in all registers, eg:

me entiendes		
se verá	BUT	**¡házmelo!**
¡no me digas!		

NOTE: in R3, and (in some dialects) in R1, the pronoun(s) may *follow*
the first verb in a clause: eg the abbreviation **u.t.c.r.** in the *Diccionario
de la Real Academia Española*, which stands for **Úsase también como
reflexivo**. Some writers have cultivated this usage in other contexts,
eg:
    **Mi compañera, nuevamente fatigada, descansó la cabeza
        sobre el hombro de la que – lo sabíamos ahora – llamábase
        Rosario...** (A. Carpentier)
    My girl-friend, who was tired once again, rested her head on the
        shoulder of the woman who we now knew was called
        Rosario . . .

The unstressed pronouns *follow* all non-finite verbs (infinitive,
gerund) and the positive imperative, eg:
    viéndolo
    al abrirla
    ¡dígamelo!

(Pronouns are *never* attached to the past participle.)

The unstressed pronouns *either precede* the main verb *or follow* the
infinitive or gerund in common verb + infinitive and verb + gerund

groups. There is no difference in acceptability or register. Groups that allow such variation are:

†**acabar de** + inf   †**querer** + inf
†**continuar** + ger   †**seguir** + ger
†**deber** (**de**) + inf   †**soler** + inf
†**dejar de** + inf   †**terminar de** + inf
†**empezar a** + inf   †**tratar de** + inf
†**ir a** + inf   †**venir a** + inf
†**necesitar** + inf   †**volver a** + inf
poder + inf

For example: **acaba de hacerlo** or **lo acaba de hacer**.

In the above constructions, groups of pronouns may not be split: eg, only **debe contármelo** or **me lo debe contar**. There are other constructions which allow the splitting of pronoun groups, since each verb has its own object, but which also allow the whole pronoun sequence to stand before the main verb:

te †**aconsejarán comprarlos**   OR   te los aconsejarán comprar
le †**hice leerlo**   OR   se lo hice leer
me †**permitió tocarla**   OR   me la permitió tocar

28.3 'Redundant' pronouns

Even when an object is expressed by a noun or a disjunctive pronoun, an unstressed pronoun is needed in Spanish in the following cases:

1   When a direct or indirect object is placed before the verb (see **18.2**), eg:
A Juan no le gustó la comida
John didn't like the food
Aquel libro lo leí en dos días
I read that book in two days

2   Very often when an indirect object is a person or animal or is felt to be personified, eg:
Le robó el collar a la chica
He stole the necklace from the girl
Se lo vendió a mi amigo
She sold it to my friend
Se lo mostró al público
He showed it to the audience
Le dio la comida al perro
She gave the dog food
(**Se**) **lo di al banco**
I gave it to the bank

NOTE: in the last example, the 'redundant' construction with **se** (= **le**) tends to be used if the people at the bank are known; without the 'redundant' pronoun, the bank is being thought of simply as an institution.

3 When a disjunctive personal pronoun is used, usually for emphasis or avoidance of ambiguity, eg:

Te llamaban a ti
They were calling you
Déselo a ella
Give it to her

28.4 Second-person pronouns

In Peninsular Spanish, four pronouns with second-person meaning are used:

	singular	*plural*
'familiar'	**tú**	**vosotros/as**
'polite'	**usted**	**ustedes**

The traditional labels 'familiar' and 'polite' do not adequately capture the circumstances in which the pronouns are used today. During the last twenty years or so it has become increasingly common to use **tú** and **vosotros/as** in 'polite' situations which might appear to require (and previously did require) the use of **usted** and **ustedes**. It is unthinkable to use anything but **tú** and **vosotros/as** in the following situations:

- addressing children or animals, or God
- among relatives, friends (of whatever ages), workmates, soldiers of the same rank, colleagues in the same profession

tú is also used in the sense of *one*, *you* (general), especially in R1.

Nowadays it is normal to use **tú** and **vosotros/as** in the following situations:

- among young people, whatever the circumstances
- among people of different ages in almost any informal situation
- addressing priests
- wherever it is desired to establish a friendly note, even in 'semi-formal' situations (shops, banks, restaurants, etc)
- in public speeches, especially by politicians to their audience
- in advertisements where a 'matey' tone is required

In fact, it is not going too far to say that **usted**, **ustedes**, are used only:

- in formal, public situations
- when writing to strangers
- to old people not known to the speaker
- wherever it is desired to show (sometimes ostentatiously) respect

Some examples

Señores primeros ministros, señor presidente del Consejo, señores presidentes de las instituciones co-munitarias, excelencias, señoras y señores, bien-

venidos a España... El pueblo español *os* **recibe satisfecho y consciente de la alta significación que este acto encierra.**

(Speech of King Juan Carlos to visiting diplomats on the signing of the EEC membership treaty)

¿Has probado el nuevo X turbo? ¡Cómprate un Ford!
(advertisements)

Cuando pases por la biblioteca recógeme todos los libros
(student to student)

O Dios, ayúdame a aprobar mi examen (prayer)

¿Podría darme tres sellos y una postal? (to shopkeeper)

Oiga, Señor, ¿sabe usted dónde está el Paseo de la Castellana?
(to stranger in street)

In American Spanish, the **vosotros/as** forms are completely absent, and **ustedes** is the only plural form. In the singular, some areas have **tú** as in Peninsular Spanish, while others use a form **vos** for the 'familiar' second person.

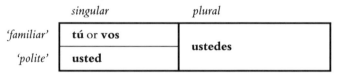

	singular	*plural*
'familiar'	**tú** or **vos**	**ustedes**
'polite'	**usted**	

The use of **tú**, **vos** and **usted** varies greatly from area to area in American Spanish. In general, the 'familiar' forms are not used in such a wide range of circumstances as in Peninsular. **usted** itself has a 'familiar' usage (parents to young children) in some areas, and is even used affectionately between husband and wife in Chile. There are register differences, too: speakers who use **vos** in R2 and below may revert to **tú** in R3.

NOTE: in areas which use the **voseo** (**vos** for **tú**), **vos** is the subject pronoun and prepositional object form; the possessives **tu** and **tuyo** survive. New verb-forms for **vos** may be used: normal in Buenos Aires, for example, are Present Indicative **tomás**, **comés**, **vivís**; Present Subjunctive **tomés**, **comás**, **vivás**; Preterite **tomastes**, etc; Imperative **¡tomá!**, **¡comé!**, **¡viví!**. For example:

No hablemos de mí: hablemos de *vos*, **de** *tus* **trabajos, de** *tus* **preocupaciones... Quiero saber qué** *hacés* **ahora, qué** *pensás*, **si has pintado o no.**

(E. Sábato, *El túnel*)

28.5 Third-person (including **usted**, **ustedes**) object pronouns

There is a great deal of variation in the use of third–person object pronouns in the Spanish–speaking world, and no real agreement on a 'standard'. The following table summarizes the present situation:

subject	*direct object*	*indirect object*
él/ellos	**lo/los** referring to things **le/les** (Pen) ⎱ referring to **lo/los** (Am) ⎰ people (increasingly **lo/los** in Pen)	**le/les** (**lo/los** 〔!〕 sometimes in R1)
ella/ellas	**la/las** referring to things **le/les** (Pen) ⎱ referring to **la/las** (Am) ⎰ people (increasingly **la/las** in Pen)	**le/les** (**la/las** 〔!〕 sometimes in R1–2: more advanced than **lo/los** above)
usted/ustedes (m)	**le/les** (Pen) **lo/los** (Am)	**le/les**
usted/ustedes (f)	**le/les**	**le/les**

However, there are many regional departures from this scheme, both in Peninsular and American Spanish.

Am Spanish-speaking Latin America
Arg Argentina
Mex Mexico
Pen Peninsular Spain
See also p 1.

〔!〕 These forms are in regular use but might be considered 'incorrect' in an examination.

29 The reflexive

The Spanish reflexive has many different functions, several of which are not paralleled in English.

29.1 Genuine reflexives

Direct object, eg:
Me afeité
I shaved
Se estaba mirando en el espejo
She was looking at herself in the mirror

Indirect object, eg:
Me he cortado el dedo
I've cut my finger
Juan se lava las manos
John is washing his hands

NOTE: this is a common way of expressing possession, and with 'possessions' which are an integral part of the 'possessor' (such as parts of the body) this construction must be used instead of a possessive adjective.

The plural reflexive may also have a reciprocal meaning which may be made clear by the use of a reinforcing phrase, eg:
Se ayudaron los siniestrados
The victims helped each other
Se ayudan mutuamente
They help one another
Los políticos no se entienden entre sí
Politicians don't understand one another
Se critican unos a otros
They criticize one another

29.2 Inherent reflexives

Some verbs exist only in the reflexive and have no genuine reflexive interpretation, eg:

†**abstenerse (de)**	*to abstain (from)*
†**arrepentirse (de)**	*to repent (of, for)*
†**atreverse (a)**	*to dare (to)*
†**dignarse** (+ inf)	*to deign (to)*
†**gloriarse (de, en)**	*to boast (of)*
†**jactarse (de)**	*to boast (of)*
†**quejarse (de)**	*to complain (of)*
vanagloriarse (de)	*to boast (of)*

29.3   The reflexive as a marker of the intransitive

Use of the reflexive may convert a transitive verb into a corresponding intransitive:

abrir	to open	†abrirse	to open (intr)
†aburrir	to bore	†aburrirse	to get bored
acercar	to bring closer	acercarse	to get closer
acostar	to put to bed	acostarse	to go to bed
†alegrar	to make happy	alegrarse	to cheer up (intr)
†avergonzar	to put to shame	avergonzarse	to be ashamed
†cansar	to tire (tr)	cansarse	to get tired
cerrar	to close	cerrarse	to close (intr)
desgarrar	to tear (tr)	desgarrarse	to tear (intr)
†enfadar	to annoy	enfadarse	to get annoyed
estremecer	to shake (tr)	estremecerse	to tremble
†fundir	to melt (tr)	fundirse	to melt (intr)
helar	to freeze (tr)	helarse	to freeze (intr)
†hender	to split (tr)	henderse	to split (intr)
†levantar	to raise	levantarse	to get up
mojar	to wet	mojarse	to get wet
pasear	to take for a walk	pasearse	to go for a walk
secar	to dry	secarse	to get dry
†sentar	to seat	sentarse	to sit down

So close is the association between intransitive and reflexive that several intransitive verbs have developed a reflexive form which is not perceptibly different in meaning. The reflexive in this function is especially preferred in R1 (Pen) and in American Spanish. Among such verbs are:

acabar (ALSO tr)/†acabarse	to finish	acabarse also = to wear oneself out in Am
		Se ha acabado la guerra (R1–2)
adelantar (ALSO tr)/adelantarse	to go forward	adelantarse preferred in Am
†aparecer/aparecerse	to appear	But **aparecerse** tends to be restricted to certain more striking expressions, eg **Se apareció el fantasma** = The ghost appeared. **aparecer** is used for more ordinary appearance, eg **Apareció a la puerta** = He appeared at the door

†**bajar** (ALSO tr)/**bajarse**	*to go down*	(**Se** (R1)) **Bajó del autobús** = *She got off the bus*
†**callar** (ALSO tr)/**callarse**	*to be quiet*	**callarse** preferred
†**casar** (ALSO tr)/**casarse**	*to marry*	**casarse** is preferred in Pen, where **casar** belongs to R3
desayunar/ desayunarse	*to have breakfast*	**desayunarse** is R3 in Pen, but preferred in some parts of Am
enfermar (ALSO tr)/**enfermarse** !⃞	*to fall ill*	Only **enfermar** in Pen, but **enfermarse** preferred in Am
entrenar (ALSO tr)/**entrenarse**	*to train*	
†**imaginar** (ALSO tr)/**imaginarse**	*to imagine, to fancy*	**imaginarse** is R1–2
†**parar** (ALSO tr)/**pararse**	*to stop*	– **¿Cuándo para el autobús aquí?** – **Para a las cinco.** = *When does the bus stop here? It stops at five.* But **El autobús se para a las cinco** = *The bus stops (for good) at five.*
pasear (ALSO tr)/**pasearse**	*to go for a walk*	
†**recordar** (ALSO tr)/**recordarse** !⃞	*to remember*	Only **recordar** in Pen
regresar/ regresarse !⃞	*to go back, to return*	Only **regresar** in Pen
reír/†**reírse**	*to laugh*	**reírse** is preferred when followed by **de** (p 212), eg: **Se rio de su estupidez** = *She laughed at his stupidity*

!⃞ These forms are in regular use but might be considered 'incorrect' in an examination.

sonreír/†**sonreírse**	*to smile*	As **reír**/**reírse**
†**subir** (ALSO tr)/**subirse**	*to go up*	As **bajar**/**bajarse**
†**tardar**/**tardarse** ⚠	*to take time*	Only **tardar** in Pen
terminar (ALSO tr)/**terminarse**	*to finish*	

29.4 The reflexive as an intensifier

With many non-reflexive verbs, both transitive and intransitive, the addition of a reflexive pronoun gives a 'stronger', though essentially equivalent, meaning. The following list illustrates some of these differences:

	Non-reflexive	**Reflexive**
†**caer**	**Cayó de rodillas** He fell to his knees **Tiró la piedra, que cayó muy cerca** She threw the stone, which fell very close by **Cayeron muchos soldados en la batalla** Many soldiers fell (= died) in the battle **No caiga en la tentación** Don't fall into temptation (fig) **Su cumpleaños cae el lunes** His birthday is on Monday	**Juan se cayó del árbol** John fell out of the tree (implies an accident) **El libro se cayó de la mesa** The book fell off the table **¡Cuidado, te vas a caer!** Careful, you're going to fall! NOTE: the reflexive is favoured with a following **de** + noun phrase.
†**comer**	**He comido bien** I've eaten well	**Se lo comió** He ate it up
†**dormir**	**Duerme unas ocho horas** He sleeps about eight hours	**Se durmió en seguida** She went to sleep immediately
†**encontrar**	**No encuentro la calle** I can't find the street	**Se lo encontró en la calle** He found it (by chance) in the street
escapar	**Escapó a la policía** He avoided the police	**Se han escapado los presos** The prisoners have got out **El gas se escapa** The gas is escaping

	Non-reflexive	**Reflexive**
†**ir**	**Voy a Nueva York** I'm going to New York	**Se fue a Argentina** She went off to Argentina
leer	**Leí cuatro libros** I read four books	**Me leí cuatro libros** (R1–2) I read four books
†**llevar**	**Llevaba una maleta** She was carrying a suitcase	**Se lo llevó a Francia** He took it off with him to France
		El ladrón se llevó todo el dinero The thief took all the money
†**marchar**	**Marcharon los soldados todo el día** The soldiers marched all day	**Se marcharon** They went off
	No marcha bien el motor The engine is not running well	
†**morir**	**Murió su padre el año pasado** His father died last year	**Se está muriendo** She's dying
†**ocurrir**	**Ocurrió ayer el accidente** The accident happened yesterday	**Se me ocurrió regresar** It occurred to me to return
†**pasar**	**Los años pasaron** The years passed	**Se pasa todo el tiempo estudiando** (R1–2) He spends all his time studying
	¿Qué pasa? What's happening?	**Se me pasó la oportunidad** The opportunity passed me by
†**quedar**	**El prado queda más allá** The field is further on	**Me quedo en el coche** I'll stay in the car
	No queda ningún libro There's not one book left	**Me quedo con el periódico** I'll keep the paper
	Quedan diez minutos There are ten minutes left	
	Queda como un señor He's shown himself to be a gentleman	
†**salir**	**Salió del parque a las siete** She left the park at seven	**Se enfadó y se salió del café** He got cross and walked out of the café
		Se salió a mitad de la película He went out in the middle of the film (may imply displeasure)
		La bombona se sale The gas bottle is leaking

	Non-reflexive	Reflexive
†**tomar**	**¿Qué vas a tomar?** What will you have to drink?	**Se tomó cuatro vasos de cerveza en cinco minutos** He gulped down four beers in five minutes
†**traer**	**Juana ha traído el lápiz** Juana has brought the pencil	**Dijeron que no, pero se trajo las tazas** They said not, but (still) he brought the cups (implies insistence)
†**venir**	**Vino a Inglaterra en 1948** He came to England in 1948	**Se ha venido a Inglaterra para abrir una nueva fábrica** He's come to England to open a new factory (implies more specific purpose)

29.5 The impersonal reflexive

The uses of the reflexive in **29.1–4** above apply to all persons. The third-person reflexive may also be used when the subject of the verb is left unexpressed: in this function it is often translatable by the English passive (but see **29.7**). Two constructions can be distinguished:

(a) The logical object of the verb appears to act as the subject, and the verb agrees with it in number, eg:
> **Se venden motos**
> Motor-bikes for sale
> **Se compran coches** (see **18.1**)
> Cars bought

(b) The verb is invariably in the singular and the logical object is also the grammatical object, eg:
> **Se les ayudó a los siniestrados**
> The victims were helped
> **Se le detuvo al hombre**
> The man was stopped

These two constructions are in practice often indistinguishable, though (b) is sometimes considered to be lower in register than (a):
> **Se me entregaron dos cartas** (R2)/**Se me entregó dos cartas** (R1)
> I was handed two letters

The impersonal reflexive can also be used with intransitive verbs, eg:
> **Cuando se tiene veinticinco años ya se está en edad para pasarse la vida tranquila**
> When you are 25 it's time to have a peaceful life

29.6 Further notes on **se**

1   The **se** which obligatorily replaces **le** or **les** in groups of more than one third-person pronoun is not a reflexive at all:

    Di el libro a Juan   **Se (= le) lo di**

2   In Spanish, not more than one **se**, of whatever kind (including 1 above), is allowed per verb. Many verb + infinitive and all verb + gerund structures also count as 'one' verb for this purpose, all the pronouns standing either before the finite verb or after the infinitive or gerund. Thus the notion *You cannot bathe here*, which might involve the 'clash' of two instances of **se** (one the impersonal reflexive, **se puede**..., the other the reflexive of **bañarse**), must be rendered in one of the following ways:

    Uno no se puede bañar aquí
    No está permitido bañarse aquí
    No se permite bañarse aquí (**bañarse** is here the subject of
       permitir, and therefore a separate clause)

29.7 The reflexive and the passive

Contrary to what is sometimes suggested, the passive (eg **fue escrito**) is very frequently used in Spanish, especially in R3. However, there are several circumstances in which, by comparison with the English passive, it either cannot be used or is not preferred. In such circumstances, it is often appropriate to use a reflexive construction instead. It is perhaps most important to appreciate where the Spanish passive and reflexive respectively *cannot* be used. In the following examples, suggested translations of the English sentences discussed are shown in brackets.

●   The Spanish passive cannot be used as an equivalent to the English passive

(a)   where the subject of the passive verb is logically an indirect object or a prepositional object, eg:

    I was taught Spanish by a Spaniard
    (**Me enseñó el español un español**)
    This bed was slept in by Henry VIII
    (**Enrique VIII durmió en esta cama**)

(b)   where the passive subject has no article, eg:

    Pianos are sold here
    (**Se vende(n) pianos aquí**)

(c)   where the past participle has a different meaning as an adjective with **ser**, eg:

    The students were bored by the lecture
    (**La clase aburrió a los estudiantes** OR **Los estudiantes estaban
       aburridos por la clase** since **ser aburrido** = *to be boring*)

(d)   in the Present and Imperfect tenses where the verb denotes a single action, eg:

Now the window is shut by the teacher
(**Ahora la profesora cierra la ventana**)

BUT the following are acceptable:

La ventana fue/será/ha sido, etc **cerrada por la profesora**
La ventana es cerrada todos los días por la profesora

and with a verb denoting a quality, eg:

Es conocido por todos
He's known by everyone

NOTE: **La ventana es cerrada por la profesora** is also possible with a 'commentary' interpretation: *The window is being shut by the teacher.* This use is more frequent in journalistic R3 than in other registers. The following are examples of captions from newspaper photographs:

Un obrero es socorrido por manifestantes en Tiananmen
A worker is aided by demonstrators in Tiananmen
Asaltantes de supermercados son detenidos por la policía argentina en la ciudad de Rosario
Supermarket raiders are arrested by Argentine police in the city of Rosario

- The Spanish reflexive cannot be used

(a)   where a literal reflexive meaning is possible, eg:

The children were taught to read
(**A los niños se les enseñó a leer**)
NOT **Los niños se enseñaron a leer**, which would mean *The children taught themselves to read.*

(b)   where an agent is expressed, eg:

These books were sold by my uncle
(**Estos libros los vendió mi tío**)
NOT **Estos libros se vendieron por mi tío**

BUT NOTE: reflexive + agent constructions appear to be becoming more used in Spanish; the following, for instance, are perfectly acceptable:

Este libro se editó por un catedrático muy conocido
This book was edited by a very well-known professor
La Academia se fundó por Felipe V
The Academy was founded by Philip V

(c)   in the third person, where another **se** is needed or implied (see **29.6**), eg:

John wasn't asked for it
(**No se lo pidieron a Juan** – se here = **le**)
NOT, of course, **No se se lo pidió a Juan**. **No se pidió a Juan** is acceptable but means *He/She didn't ask John for it.*

30 Comparison

30.1 Comparison of inequality (*more/less/fewer than*)

- If a single part of speech is being compared, **que** is used, eg:
  Pedro es más/menos alto que Juan
  Pedro is taller/shorter than John
  La biblioteca tiene más/menos periódicos que revistas
  The library has more/fewer newspapers than magazines
  Da más que recibe
  She gives more (= to a greater extent) than she receives
  Es más/menos pequeño (ahora) que antes
  It's smaller than/not as small (now) as before

NOTE: in R1, a 'redundant' **no** is sometimes used after **que**, eg:
  Tiene más libros que no ⏢ yo
  He has more books than me

Where the comparison is with an element in another clause, **de** +
pronoun + **que** is used. If the pronoun refers back to a noun, it
agrees with the noun; if it refers to a clause, **lo** is used, eg:
  **Aquí hay más ⏢libros⏢ de ⏢los⏢ que se puede leer (se puede leer
  ⏢libros⏢)**
  There are more books here than can be read
  Es más alto de ⏢lo⏢que yo pensaba (pensaba ⏢que. . .⏢)
  He's taller than I thought

Contrast the following pairs of examples:
  Tiene más dinero de ⏢lo⏢ que dice (dice ⏢que. . .⏢)
  She has more money than she says
  Tiene más ⏢dinero⏢ d ⏢el⏢ que yo le di (Le di ⏢dinero⏢)
  She has more money than I gave her
  **Necesita más atención de ⏢lo⏢ que se sospechaba (se
  sospechaba ⏢que. . .⏢)**
  It needs more attention than was thought
  **Necesita más ⏢atención⏢ de ⏢la⏢ que se puede dar (se puede dar
  ⏢atención⏢)**
  It needs more attention than can be given

Notes

1 In R1, **de lo que**, **del que**, etc are sometimes replaced by **que** alone
  ⏢⏢ .

2 **que lo que**, etc are used in comparisons not involving a clause, eg:
  **Los libros que acabo de leer son más interesantes que los que
  tengo que leer ahora**
  The books I've just read are more interesting than those I've got to
  read now

With a numeral

With a numeral, **de** is used, eg:
Ha ganado más/menos de cien mil pesetas
He's earned more/less than a hundred thousand pesetas
Quedaron más/menos de dos meses
There were more/less than two months left

But **no más que** = *only*, and **que** is generally used before a numeral when a negative is present, eg:
No me quedan más que dos meses
I've only two months left OR I haven't more than two months left

30.2 mayor/más grande, menor/menos grande

These forms of the comparative are interchangeable *except* when they refer to people, when **mayor** and **menor** relate exclusively to age:
Es mayor que yo
He's older than me
BUT
Es más grande que yo
He's bigger than me
Esta calle es mayor/más grande que aquélla
This street is bigger than that one

NOTE: **mayor** also has the non-comparative sense of *elderly*: **una persona (muy) mayor** = *a (very) elderly person*.

30.3 Comparison of equality

tanto + noun/**tan** + adjective or adverb **como. . .**:
Me hace falta tanta comida como a él
I need as much food as he does
Este pueblo no tiene tantas casas como el otro
This village doesn't have as many houses as the other
Este chico me parece tan listo como su hermano
This boy seems to me as intelligent as his brother
Escribe tan bien como yo
He writes as well as I do

Notes

1   There is an alternative pattern with adjectives:
Es blanco como (R2)/**cual** (R3) **la nieve**
It's as white as snow

2   **tanto… como…** is also frequently used as the equivalent of English *both . . . and . . .*, eg:
tanto los ingleses como los españoles
both the English and the Spanish
(See ch. **13**.)

Contrast the non–comparative **tan/tanto...que...**:

Hacía tanto frío que no queríamos salir
It was so cold that we didn't want to go out
Era tan alta la torre que no quería subir a ella
The tower was so high that he didn't want to go up it
Llovía tanto que la carretera quedó inundada
It was raining so much that the road became flooded

30.4   Comparison of clauses

Cuanto más lee, (tanto) más se divierte
The more he reads, the more he enjoys himself
**Yo estuve tanto más contento cuanto que me resultó
    gratuita la comida**
I was all the happier because the meal was free

31 Usage with names of countries

The vast majority of countries do not take the definite article unless they are qualified by an adjective or adjectival phrase:

Voy a España
I'm going to Spain
Es de México
He's from Mexico

BUT

en la Italia de hace cincuenta años
in the Italy of fifty years ago
en el Chile contemporáneo
in contemporary Chile

However, there are a number of countries, both masculine and feminine, which may be preceded by the definite article. They are indicated in ch. **7** as follows: (**el**) **Japón**, (**los**) **Estados Unidos**, (**la**) **Argentina**. Generally speaking, the use of the article is more typical of the written registers. One or two countries, notably **El Salvador**, have a definite article as part of their name, and it must always be used. As with names of towns (eg, **El Ferrol**) where the article forms an integral part of the name, the article does not combine with **de** or **a** in very formal usage, eg:

en el norte de (la (R2–3)) **Argentina**
in the north of Argentina
el Primer Ministro de(l R2–3) **Japón**
the Prime Minister of Japan
la capital de El (R3)/**del** (R1–2) **Salvador**
the capital of El Salvador

Spanish word index